Goethe contra Newton

GOETHE CONTRA NEWTON
Polemics and the project
for a new science of color

DENNIS L. SEPPER
Department of Philosophy
University of Dallas

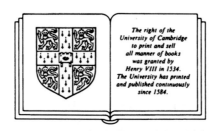

The right of the
University of Cambridge
to print and sell
all manner of books
was granted by
Henry VIII in 1534.
The University has printed
and published continuously
since 1584.

Cambridge University Press
Cambridge
New York   New Rochelle   Melbourne   Sydney

PUBLISHED BY THE PRESS SYNDICATE OF THE UNIVERSITY OF CAMBRIDGE
The Pitt Building, Trumpington Street, Cambridge, United Kingdom

CAMBRIDGE UNIVERSITY PRESS
The Edinburgh Building, Cambridge CB2 2RU, UK
40 West 20th Street, New York NY 10011–4211, USA
477 Williamstown Road, Port Melbourne, VIC 3207, Australia
Ruiz de Alarcón 13, 28014 Madrid, Spain
Dock House, The Waterfront, Cape Town 8001, South Africa

http://www.cambridge.org

First published 1988
First paperback edition 2002

A catalogue record for this book is available from the British Library

Library of Congress Cataloguing-in-Publication Data
Sepper, Dennis. L.
Goethe contra Newton: polemics and the project for a new science
of color /by Dennis L. Sepper.
p. cm.
Bibliography: p.
Includes index.
1. Color. 2. Color – History. 3. Goethe, Johann Wolfgang von,
1749–1832. 4. Newton, Isaac, Sir, 1642—1727. I. Title.
QC495.S43 1988
635.6 – dc19 87 – 21463
CIP

ISBN 0 521 34254 6 hardback
ISBN 0 521 53132 2 paperback

To my family

Have thought about fiction and science. The disaster they cause comes from the need of reflective reason, which creates for its own use a sort of image, but thereafter sets it up as true and concrete.

– Goethe

To explain all nature is too difficult a task for any one man or even for any one age.

– Newton

Men who like him had taken up the entire abundance of the elements of their age's culture without being constricted in the natural independence of their sensibility, who as ethically free individuals in the noblest sense of the word needed only to follow their fervent, inborn sympathy for all stirrings of the human spirit in order to find the right way amidst the cliffs of life, already in our times have become very rare and will likely become rarer.

– Helmholtz

Contents

Preface

People say: between two opposed opinions the truth lies in the middle.
Not at all! Between them lies the problem, what is unseeable, eternally
active life, contemplated [*gedacht*] in repose.

— Goethe (*MR*, no. 616)

Johann Wolfgang von Goethe's Farbenlehre[1] has produced bitter controversy for almost two centuries. Consequently, a work that presumes
to illuminate its most controversial aspect, the polemic against Sir Isaac
Newton's theory of white light and colors, should indicate at the outset
its position with respect to the controversy. The first and most important
point is that there is no simple answer to what seems the basic question,
"Who is right, Newton or Goethe?" Attempts to answer the question
involve more than sorting out the details. The different fundamental
aspects under which the question must be posed — phenomenal, theoretical, methodological, historical, and philosophical — must also be
clarified.

Common opinion, including the consensus of the physical literature,
holds that the Goethe–Newton conflict can be resolved by simple fact.
It is interesting that even many of the partisans of Goethe's science have
agreed, but they think the facts speak for Goethe rather than Newton!
This circumstance made me realize that the issue of fact itself had to be
raised, because the question of what factuality is lies at the heart of
Goethe's color science and his repudiation of Newton. Goethe charged
that Newton had portrayed as fact — or, to use terms preferred by Goethe,
phenomenon or appearance — what was hypothesis, and thus that Newton
had injected a fundamental epistemological confusion into the very core
of the science of colors. Goethe's first intention, then, was to pay the
most careful attention to the phenomena of color and to be scrupulously
untendentious in presenting them publicly; his second intention was to
unravel the complex relationship between these phenomena and the ways
in which we speak and speculate about them.

Three centuries ago, Newton established the foundation of modern
optics and revolutionized the study of color. These have been lasting
achievements, and I have every reason to expect them to endure even as

they continue to be modified through the progress of research. Nevertheless, we must realize that the enduring substance of Newton's discovery is not identical with Newton's presentation of his experiments and theory; the former is the result of three hundred years of critical revision, the latter is fixed in Newton's writings and in the particulars – not always unassailable – of his approach and goals. To us, Newton's basic theory of light and colors is a good hypothesis, but to Newton it was much more: a fixed and foundational truth that might perhaps be more exactly specified but never refuted. Moreover, we must realize that Newton did not always distinguish carefully what we might call the "physics" underlying color, which is a physical optics of radiation, from the "psychophysics" of color, which tries to correlate the kind and amount of radiation with what is seen and which therefore inevitably draws into the ambit of color science matters of psychology, physiology, and perception. Insofar as he even raised the question, Newton for the most part tried to give the psychophysics of color a purely physical basis, and thus he really did not provide a comprehensive foundation for the science of color qua color. Newton's partial success, compounded by subsequent deformations of his theories in the course of eighteenth-century optics, created a situation that justified Goethe's criticisms and his attempts to lay a new foundation grounded upon a more scrupulous regard for articulating the proper approaches to the phenomena of color.

Yet to argue that Goethe's Farbenlehre and his polemics have been largely misunderstood is not to argue that they are unproblematic or simply right. I have come to believe that Goethe has an ampler conception of science than Newton, that he has a sounder notion of what an empirical methodology requires and a firmer grasp on the epistemological and philosophical issues involved; however, in the competition for scientific achievement Newton must take the palm of victory. (I do not, by the way, expect that everyone who reads this book will agree with my assessment of Goethe, but I do think most will understand that these claims are not groundless.) Although Goethe is not as amathematical as people think, he nevertheless did not resolve the question of how mathematical conception and calculation are to be reconciled with seeing and experiencing the appearances, and thus despite his intention to present an all-encompassing science of color – and not a merely qualitative science (whatever that might be), as some enthusiasts have claimed – we must conclude that, even on his own terms, he failed to realize this project.

If Goethe were alive to see the sciences of color today, he would approve of the vast cooperative effort, the manifold approaches, the theoretical variety, the exact specification of experiments, the refinement of instruments, and the vigor of scientific communication and debate. In short, he is not the proponent of antimodern science he is often portrayed as;

in fact, I believe that the natural sciences have in some respects been reorganized in ways that he hoped would come about (most important, perhaps, being the intensive cooperation of communities of researchers). But it is clear, too, that Goethe, looking upon present-day work, would remind us not to let theories obscure what we actually see or forget that our ultimate goal is comprehensive fidelity to nature.

Scholars interested in Goethe and cultural history may miss in this book a sustained effort to explain the relationship between Goethe's science and his literary works, or between his science and broad cultural currents, such as Neoplatonism and Spinozism. My apology is that to begin to do justice to the Goethe–Newton controversy it is necessary to delve into textual, experimental, historical, and philosophical issues; this seemed work enough (and even this only begins to scratch the surface of the positive teachings of the Farbenlehre, the elucidation of which would seem to be the next order of business). Although I have not ignored such issues as philosophical connections and cultural influences, I have for the most part followed the principle that one must initially avoid explaining Goethe's scientific work according to what historians of science call externalist categories in order to provide a good internalist account of it. At any rate, I believe I have followed a thoroughly Goethean method in imposing on myself the primary obligation of securing a basis that might ultimately lead to a more speculative sequel.

While taking into account historical factors, I treat Goethe and Newton in some sense as contemporaries, trying to come to terms with a common object of investigation. I do this by carefully examining in context what Goethe and Newton wrote, and also by elaborating from this examination some notion of their characteristic ways of conceiving the phenomena (*Vorstellungsarten*, a term that will become thematic at the end of Chapter 2). Although we may not achieve complete commensurability between their different ways of conceiving things, we can establish a common ground that presupposes not consensus but rather the ability of human beings to talk with and learn from one another. I emphasize this common ground because it is something that the opposing sides in the controversy have rarely, if ever, achieved. Indeed, one might reasonably argue that the eclipse of the Farbenlehre was assured by Goethe's failure to establish a common ground on which both Goetheans and Newtonians could stand, and that the polemic served to obscure what was at issue rather than illuminate the differences between the two approaches to color. The polemic was not only a strategic blunder for Goethe personally, it was also a calamity for his scientific project.

To understand this project, it is essential to see how and where Goethe differed with Newton and to make clear that Goethe was fully aware of the character and bearing of the differences. To shed light on these matters and the reasons for them, I have scrutinized in Chapter 3 the letter in which Newton announced his theory to the Royal Society of London. To those who might object that in virtually dissecting this work I am unfair to Newton, I say that the classics of science are at least as much a part of our heritage as the *Iliad*, *Hamlet*, or *Faust*. Meticulousness is perhaps not necessary for a first appreciation of classic works, nor is it sufficient for pronouncing the last word on them; but at some point we must approach them with the presumption that their authors wrote precisely what they did for precise reasons. Moreover, I have tried to be scrupulous with Goethe's writings as well. If at times I seem to treat Goethe more indulgently, it is because this book is chiefly about a scientific work that has been subject to a more persistent neglect and misapprehension than Newton's and that is therefore in need of an at least provisionally sympathetic reading; moreover, Newton made the more extreme claims of truth, so it is perhaps just to hold him to a very strict accounting. But I do not spare Goethe when evaluating his accomplishments and failures; least of all do I approve of his having initiated the polemics and partisanship that have marred the controversy from the beginning and, even worse, have obscured the questions of science and truth. I have tried to avoid partisanship myself, but undoubtedly have not fully succeeded; yet I can still hope that the defects of my work are not so severe as to prevent readers from seeing what needs to be seen in the affair of Goethe against Newton.

As I conclude this preface, I realize that there is no way of adequately expressing my gratitude to the scores of those who have helped me bring this work to fruition. Not least do I owe thanks to the librarians who have so ably and readily given their assistance: I should like especially to thank the staffs of the Bayerische Staatsbibliothek, the Deutsches Museum, and the Ludwig-Maximilians-Universität in Munich; and the library staffs of the University of Chicago, Stanford University, and the University of Dallas, in particular Mrs. Alice Puro. The Deutscher Akademischer Austauschdienst (DAAD) generously supported me during my year-and-a-half-long stay in Germany, and Frau Margret Kassian and her family sheltered me from the worries of everyday living so that I could devote myself to "meta-worries" instead.

Although I never had the opportunity to meet or speak with him before his death, I wish to express my gratitude to Rupprecht Matthaei, the principal editor of the volumes on color science in the Leopoldina-Ausgabe of Goethe's scientific writings and a color scientist in his own right, for doing more than anyone in this century to bring Goethe's Farbenlehre to the public in a full and comprehensive way, and for helping guide readers to an understanding of it.

The original insights that led to this book first glimmered in University of Chicago seminars on Goethe conducted by Manfred Hoppe, at whose instigation I first read the Farbenlehre; a more challenging teacher I have not met. Although I did not meet Erich Heller until the dissertation underlying this book was well advanced, his essays on Goethe inspired me to pursue my insights. When I finally met him in person I profited from his generous comments and his kindly admonitions not to be carried away by enthusiasm. In Germany Reinhard Löw and Ivo Schneider gave me encouragement and sound advice, and were always a responsive audience. Among those who have read and commented on my manuscript I give special thanks to John Cornell, whose conversations have been a constant source of intellectual stimulation.

I want also to thank the University of Chicago's Committee on Social Thought, which encourages risky ventures where more orthodox academic departments might not let their students tread, and especially Stephen Toulmin, whose continued support and uncanny ability to find the proper word of encouragement and to point out where things are going astray helped turn an idea and a hope into reality.

Jonathan Sinclair-Wilson at Cambridge University Press has been every bit the professional that those who know him told me he is; I offer a special thank you for his assistance in bringing this book to the public. Thanks also to Helen Wheeler, Janis Bolster, and Rhona Johnson for their aid; and I especially thank Brian MacDonald for his fine editing, which helped this book find a more consistent tone. The defects that remain are doubtless the result of resisting his advice or the counsel of others. Let them be held blameless.

I could hardly list the names of all those who have labored over my manuscripts, but I must not omit thanking publicly at least Gloria Valentine, Vicky Boubelik, Tina Lemon, Mary Jensen, Joanne Baird, Laura Braith, Regina Gomez, and Liota Odom.

I especially thank my parents, Joseph and Marge Sepper, for the help and support they have given over the years.

To Kathleen Wellman I owe not just the thanks of husband to wife for her love and encouragement, but also the gratitude of philosopher to historian. Finally, I cannot say that Elizabeth Wellman Sepper and Matthew Wellman Sepper have offered criticism or advice, but they have been encouraging in their very own way, and they, and their mother, have made the whole process more humanly bearable. May they someday read this and understand.

Abbreviations

The following abbreviations are used in text and note references for works I cite frequently. Unless otherwise noted, citations are by page numbers. Author-date citations refer to the reference list at the end of this volume.

Works by Goethe

BzO	*Beiträge zur Optik*, part 1 (1791) and part 2 (1792); found in *LA* I, 3:6–53. Cited by standard paragraph numbers.
FL-D	The first, didactic part of *Zur Farbenlehre* (1810); found in *LA* I, 4. Cited by standard paragraph numbers.
FL-P	The second, polemical part of *Zur Farbenlehre*; found in *LA* I, 5. Cited by standard paragraph numbers.
HA	Hamburger-Ausgabe (*Goethes Werke*) = Goethe 1948–60. Cited by volume and page.
LA	Leopoldina-Ausgabe (*Die Schriften zur Naturwissenschaft*) = Goethe 1947–. Cited by division, volume, and page.
MR	*Maximen und Reflexionen*, ed. Max Hecker = Goethe 1907. Cited by aphorism number.
WA	Weimarer-Ausgabe (*Goethes Werke*) = Goethe 1887–1919. Cited by division, volume, and page.

Works by Newton

Corresp.	*The correspondence of Isaac Newton* = Newton 1959–76. Cited by volume and page.
LO	*Lectiones opticae* = Newton 1729.
OL	*Optical lectures* = Newton 1728.

Opticks   = Newton 1952.

Shap.   Alan E. Shapiro, ed., *The optical papers of Isaac Newton,* vol. 1 = Newton 1984.

Other works

Eck.   Johann Peter Eckermann, *Gespräche mit Goethe in den letzten Jahren seines Lebens* = Eckermann 1949. Cited by date of conversation.

1

Defining the questions of the Farbenlehre

Should I not be proud, when for twenty years I have had to admit to myself that the great Newton and all the mathematicians and noble calculators along with him were involved in a decisive error with respect to the doctrine of color, and that I among millions was the only one who knew what was right in this great subject of nature? With this feeling of superiority, then, it was possible for me to endure the stupid presumption of my opponents. They sought in every way to persecute me and my doctrine and to make my ideas ridiculous; but I nonetheless took great pleasure in my completed work. All the attacks of my opponents only served to help me see human beings in their weakness.

                                – Goethe (Eck., 30 December 1823)

The critical dilemma

The name Johann Wolfgang von Goethe (1749–1832) evokes the image of a giant of world literature. Although the epoch of adulation is past, and although his association with the bourgeois and petty aristocratic cultures of late eighteenth- and early nineteenth-century Germany has impaired his reputation, his greatness as a writer and his central role in the history of German literature are indisputable. Already in his youth he took the world of German letters by storm with his lyric poems, his drama *Götz von Berlichingen*, and his novel *Die Leiden des jungen Werther* – achievements that would have assured him an important chapter in literary histories. But it is the works of his maturity that truly guaranteed him human immortality as a writer and sage. Goethe's *Faust* is the most famous and greatest version of a story that has been taken as archetypal of the Western spirit. When we consider in addition novels like *Die Wahlverwandtschaften* and the two parts of the *Wilhelm Meister* saga, his autobiography *Dichtung und Wahrheit*, the *Italienische Reise*, the *West-östlicher Divan*, and countless other poems, stories, dramas, essays, translations, and letters, all written with masterly art and insight, we appreciate that, beyond whatever justice there is in comparing him with Shakespeare and Dante, the sheer variety and richness of his literary production make him a writer sui generis.

Goethe was also active as a painter, a scholar, and a theater director and manager. He served as a director of universities and museums; an administrator responsible for parks, forests, mines, and roads; and a diplomat and minister of state. He was a scientist and patron of science and technology, with notable publications in anatomy, botany, and chromatics. Through this partial list of Goethe's activities and accomplishments, we begin to appreciate that this man was a German, or rather European, phenomenon with hardly a parallel. It is not at all surprising that to the civilization of nineteenth-century Europe he represented a pinnacle of human achievement. He was described already in the last years of his life as the Olympian, the calm, perfectly self-possessed, all-comprehending spirit who was the true heir of the entire legacy of the West and the fulfillment of the ideal of universal culture. He seemed to incarnate the spirit of antiquity and of the Renaissance, yet also to be a modern man whose powers were ample enough to range from rococo delicacy to the turbulence of *Sturm und Drang* romanticism, from the stern demands of natural science to the forms, depths, and delights of lyric – all without losing his unique individuality or undermining the masterful authority of his fundamentally classic spirit.

Goethe appeared to have followed the stirrings of his spirit even in science, but precisely here the universality of his genius is at issue. For Goethe believed that his major contribution to the sciences of nature, indeed the most important of all his works, was his Farbenlehre, his doctrine of color; yet, at least according to conventional wisdom, the poet was fundamentally in error. He appears to have committed an incredible blunder at the outset of his physical studies of color by rejecting Isaac Newton's theory of white light and colors as demonstrably false. A few casual observations with a prism appear to have settled his opinion: Observing that a white wall viewed through the prism remains white, and that colors appear only where there are contrasts of dark and light, he concluded that the notion that white light is separated into the various colors that compose it was wrong. Yet the phenomena he observed were not unknown to Newton, and so it seems that his insight amounted to nothing more than a misunderstanding of the theory. Although not a few scientists, both friends and strangers, tried to put him right, in person and in print, Goethe nevertheless held fast to his belief and continued his studies outside the traditional framework of optics and color science. As a result, he developed a theory of color that had little to do with physics and mathematics and that included a sustained attack on one of the greatest scientific achievements ever, Newton's optics. Thus Goethe's Farbenlehre seems at best a curiosity, at worst a willful perversion of the human faculties.[1]

An oddity already in its own day, Goethe's Farbenlehre has grown stranger and more in need of explanation and apology with the passage of time. Occasional defenders, some eminent scientists, have been able to show at best that the work is not entirely peripheral to the concerns of modern optics and color science (e.g., Jablonski 1930). A few historians of science have been willing to resurrect it for its insights into the pre-modern conception of color rather than for any intrinsic scientific merit (see Wasserman 1978 and Judd 1970). Despite the time and labor that Goethe lavished on it, the Farbenlehre seems not to be informed with any genuinely scientific spirit or fundamental achievement. After more than 175 years the judgment of the eminent French physicist Etienne Malus still seems to hold:

[There is] a striking contrast between the precise and simple manner in which Newton retails his experiments and conclusions, and the inflated, vague, and ironic tone with which Goethe denies the best known facts and the most evident consequences....

... He treats the Newtonians as though they were Cossacks, their opinions as though they were incredible idiocies....

... It is astonishing to see Goethe employ such arguments in a work of physics, and it is to be only too often perceived that he is not in the state of mind appropriate to those who sincerely seek the truth. (Malus 1811, 213, 218–19)

Aggressive and even insulting remarks about Newton and his followers can indeed be found in the second, polemical part and in the third, historical part of *Zur Farbenlehre*. Goethe variously calls Newton's theory contrafactual, a fairy tale, hocus-pocus, and word-rubbish (*Wortkram*); he accuses Newton of sophistry, stubbornness, and shamelessness, even of self-deception bordering on dishonesty. For the followers of Newton he shows even less tolerance. He berates them for being captious and dishonest, uttering thoughtless idiocies, spending their time gluing, mending, patching, and embalming Newton's theory. He calls them incompetent and obscurantist, lazy, self-satisfied, merciless, and persecutorial; they are mere copyists of error who constantly repeat the words of the master, record only what is favorable to the theory, and proceed in opposition to nature, intelligence, and common sense (see *FL-P*, par. 45, 76, 205, 356, 360, 471, 472, 582, 584, 635; and *WA* II, 4: 40, 64, 82, 101, 105, 106, 165).

To Goethe's early critics, the fact of his errors and intemperance was beyond doubt. Pointing them out was of course important, but attempts to understand the reasons behind them were far more revealing. By his own confession, Goethe had misunderstood Newton's theory and did not have enough training in mathematics to judge its true rigor. Because Goethe was interested primarily in the artistic, poetic, and psychological uses of color, he did not properly evaluate the physics of color. His very talent, his poetic gift, inclined him more to romanticism, speculative *Naturphilosophie*, and the overvaluation of mere appearances, than to theoretical science and objective reality. The critical literature that followed, especially after Goethe's death, sought to explain why Goethe had committed his grave error and why he persisted in it.

Although there are signs that in the 1830s the controversy between scientists and supporters of Goethe was still topical (see Dove 1853, 15–16; cf. Schmid 1940, 347–50), by mid-century the debate had turned into a question about Goethe rather than about science. A milestone in this change was Hermann von Helmholtz's 1853 lecture on Goethe's scientific works. According to Helmholtz the facts of the matter are clear. In the *Beiträge zur Optik* Goethe describes what is seen when one looks through a prism at white figures on a black ground; black figures on a white ground; and colored figures on black, white, and colored grounds. He depicts the perceived phenomena "circumstantially, rigorously true to nature, and vividly, puts them in an order that is pleasant to survey, and proves himself here, as everywhere in the realm of the factual, to be the great master of exposition" (Helmholtz 1971, 28). Goethe thinks that the perceived phenomena are sufficient to contradict Newton, especially his two observations that, when viewed through a prism, the central portion of a broad white figure on a dark background remains white, and a narrow black stripe on a white ground is completely dissolved into colors. According to Helmholtz, however, the assumption in Newton's theories that white light is composed of differently refrangible, different color-producing lights can explain these phenomena very well.

Helmholtz suggests that at first Goethe remembered too little of Newton's theory to come upon this physical explanation of the facts; however, Goethe's subsequent discussions of the theory make clear that he did come to understand it. Nevertheless, he continued to insist that the incorrectness and absurdity of Newton's theory ought to be evident to all who have eyes to see, but without once plainly indicating exactly how it was unsatisfactory. Helmholtz expresses his perplexity: "And I for one do not know how anyone, regardless of what his views about colors are, can deny that the theory in itself is fully consequent, that its assumptions, once granted, explain the facts treated completely and indeed simply" (ibid., 30). Helmholtz remarked how disturbing Goethe's idiosyncratic stubbornness about Newton's theory is to all who consider the German poet to have been a man of the rarest spiritual capacities. Yet this opposition, Goethe versus the physicists – in agreement about the facts but in violent contradiction about their meaning – Helmholtz considers to be revealing of a far deeper opposition, one which must be sought in the differences of character and ability that distinguish the poet from the scientist.

The poet-artist thinks that ideas must be immediate rather than abstract, and just as a work of art must not be subjected to any rending analysis that destroys it, neither should nature be rent by torturing experiment and abstraction. White is a simple sensation, regardless of what the scientist does with his prism, and so white cannot possibly be composite. A beam of light forced through prisms and lenses and apertures in dark rooms is nature put on a rack. Helmholtz grants that a poet-artist may have a genius for scientific description, as Goethe proved in osteology and botany, but nevertheless the artistic sensibility tends toward murky and ill-defined concepts that are essentially useless in exact physical science. Goethe, the poet par excellence, was unable to grasp precisely that abstract concepts are necessary to all real science. Direct, sensuous observation cannot substitute for well-defined concepts worked out by the intellect. Lacking geometry and an exact, theoretically guided experimental technique, Goethe could not penetrate to the ultimate forces of nature that are the proper realm of physical science. The poet, in his enthusiasm, in his longing for the realm of spirit, fails to recognize the legitimate claims of the material world. The duty of the scientist, on the other hand, is to discover the mechanisms of matter behind the appearances. This pathway is quite different from the poet's; yet it is not entirely blind to the inspiration of genius, and ultimately physical research is justified by enlarging the culture of humankind through subordination of the mechanisms of matter to the purposes of the ethical spirit (ibid., 30–43).

Helmholtz's understanding of Goethe's scientific work thus rests on his theory of the dichotomy of poet and scientist. A characterological or typological trait of the poet prevents him from grasping the real essence of science. On the other hand, the scientist must, to some extent, be open to the demands of spirit, and science is fundamentally part of a grand ethical quest. Earlier critics of the Farbenlehre had almost invariably raised the point that poets and scientists have different concerns and talents, but it was Helmholtz who made this distinction programmatic for understanding not only Goethe but also the very nature of science. Goethe's apparent inability to grasp the essence of Newton's science reveals the chief differences between those who cultivate imagination and human truth and those who pursue objective truth in nature. For the next seventy-five years both scientists and scholars followed Helmholtz's lead in their criticism of the poet-scientist Goethe.

The essay suffers from a curious imbalance, however. Although Helmholtz unified the themes of the earlier criticism, he also minimized an important concession that his predecessors had allowed: He concentrated on the physical aspects of the Farbenlehre to the exclusion of the physiological and the psychological–aesthetic portions. He unrelentingly insisted that Goethe's science was intrinsically unphysical or antiphysical, a fact made evident by Goethe's opposition to Newton. Goethe's assault on Newton seemed to betray an incomprehension of all modern science per se. His apparent incapacity to understand physical science demanded not a scientific inquiry into the subject of color but rather a psychological inquiry into the mind and soul of Goethe as individual and poet. Helmholtz praised Goethe's descriptive powers, but in an age when the successes of abstract theoretical and applied physics seemed limitless this was hardly calculated to inspire trust in Goethe's scientific abilities. By disallowing the Farbenlehre's claim to be a genuinely physical science, Helmholtz undermined essentially its claim to being scientific. Thus there could be no good reason to take seriously either the work itself or its implicit attempt to discover a theoretical unity of physiology, physics, chemistry, and the perception of and reaction to color.

At the turn of the century there occurred a partial rehabilitation of the Farbenlehre when physiologists investigating the processes of color perception, chiefly advocates of Ewald Hering's color research and theories, rediscovered Goethe's so-called physiological colors. They came to regard the Farbenlehre as a legitimate progenitor of the physiology of the color sense, and scholars and scientists began to examine the work for anticipations of modern discoveries (Jablonski 1930). Although they viewed the work as a beginning science – pointing to the relevant phenomena and, to a certain extent, anticipating several important theoretical concepts – rather than a full-fledged science, this renewed credibility won the Farbenlehre a larger audience among laymen and scientists. The philosophical implications of Goethe's science also attracted increased attention and research, and literary historians no longer needed to feel embarrassed about Goethe's putative gaffe, because now they could cite praise from eminent researchers. By the 1920s and early 1930s the Farbenlehre was stirring even greater interest in the aftermath of the birth of the new physics, an interest reflected in the influential 1941 lecture on the doctrines of Goethe and Newton in light of modern physics by Werner Heisenberg.

Heisenberg agreed with traditional critics that Goethe's "fight for a more 'living' science in the field of color theory" was over; "the decision on 'right' and 'wrong' in all questions of detail has long since been taken. Goethe's colour theory has in many ways borne fruit in art, physiology and aesthetics. But victory, and hence influence on the research of the following century, has been Newton's" (Heisenberg 1952, 60). Nevertheless, Heisenberg admired what Goethe had accomplished. A chance observation had spurred Goethe to contradict Newton and begin an intensive investigation of the origins of color, which Goethe attributed to "the combination of light and dark" in what he called the "Urphenomenon" of color. "This concept brings together into a unified, orderly whole the many effects of colours in our world of the senses rather by way of a guiding idea, based not on reason but on experience" (ibid., 62). In the Newtonian scheme, on the other hand, the simplest phenomenon is of a completely different order, "the narrow monochromatic ray purified by complicated mechanisms from light of other colours and directions" (ibid.). This phenomenon enables us to measure and predict optical phenomena, and every color can be associated with a number. What is simple in Newton's system, the monochromatic ray, is a complex phenomenon according to Goethe, and the simplicity of white light that was so evident to Goethe is denied by Newton.

Although Goethe's complaint that Newtonian physics does not encounter nature may be well taken, "on the other hand, the physicist can legitimately reproach Goethe in that his theory cannot be regarded as scientific since it cannot lead to a real control of optical phenomena" (ibid., 63). His theory tries to link together phenomena that to the physicist's mind must be kept separate and does not observe a careful distinction between subjective and objective. "It is just the very unity of Goethe's theory which [the physicist] cannot accept" (ibid., 64). Heisenberg's preliminary sketch then concludes with a judgment that leads to a new question.

It is clear to all who have worked more recently on Goethe's and Newton's theories, that nothing can be gained from an investigation of their separate rights and wrongs. It is true that a decision can be taken on all points of detail and that in the few instances, where a real contradiction exists, Newton's scientific method is superior to Goethe's intuitive power, but basically the two theories simply deal with different things. (Ibid.)

The rest of the lecture is devoted to defining the domains proper to Goethe's kind of color science and to Newton's. Heisenberg disagrees with those who find no mathematics in the Farbenlehre (he believes Goethe's contrasts and symmetries recall the modern mathematical theory of symmetry), questions the adequacy of the poet–scientist dichotomy, and emphasizes that to say Goethe deals with color subjectively but Newton objectively is to forget that modern physics itself has blurred the distinction between subject and object. Although Goethe blundered when he entered the realm of Newton's physics, the very dilemma of modern physics is that it deals with a shadowy underworld rather than with the world of direct experience, that it depends on human decision and intervention that forces this underworld to appear, and that it is subject to all the fundamental limitations of human understanding. Heisenberg therefore concludes that it is necessary to continue Goethe's struggle against the physical theory of color on an extended front. Science singles out from the manifold physical phenomena a finite and limited field. The most serious task facing science today is to find the appropriate sciences for the various fields and aspects of reality. "Dividing reality in this way into different aspects immediately resolves the contradictions between Goethe's and Newton's theories of colour. In the great structure of science, the two theories take up different positions" (ibid., 75).

Heisenberg's conclusions appear conciliatory but are not revolutionary: They do not rehabilitate Goethe's physical science but only his sense of the limitations of physical science. Heisenberg's argument is important not because it defends Goethe from the accusation of being unscientific – the physiologists had already done this decades earlier – but because an eminent representative of physics retreated from the Helmholtzian opinion that the Farbenlehre, being not truly physical, was not truly scientific. Although some may argue even with Heisenberg's formulation (e.g., Jaki 1969), his 1941 lecture still expresses the mainstream of scientific opinion about Goethe's Farbenlehre vis-à-vis Newton and modern science. The question of how Goethe's struggle might be continued has nevertheless received very little attention.

In addition, by casting doubt on the common explanations for Goethe's failure in physical science – his lack of mathematics, his failure to be objective, the difference between the poet and the scientist – without disagreeing with the idea that Goethe failed, Heisenberg leaves us without any explanation of the reasons behind Goethe's mistakes. For granted that there are many different aspects of the world that demand different kinds of sciences, and that the Newtonian theory claimed to account for aspects of the world that it cannot really explain, why did Goethe not state this criticism and then begin developing an appropriate science for that aspect of reality he was truly concerned with? That is, why did Goethe criticize and try to displace the theory of Newton in the first place? Surely this ought to be one of the initial questions we ask when studying the Farbenlehre; but it is doubtful that we can answer it with any rigor if we proceed immediately to vague generalities, such as the typology of poet and scientist or the various aspects of reality, or to peripheral issues, such as the inner workings of Goethe's psychology or his resentments. Yet by asserting that the matters of detail have been settled in Newton's favor and that nothing can be gained from an investigation of the separate rights and wrongs, Heisenberg seems to deny access to what, on the face of things, is the most natural way to determine the reasons for Goethe's apparent failure in physical science – that is, by ferreting out the errors in the works on color, by analyzing the arguments he produced against Newton, and by examining how exactly he justified his alternative science. On the contrary, the writings of Newton and Goethe should be examined to define as exactly as possible the issues involved and to determine where the proper boundaries of the science of color fall according to their interpretations.

If Heisenberg's critique of the traditional explanations of Goethe's failure is valid, then what remains of the tradition is chiefly the conviction that Goethe committed a fundamental error; a clear notion of what produced the error is absent. Yet in the controversy over Goethe's Farbenlehre, despite the constant refrains that Goethe's errors are clear and essentially all matters of detail are settled, very few writers have considered the errors in detail. The accusation is an assertion, not a demonstration. The literature about the Farbenlehre is full of wonderment that only rarely leads to circumspect investigation.

The Farbenlehre is still shrouded in a number of mysteries, none of which is more perplexing than the question of why Goethe felt compelled to diverge from the Newtonian theory. If we could give a reasonable, well-documented answer to this question, we might also gain insight into what Goethe hoped to achieve with his alternative science. On the other hand, some kind of adequate understanding of what Goethe was attempting positively may be prerequisite for grasping fully the motives that led him to reject Newton's optics. At least in principle, we ought to be able to pose the questions separately, even if we are ultimately compelled to acknowledge that they are intertwined. Furthermore, it is improbable that every aspect of Goethe's criticism of Newton depends on the whole of the Farbenlehre and vice versa, so that at least some of his polemic may be salvageable whatever one thinks of the adequacy of the Farbenlehre. Once we are in a position to judge better the right and the wrong, the just and the unjust, perhaps we can understand why Goethe resorted to polemic in the first place. To reach that end, we must set aside, as much as we are able, the excesses of passion that have unfortunately ruled so much of the controversy. Goethe and Newton were both men of prodigious intellect and ability. It would serve us well to keep this in mind and, at least provisionally, to assume that both understood what they were doing. Even if ultimately we conclude that it is proper to ascribe their differences to the one's being a scientist and the other's being a poet, we must beware of denying to either a share in capacities that are characteristic of all human beings.

Color theory, color phenomena

Replicating Newton's discovery in a rough and ready way is fairly easy. If you take a triangular glass prism with a large refracting angle (close to 60 degrees), you can catch a beam of sunlight entering a window and observe the spectrum (or spectra, since there are several reflected and refracted images) cast on the wall, ceiling, or floor. To be more exacting, we would need to exclude as much as possible all sources of extraneous light, so that only direct sunlight would be admitted. The light would shine into a long room (15 to 20 feet from window to wall) through a small circular aperture at the window. (Of course, the aperture needs to face the sun.)

Reproducing what Newton called his crucial experiment, however, requires considerably more effort. We need two boards with small apertures, two prisms with large refracting angles, and a way to fix one of the prisms rigidly in place. The first prism would be held at the window-shut aperture; part of the refracted light would pass through a small aperture in a board fixed close to the first prism; perhaps twelve feet further along would be fixed another board with a small aperture; immediately beyond this there would be a second prism fixed rigidly in place to receive the ray of light and refract it in the same direction as the first prism (see Fig. 1.1). With practice we can learn to rotate the prism so that different colors are cast on the hole in the second board and thus refracted a second time. Because the two boards and the second prism are fixed in place, the angle at which the light strikes the second prism will be constant, no matter what color light from the first refraction we cast upon the aperture in the second board; despite this equality of the incident angle, the light will be refracted to different degrees by the second prism. Light that comes from the violet extreme of the first refraction's spectrum will be most refracted, from the red extreme least refracted; the intermediate parts will be refracted intermediately. Consequently, white light consists of many different colors of light that have different degrees of refractibility or, to use Newton's term, refrangibility.

Another demonstration entails reproducing the first experiment of Newton's *Opticks*, in which we need only put side by side against a black background two rectangles, one an intensely saturated (dark) blue, the other an intense red, and observe them through a prism. We will see that they are no longer side by side, the blue rectangle being apparently moved further away from the line of sight than the red. Once more we see that light is differently refrangible, and according to color.

This doctrine of differential refrangibility appears to have some decisive consequences for the science of color. One is that color, or more precisely the quality of producing color, is inherent not in physical bodies or in the eye but in the rays. First, the colors of the spectrum are not the colors of any body; rather, they are produced from what seemed originally to be white light. Second, if we illuminate a body with homogeneal light (what we usually call monochromatic light, radiation of a single wave-

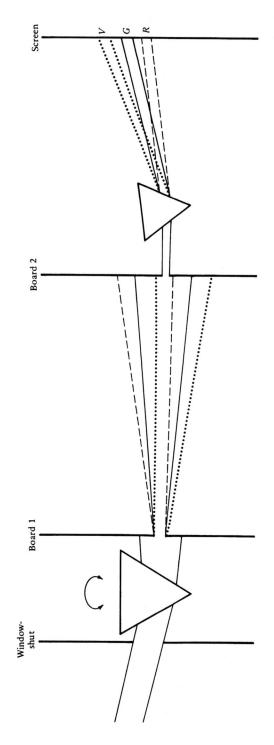

Figure 1.1 Newton's experimentum crucis. Rotating the first prism (on the left) while keeping the other prism and the two boards with apertures stationary makes the complete spectrum cast on the second board move up and down, so that different colors fall on the aperture and pass through. The violet portion is refracted most (to V), the red the least (to R), green and other colors intermediately. (This figure is not drawn to scale.)

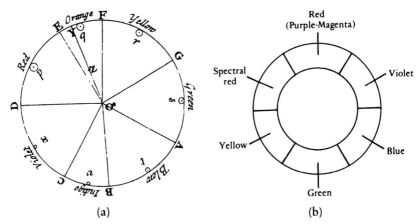

(a)   (b)

Figure 1.2   a) The color circle of Newton. (From Newton, Opticks, 1st ed. [London, 1704], Book 1, Part 2, Figure 11 from Plate 3. Photograph courtesy of History of Science Collections, Cornell University Libraries.) b) The color circle of Goethe.

length), that body will appear to be of the color that such light produces or, if the body absorbs all the light, black. Moreover, reflection, refraction, diffraction, and so forth do not alter the color-producing qualities of rays. Thus the so-called color of a natural body is nothing more than a function of its predisposition to reflect or absorb the various components of white light. This means that if we are given a specification of the percentage of light that a body reflects for every wavelength in the visible spectrum and know the exact composition (in terms of wavelength and intensity) of the illuminating light, we can predict exactly what the intensities will be at the various wavelengths in the reflected light and thus what the perceived color – presuming that our observer has unfatigued, normal vision – will be.

Newton offered a color circle or disk as a device to predict approximately the outcome of such mixtures of rays *(Opticks, 155)*. A line representing the spectrum is bent around into a circle so that the extreme violet point and the extreme red coincide (Fig. 1.2a). The circle then is used as follows. If we know that a given light consists of three parts red, two yellow, one green, and four blue, we position three markers on the circle in the red, two on the circle in the yellow, one in the green, and four in the blue and then determine the resulting center of gravity for the disk. If the center of gravity is the exact center of the disk, the color will be white; if not, the color is of the same hue as the spectral color on the radius drawn through the center of gravity, and more or less intense according to its distance from the white center.

Thus, the foundations of the Newtonian theory of color involve a doctrine of differential refrangibility and a function to account for the results of mixing the various kinds of rays. Since Newton's day there has been much empirical study and theoretical improvement of the ray-mixing function, but the roots go back to Newton; only occasionally has the doctrine of differential refrangibility been criticized. Goethe nevertheless directed his attacks chiefly against the formidable redoubt of differential refrangibility. Although the consensus of scientists and most scholars has always been that Goethe was dreadfully wrong, Goethe was on solid ground, and his polemics point up serious factual and methodological shortcomings in the work of Newton and his followers. Before going into the details, however, I wish to provide concrete evidence drawn from more reputable sources than Goethe that Newton's theory of differential refrangibility may be reasonably called into question and that his theory of color does not offer an adequate basis for a comprehensive chromatics.

When Newton first published his new theory of light and colors he made proof claims that several critics thought were excessive. One of the disputed matters was whether the prism in some way produced or manufactured the colors out of the white light (as so-called modificationist theories of color contend). As discussed in Chapter 3, Newton prevailed without ever justifying his claims to have proved the theory. For nearly two hundred years, however, it was thought that Newton had refuted his opponents and established the fact of differential refrangibility of rays already present in unrefracted white light, regardless of the nature of the rays (e.g., whether they are corpuscles or waves; see *Corresp.* 1: 177). Even in Goethe's lifetime this claim seemed to gain additional confirmation from the breakthrough to the modern wave theory of light. The older prevailing theory, that light consisted of small particles or corpuscles, was popularly attributed to Newton and, although he was never as explicitly a corpuscularist as his later followers, the triumph of the wave theory was generally seen as a defeat for the Newtonian view. Yet no one thought it necessary to revise the theory of white light and colors, for it was simply a matter of substituting one kind of ray for another, aetherial vibrations for corpuscles, and wave frequency and amplitude could stand for properties like particle mass and quantity.

In the latter part of the nineteenth century, however, the French physicist Louis-Georges Gouy showed that on the basis of the mathematical theory of waves it was not necessary to suppose that white light actually contained waves of all spectral frequencies, but rather one could argue that the prism or diffraction grating produced the differentiation. As A. I. Sabra has pointed out (1967, 280–81), the ensuing debate between Gouy, Lord Rayleigh, and Arthur Schuster on the one hand and Henri

Poincaré on the other reenacted, at a much higher level of sophistication, the debate of Newton and his critics over the original compositeness of white light. But the nineteenth-century dispute had a quite different outcome: the empirical and theoretical evidence came to be interpreted as more favorable to the modificationists. This makes it highly improbable, then, that Newton had truly swept from the field all modification theories. This renewed support for the modificationist view of white light

> raises the question whether Newton's experiments on refraction by prisms, which are usually said to prove the composite nature of white light, were of much significance in this respect. Since white light may be regarded as consisting merely of a succession of random pulses, of which the prism performs a Fourier analysis, the view that the colors are manufactured by the prism, which was held by Newton's predecessors, may be regarded as equally correct. (Jenkins and White 1976, 249–50)

That is, Newton's doctrine of differential refrangibility must be radically qualified; for although both schools acknowledge that a differentiation exists after refraction, the modificationists deny that before refraction there are already present all the rays to which Newton assigns the quality of differential refrangibility.

The other major constituent of Newton's theory, color as a function of ray mixing, is also open to question. Already in 1948 Gehrcke had shown that, by rotating appropriately patterned black-and-white disks illuminated only by light from a sodium lamp (which has just two spectral lines very close together in the yellow portion of the spectrum, at 5890 and 5896 Angstroms), one can obtain colors other than yellow; in fact, he was able to produce, under various circumstances, lilac, blue, green, yellow, orange, and red (Gehrcke 1948). More recently, Edwin Land and others have shown that a nearly full range of colors can be achieved by employing just two so-called monochromatic lights, in some instances even when both are of the same basic hue (yellow, in particular; see Land 1959a, b); and, in refutation of some of his early critics who claimed that the results, obtained with representations of natural settings, depended on color memory or eye fatigue, Land produced the same variety of colors with abstract patterns illuminated by flashes as brief as one-tenth of a second (Land 1977). In place of the notion that color is a function of radiation, he proposed that "colors in images arise not from the choice of wavelengths but from the interplay of longer and shorter wavelengths over the entire scene" (Land 1959b, 88). Color would thus be a function of a duality within a totality: The interrelation between the long-wave and the short-wave components is more significant than the exact wavelengths reflected to the eye. The Newtonian spectrum, far from revealing the essence of color, is rather an anomaly: "For all its beauty the spectrum is simply the accidental consequence of arranging stimuli in order of wavelength. The significant scale for images runs from warm colors through neutral colors to cool colors" (ibid., 91). Thus studying the spectrum and simple images produced in camera obscura may not reveal as much about color as the study of vision under natural conditions, where images appear in an illuminated field rather than as spots in dark surroundings (cf. Mundle 1971, ch. 9; and Hurvich 1981).

All modern color research of course relies heavily on spectral analysis, following the tradition of Newton; illuminants need to be carefully controlled for the sake of accuracy and reproducibility. Whether there is a simple relation between wavelength and perceived color, however, is not at all clear. Yet despite the new theories and phenomena, we continue to talk of light of a single wavelength as monochromatic, single colored, even though it is well known among color researchers that the perceived hue of so-called monochromatic light varies with luminance, duration of perception, and ambient illumination (Wasserman 1978, esp. chs. 5–8).

Certain problems accrue to the standard ray theory by virtue of the very appearance of the full spectrum. The rate of variation in hue as we proceed from one end of it to the other is not constant; there are broad stretches of basically uniform color separated by narrow bands in which the transition is rapid. If color change were strictly proportional to change in wavelength or frequency, this pattern would be impossible. One might be tempted to conclude that the eye is an imperfect detector. But, as Land in particular argues, the eye evolved not to serve for spectroscopic analysis but as an instrument of vision, for which purpose it would be unsuited if it were a passive receiver. The relative homogeneity in the spectrum of the different fields of color, to which we assign the generic names red, yellow, blue, and so forth, and the corresponding difficulty in discriminating any large number of variations of hue[2] show that color cannot be simply equated with specific wavelengths. Although we cannot do without the spectroscopic analysis of radiation in a comprehensive science of color, we cannot expect it alone to provide a theory that exhausts the chromatic phenomena.

Interestingly, the arguments of Gouy and Land relate to some of the themes and phenomena that were central to Goethe's case against Newton (a case that was formulated, of course, without the aid of a mathematical apparatus, which was essential to Gouy, whose argument depends on showing the indifference of the mathematical theory of waves to the preexistence in white light of all possible wavelengths). The phenomena of colored shadows were the catalyst for Land's original work; approximately 165 years earlier they had impelled Goethe to recognize that these same phenomena are caused not by the ray composition of light but by the lawful workings of the eye. Goethe like Land argued that color is due to a polarity; that the warm–cool schema more nearly reveals the nature of colors than the spectral scale of five or seven colors; that colored objects tend to retain their "natural" colors under various illumination (and for this and related reasons Goethe believed that it made good sense to speak of a body's natural color); and that the primary task of color science is to investigate colors as they appear under normal circumstances. In general accord with Gouy, though on the basis of a logical–rhetorical analysis of Newton's proofs rather than a mathematical one, Goethe insisted that colors might be produced from white light by the action of the matter of the prism on the light (see Appendix). Perhaps more than anything else, however, Goethe challenged Newton's theory on the grounds that it was not truly comprehensive, although it had been given the appearance of being so. This claim anticipates the next major point: Goethe was not so much interested in opposing "his" theory to another as in reopening the science of color to new kinds of investigations, recalling researchers' attention to the phenomenal basis of their theories, and reforming the method and purpose of scientific argumentation.

An overview of the argument

Because the background and rationale of Goethe's studies of color and his polemic against Newton's theory are complex, it may be useful to give now an overview of my argument, which will be substantiated in later chapters.

Although Goethe began as a dilettante in the science of color, within a few years of his first optical experiments (ca. 1790) he had achieved a unique position from which to assess Newton's theory. Probably none of his contemporaries had studied Newton's optical writings more intensively; certainly no one could approach him in the depth and breadth of his knowledge about the history of color science; nor was any other researcher as aware as he of a subtle decline and corruption that had occurred in chromatic science during the eighteenth century, not least in the teaching of Newton's theory. Furthermore, as a result of his attempt to survey and comprehend experientially the entire domain of color, including the phenomena not simply reducible to physical effects (e.g., colors produced by applying pressure to the eye, or the apparent harmonies and contrasts of colors), no one knew better the intrinsic limitations of the prevailing theory. The attacks on Newton's theory and his followers certainly do betray an offended amour-propre and sometimes contain errors and distortions; nevertheless, they proceed from a coherent conception of the nature and prerequisites of scientific theorizing and form part of a sustained and reasonable critique of Newton's method and his faithfulness to the phenomena of color. Moreover, although Goethe's initial rejection of the theory looks as though it was based on a misunderstanding of Newton, it more probably reflected what Goethe had learned about the theory from an error-marred account in an otherwise reputable textbook. This may seem to suggest that Goethe directed his criticisms at the wrong target, Newton rather than the corruptors of Newton, yet many of his criticisms apply to Newton as well.

Ironically, Goethe's first publications on color, the *Beiträge zur Optik* (1791–92), contain chiefly an implicit critique of Newton. The positive doctrine they present is as much a method (which, in aiming at comprehensive coverage of the phenomenal field, was directed toward overcoming what Goethe saw as the chief defect of the scientific work of many of his predecessors and contemporaries in experimental science) as it is a description and interpretation of the phenomena. But even in this positive teaching, Goethe left too many things implicit. Holding, as he did in the early 1790s, to a rigorous, even naive version of Baconian inductivism, which required him to withhold expressing his theoretical convictions so that the reader might come to the same conclusions by pure induction from the phenomena (a method which Goethe erroneously believed his contemporaries practiced), he ended by seeming to do little more than offer a series of experiments already well known, at least in principle; consequently, the few passages that broke through the Baconian reserve to point out a contrast with Newtonian theory made the work's chief purpose seem to be the refutation of Newton.

It has not been widely understood that *theory* does not have the same meaning for Goethe and Newton, and therefore direct comparisons based on the assumption that they are (or should be) guided by similar principles and methods and concerned with identical domains are misleading. Theory for Goethe is not a set of propositions or a mathematical modeling; rather it is more akin to something suggested in the root meaning of ancient Greek *theoria*, which was the activity of the spectator, a seeing and recognizing, a sense also conveyed by the German *Anschauung* ("onlooking," a perhaps simpler and more faithful rendering than the usual "intuition"). *Anschauung*, the direct and thoughtful viewing and experience of the phenomena, is the foundation of Goethe's science, although certainly not the whole of it. Moreover, it has not been sufficiently recognized that the approach of the later Farbenlehre is, in comparison with the *Beiträge*, greatly more ambitious and comprehensive in its articulation of the phenomenal domain, more modest in its epistemological claims, more sophisticated in its understanding of methodology, more explicit in its treatment of the interplay of subjectivity and objectivity, and more aware of the complex historical factors at work in the development of the sciences. The later Farbenlehre (which originates in the latter part of the 1790s and culminates in the 1810 publication of *Zur Farbenlehre*) did not supplant the earlier work; rather, the subsequent investigations remained faithful to its basic method but elaborated its methodological, historical, and philosophical presuppositions and placed it within a larger context.

Goethe started out with the hope of proceeding from absolutely certain propositions of limited scope toward equally certain propositions of ever greater generality. Like Newton, he believed that the goal of science was to find out the objective basis of the phenomena by using reason and experiments. Unlike Newton, however, he did not aim immediately at a comprehensive and ambitious theory but insisted on an exhaustive review of the relevant instances, whether provided by nature or experiment, and on a systematic attention to the modes and circumstances in which the phenomena appear and disappear. Goethe was highly critical of how Newton and his followers went about proposing and proving their theories, and more than anything else he intended to reform the ways in which scientific evidence was gathered, marshalled as proof, and presented for the edification of the scientific and nonscientific public. That is, his major aims from the beginning were methodological and pedagogical. His scientific contemporaries, however, seeing in his expositions little more than a rehash of well-known results and nonplussed by the apparent disagreement with Newton, completely overlooked these aims and for the most part let his writings pass without comment. The continued neglect by physicists compelled him to go back to the sources of color science; out of this historical regress developed both a profound philosophical understanding of science as bound by its history and a realization that inductive certainty is untenable because facts and phenomena are laden with theories. This at least partial constitution of factuality by theory opened the domain of phenomena to a variety of interpretations and constitutions, few of which could be dismissed out of hand.

It may seem astonishing that the mature Farbenlehre, with its explicit polemicizing against Newton's theory, was intrinsically pluralist. Indeed, Goethe was in a sense a limited pluralist in his work ca. 1790, for he believed even then that the best and most profound science would result only from the cooperation of researchers in many different disciplines, from the convergence of different approaches on a single object. Such cooperation might occasionally even require certain kinds of scientific polemic, for the convergence of approaches implies not the side-by-side cultivation of mutually indifferent points of view but rather a constant criticism, comparison, appraisal, and reappraisal of the various positions with respect to the phenomena and to one another, so that the single truth Goethe initially hoped for might emerge in perfect clarity. Yet at this early stage Goethe was not inclined to polemicize publicly. Only after the emergence of his mature pluralism – in which there is no longer a single, unambiguous propositional truth, in which there is even room for a Newtonian approach – did he openly polemicize against the Newtonian theory. As ironic as this may seem, that mature pluralism was accompanied by polemics, it was precisely the pluralistic spirit, rooted in an understanding of the theory-laden nature of the phenomena, that virtually mandated a public confrontation with a generally prevailing theory that ruled over the minds and experience of scientists and laymen alike.

From the results of his initial foray into optics Goethe saw the need to make color the object of an independent discipline, which required that a science of chromatics be instituted in its own right, free of dependence on the ray theory of Newton. By realizing that the rigorous inductivism professed by his contemporaries was an ideal more breached than practiced, and by reflecting on the predominant indifference to and rejection of his earliest efforts, he was gradually impelled to rethink the principles of his chromatics and to broaden the scope of his investigations to encompass history, philosophy, and a host of other factors. He thus progressed from being an amateur of several sciences who occasionally reflected about method to a full-blown practitioner who had become a historian and even a philosopher of science. Through his writings and his example, he hoped to help bring about a major reformation of the scientific approach to nature.

Only by combining the perspectives of the history of science and the philosophy of science, and by bringing to bear some understanding of the diversity of the phenomena and theories of color, can a fair assessment of Goethe's Farbenlehre be made; only against this backdrop can the scope, achievements, and failures of both Goethe's and Newton's color sciences become apparent. In particular, it is precisely the manifold richness of Goethe's Farbenlehre that has made it so difficult to evaluate, because no single discipline, whether natural scientific or humanistic, is in a position to see it as a whole.

Neither critics nor proponents have been especially fortunate in choosing their perspectives. Those who have concentrated on details – like Goethe's unhappy attempt to explain the colors of refraction by appealing to the effect of a putative secondary image (see Appendix) – have cultivated the impression that the Farbenlehre can be rejected out of hand (mutatis mutandis, the same can be said of the treatment of Newton's optics by Goethe's proponents). On this view, the "facts" refuted the theory. But this approach at the very least overlooked completely that Goethe had challenged the factual nature of what was offered as fact and had rejected the primacy of the method of crucial experiments.[3] The essentially erroneous belief that Goethe was wrong about the facts inevitably undermines attempts to give an overall assessment of his science. The emphasis on the supposedly unequivocal verdict of the facts doubtless also makes any effort to articulate the historical circumstances in which Goethe (and Newton) worked seem wasted. But the lack of historical perspective eliminates dimensions that might have made the Farbenlehre and the accompanying rejection of Newton much more plausible. Again I refer to Helmholtz. In his 1853 lecture he said that "Newton's color theory is based on the assumption [*Annahme*] that there is light of different kinds, which also differ, among other things, in the impressions of color they make in the eye," and he could not understand "how anyone, regardless of what his views about colors are, can deny that the theory in itself is fully consequent, that its assumptions, once granted, explain the facts treated completely and indeed simply" (Helmholtz 1971, 30).

Without realizing it, Helmholtz conceded with these words one of Goethe's cardinal points. Newton had insisted that his theory was no mere assumption, a hypothetical instrument that correlates facts. He and most of his eighteenth-century followers claimed that the theory had been shown to be self-evidently true by experiment; the theory itself was fact, and assumptions were not involved. It was this claim of factuality, of freedom from hypothesis, of direct and immediate proof by experiments, that Goethe found most problematic of all. Had he been able to wrest from his contemporaries Helmholtz's tacit admission of the hypothetical nature of Newton's theory, he could have declared a major victory in his campaign. He would have accomplished his first goal, to make preeminently clear that the theory itself was a hypothesis and not a fact.

Because of the character of Goethe's chromatic science, because of his disagreement with Newton over the nature of theory, we must do more than summarize Goethe's results, for that would actually distort his science by ignoring its multidimensionality; rather, we must experience, through words if not through actual experiment, the phenomena out of which the Farbenlehre grew, and thus grasp the sense in which his way of looking at color is theoretical, yet not theoretical in the manner of Newton. To establish this we shall need to examine not only writings by Goethe and some of the phenomena of color, but also Newton's writings and some other documents and episodes in the history of science. We shall not undertake a comprehensive analysis of Goethe's entire doctrine of color – the present work is a necessary preliminary to such an undertaking – but we shall try to command sufficient background to understand how Goethe's Farbenlehre came about, what its major themes and principles are, and why it failed; this inevitably requires that we properly understand the focus and motifs of his critique of Newton and

Newton's followers. As we shall see, Goethe contributed to his own failure. Yet we shall also see that the age in which he worked had narrowed the conception of what legitimate science was so that hostility, and often an inability to comprehend, were the principal responses toward someone who, in an often idiosyncratic way, tried to show the one-sidedness of the theory of differential refrangibility according to color and the fatefulness of historical decisions that had been taken without proper reflection.

In reading Goethe as scientist, as philosopher of science, and as historian of science, we shall occasionally find ways in which he anticipated later work. But it would be a mistake to try to rehabilitate Goethe merely by turning him into a twentieth-century scientist or historian or philosopher before his time. We shall try instead to uncover the logic and project of Goethe's science. We shall concentrate on his efforts to amplify, by comprehensively outlining the scope of color phenomena, the narrow base on which the modern science of color had been founded; on his attempts to discipline the use of imagination and hypotheses in science; and on his hopes to incorporate a historical dimension into modern science that would help preserve a sense of the accomplishments of the past as well as keep alive the sense of future possibilities through the use of the past.

Goethe recognized that the natural sciences are among the most noble and ambitious undertakings that have ever been conceived, but that even in the best of circumstances there would always be temptations and dangers accompanying the benefits and achievements they had to offer. He was convinced that the sciences demand the use of all the faculties of human beings, not least of which is human judgment, which views the present and anticipates the future through its experience of the past. For Goethe the measure of science was thus to be found in the ampleness of human judgment, which in turn points to the ampleness of human culture or, to use a term that needs to be understood in its full scope, politics. An essay into the Farbenlehre is an essay into the politics of science, not in a narrow, pejorative sense, but in the sense that is as old and large as the tradition of political philosophy itself: a politics that determines

which of the sciences ought to be studied in the state, and which ones each class of citizens should learn, and how far....
Further, it uses the other sciences concerned with action, and moreover legislates what must be done and what avoided. Hence its end will include the ends of the other sciences, and so will be the human good. (Aristotle, *Nicomachean Ethics* 1094a28–1094b7)

2

The Farbenlehre in its origin

Before reviewing the early history of Goethe's interest in color and the beginnings of his own Farbenlehre, we must first consider the flawed presentation of Newton's theory in scientific textbooks and encyclopedias of the eighteenth century, in order to recognize the full scope of Goethe's intentions, and then briefly examine the method Goethe had already followed in his scientific work of the 1780s. After investigating Goethe's first publication on color, including its implicit criticism of prevailing doctrine and method, we shall consider the failure of this work to gain an audience and the reasons for his delaying further publication until 1810.

Goethe's writings on color

In the years 1786–88, Goethe began investigating whether one could ascertain rules to govern the artistic use of color. Later (probably in early 1790; see Matthaei 1949), in the hope that the physical theory of color would provide a guide, he performed his first experiments with prismatic colors. More extensive work with the prism led to the two *Beiträge zur Optik* (contributions to optics) that appeared in 1791 and 1792; they retail in comprehensive fashion phenomena observed by looking through prisms at objects and prepared displays. Although Goethe intended to continue the series of *Beiträge* until he had run the gamut of color phenomena, and although he continued for several years to work toward this end, he did not publish anything more on color, apart from some verse epigrams, until 1810, when *Zur Farbenlehre* appeared.[1] This multivolume work incorporated the early *Beiträge* with some modification, but it was in essence a renewed attempt to approach the phenomena of color.

Zur Farbenlehre consists of four parts, in three volumes. Best known is the first, didactic part, "Entwurf einer Farbenlehre" (project or plan of a color doctrine), which itself is divided into six sections. The first three present the known (ca. 1800) phenomena of color organized under the principal headings of physiological, physical, and chemical colors. The last three sections provide an overview of general notions derived from the particular phenomena presented in the first three sections; an analysis of the relationships of other scientific, technical, and cultural disciplines to color science; and an examination of the psychological and aesthetic effects of color, what Goethe called the "sinnlich–sittliche Wirkung der Farbe." The second, polemical part of Zur Farbenlehre, "Enthüllung der Theorie Newtons" (the unveiling of Newton's theory), is in essence a commentary on the first book of the Opticks. The third, historical part, "Materialien zur Geschichte der Farbenlehre" (materials for the history of color science), is but a fragment of the history Goethe originally planned; nevertheless, it provides an ample survey of the ideas, opinions, reflections, and methods, from ancient to modern times, that have constituted the science of color. It treats color science both internally and externally, both as a discipline arising from intrinsically scientific questions and as a human activity shaped by factors that go beyond the boundaries of science, from individual psychology to broad currents of history. The work ends with the fragmentary fourth part, which consists of a supplemental essay (by Thomas Seebeck, on the chemical effects of colored light) and colored illustrations and figures with commentary.

After 1810 Goethe continued to read the current literature on color but published only occasionally, chiefly by way of supplements to Zur Farbenlehre. In 1813 and 1820 there appeared essays on polarization colors; in 1822 he published a collection of brief articles keyed to the divisions of the 1810 work; and in the last decade of his life he began planning a revision of the Farbenlehre, although no publication resulted.[2]

Goethe's work in color science: the beginnings

The "Konfession des Verfassers," the last section of the "Materialien zur Geschichte der Farbenlehre" and the conclusion of the entire Zur Farbenlehre, gives an account of how Goethe came to his studies on color and of the path he subsequently followed. According to this narrative, he first approached the subject with the hope of discovering principles for the use of color in art. During his first journey to Italy (1786–88), he noticed that artists were able to enunciate rules for virtually all the elements of painting and drawing except color and coloring. The artists he associated with were unable to explain their practice to his satisfaction. A reference work also gave little useful information, so he began his own investigation. A friend painted pictures to test some of Goethe's ideas, but without any definite results. He also recorded observations of colors in nature, but nothing coherent emerged from these occasional impressions.

After returning to Weimar, he determined to find out what natural science had to say about color.

Ultimately I recognized that one has to approach colors, considered as physical phenomena, from the perspective of nature first of all, if one wants to gain something about them for the purposes of art. Like everyone in the world I was convinced that all the colors were contained in light; I had never been told otherwise, and I had never had the slightest reason for doubting it, since I had taken no further interest in the matter. At university I had had physics like everyone else and had been shown experiments. Winckler in Leipzig, one of the first to achieve merit in the study of electricity, treated this specialty very minutely and lovingly, so that even now I can recall almost completely all the experiments with their attendant circumstances....On the other hand I do not recall ever having seen the experiments by which the Newtonian theory is supposed to be proved; after all, in experimental physics courses they are usually postponed until there is sunny weather, and they are shown out of the running sequence of the lectures.

As I was now thinking about approaching colors from the perspective of physics, I read in some compendium or other the customary chapter, and, since I could not derive anything for my purposes from the theory as it stood there, I undertook at least to see the phenomena for myself. (HA, 14: 256–57)

To reproduce the basic experiments, Goethe borrowed equipment from a friend. He set up a room as a camera obscura but never had time to conduct his experiments. When the friend demanded the return of his equipment, Goethe decided to take at least one look through a prism – something he had not done since his youth.

I remembered well that everything appeared many-colored, but in what manner was no longer present to my mind. At that very moment I was in a room that had been painted completely white; I expected, mindful of the Newtonian theory as I placed the prism before my eyes, to see the light that comes from there to my eye split up into so many colored lights.

How astonished I was, then, when the white wall, observed through the prism, remained white just as before; that only there, where darkness adjoined on it, did a more or less determinate color appear; finally, that the window bars appeared in the liveliest colors of all, whereas no trace of coloring was to be seen in the light gray sky outside. It did not take much deliberation for me to recognize that a boundary is necessary to produce colors, and I immediately said to myself, as if by instinct, that the Newtonian teaching is false. (HA, 14: 259)

Scientists have always recognized the import of this moment, for it betrays an inadequate conception of what Newton's theory requires. What Goethe saw is explicable according to Newton's doctrine that light is differentially refrangible according to color. A ray of light upon encountering a refracting surface is "decomposed" into a virtually infinite number of component color rays[3] (see Fig. 2.1). In the case of direct vision through the prism we need only consider what happens along

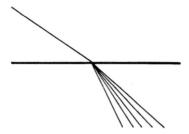

Figure 2.1 *A commonly used illustration exemplifying Newton's theory.*

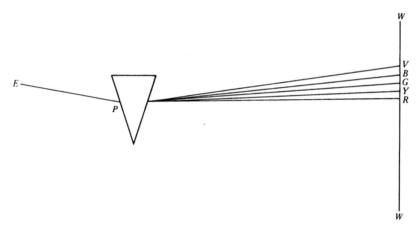

Figure 2.2 *Because of differential refraction, the various color-producing rays must come from different parts of the white wall (WW) in order to be refracted into the line PE, so that the eye at E might perceive white.*

the line of sight *EP* (see Fig. 2.2). If, for example, *EP* is a ray of white light traveling *toward,* and refracted by, the prism, and if this ray could be isolated in camera obscura, the result would be a continuous spectrum *VBGYR,* with violet the most refracted, red the least. Because the paths of light rays undergoing refraction are in principle reversible, if a violet-producing ray followed the indicated line from *V* to the prism, it would travel the line *EP,* as would the blue-producing ray following the line from *B,* and so forth across the spectrum for points *VBGYR* and all intermediate points.

Thus *EP* will be a white-producing ray if we can manage to get all the components of white to follow their respective paths so as to be refracted into *EP.* This is precisely what happens when the wall is white; for although all the unrefracted rays coming from the wall *WW* produce

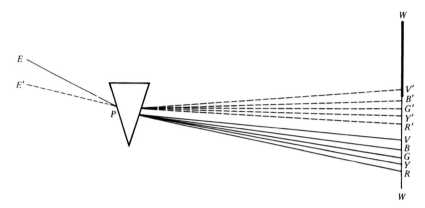

Figure 2.3   The upper part of the wall (WW) is painted black. An eye at E will see white along the ray EP (the components of which come from RYGBV), whereas along E'P the component that needs to come from V' is missing, so that the light will appear colored.

white, the differential prismatic refraction assures that the only component of the ray from V refracted along *EP* is violet-producing (the other components are refracted at slightly different angles), the only component from B so refracted is blue-producing, and so forth, and for every other possible line of sight a similar conclusion holds.

If there is some boundary in the field of vision (e.g., an area of black), the result is somewhat different. As one gets close to the boundary, the superposition of rays will no longer be complete. In Fig. 2.3, for certain lines of sight such as *EP*, all the components of white can be gathered from the segment *VR*. But lines of sight such as *E'P* will lack some of the components; the violet constituent must come from point *V'*, but no light is coming from this point, so that the color of the light along *E'P* will be the "sum" of red, yellow, green, and blue, but not violet (the result is presumably a shade of yellow). For lines of sight below *E'P*, even more components will be lost. Eventually, the process reaches a point at which only red will contribute a component to the line of sight and, finally, a point from which no light travels along the line of sight.

Thus the result of Goethe's experience is not surprising. What is surprising is that such scanty experimentation provoked the bold conclusion that Newton's theory was wrong. Goethe even admitted in the "Konfession" that a physicist subsequently tried to convince him that Newton's theory was capable of explaining what he had seen (*HA,* 14: 260–61), but Goethe would not give up his conviction.

As it stands, Goethe's account does not lend much support to the argument that some extrascientific prejudice was at work – for example, a conviction that white light, which appears so simple and pure, cannot be a compound of all the different colors. According to his earlier remarks, he was convinced like everyone else that the colors were contained in the light. Moreover, it is on very specific grounds that he rejects the theory: he claims that it had overlooked an essential circumstance, the boundary between light and dark.

Why did Goethe expect what he did? Why did he so swiftly draw the conclusion about Newton? Perhaps we should note that the narrative suggests the passage of a certain, though relatively short, period of observation and experiment; that is, his outburst was not quite instantaneous. Nevertheless, he must have been very sure of what would, but did not, happen. He clearly did not anticipate that a border or contrast in the field of vision would be necessary for color to appear.

The continuation of the account makes clear that Goethe did not read any of Newton's writings until he was already far advanced in his early work (HA, 14:263). The evidence suggests that he first examined Newton's optical writings at about the time part 1 of the Beiträge zur Optik was published. Apparently his original misimpression did not come directly from Newton. Nor are the physics lectures Goethe attended in Leipzig (when he was in his teens) a likely source of his expectation. Two passages in the "Konfession," however, provide important clues: He turned to Newton's writings after having been put off by "the obsequiousness of the compendia" (HA, 14: 263), and upon first deciding to consider the physical nature of colors he "read in some compendium or other the customary chapter" (HA, 14: 257). What textbooks might Goethe have consulted and what would he have found there?

The German scientific compendia and their problems

In the historical part of Zur Farbenlehre Goethe included a section devoted to eighteenth-century compendia and textbooks of natural and experimental philosophy, chiefly those used as texts in German schools and universities or as reference works; in all he lists upward of twoscore works (HA, 14: 206–15). These textbooks, with titles such as physics, experimental physics, physical library, physical institutes, elements of physics, and theory or doctrine of nature, are compilations and condensations of information on the elements of inanimate nature. Topics would include magnetism, electricity, light, force and motion; chemistry was likely to be excluded. By their nature, these works were not calculated to make extraordinary technical demands on the reader (in general they did not require any sophisticated mathematical knowledge), nor would they ordinarily include recent discoveries or theories. As such, they are not always reliable indicators of the actual state of work in natural philosophy at the time of their publication; however, they do reflect the state of the basic teaching of natural philosophy to the best-educated young students of the era. As we shall see, references to optics and color in these books indicate that their authors – most of whom were natural philosophers, some quite distinguished – did not completely understand Newtonian theory and its consequences.

Goethe examined most of the texts in his listing of eighteenth-century compendia comparatively late in his color studies, while preparing the historical part of *Zur Farbenlehre*. Ascertaining which texts he consulted when doing his earlier research is difficult, because his activities during the late 1780s and early 1790s are not consistently documented by contemporaneous records. Despite this problem, there is strong evidence that the compendium Goethe referred to in the "Konfession des Verfassers" was Johann Christian Polykarp Erxleben's *Anfangsgründe der Naturlehre*.[4] Goethe more than once acknowledged his high regard for this work and its importance in his scientific education. In an outline of his scientific development, a comment on the decade of the 1780s referred to "the various editions of Erxleben at Wittenberg, a decisive advantage" (*WA* II, 11: 301). A passage in the fragment "Aphoristisches, Zur Morphologie" is even more explicit:

[A]nd so my nature studies rest on the pure base of living experience; who can take away from me that I was born in 1749, that I (to overleap a great deal) faithfully instructed myself out of Erxleben's *Naturlehre* first edition, that I did not so much first see in print the expansion of the other editions, which piled up without limit owing to Lichtenberg's attentiveness, as rather hear of and experience immediately in progress each new discovery. (*WA* II, 6: 218–19)

Moreover, the only footnote in the first installment of the *Beiträge zur Optik* was a citation of the fifth edition of Erxleben.

Erxleben's treatment of color is found almost entirely in one chapter, "Of Light." After sections on the basic principles of geometric optics and vision, theories of light, the eye's way of judging the distance and size of objects, and the laws governing reflections and refractions by means of mirrors and lenses, Erxleben considers color in "The Colors of the Prism" and "How Bodies Display Colors," as well as in a single paragraph of the section "Of Optical Instruments: The Eye, and Its Defects." He begins with the spectrum obtained by refracting a beam of light in camera obscura:

If in a darkened room one intercepts with a triangular glass prism the bundle of parallel rays of the sun falling through a small round hole, after refraction the rays are no longer parallel but instead diverge more and more. If one intercepts these refracted rays with a screen, they will form thereon an oblong rectangular image that is bounded above and below with curved lines and that consists of the following colors lying one above the other and flowing into one another: red, orange, yellow, green, bright blue, dark blue, violet. (Erxleben 1787, par. 362)

In eighteenth-century science texts, this statement stands as one of the more complete descriptions of how the spectrum is formed and what it looks like, and even today it can be accepted as an adequate description of what occurs when reproducing Newton's experiment. Nevertheless, it is not as complete as it might have been. For example, the spectrum does not appear in the form described unless the screen is placed at a sufficiently large distance from the prism. By completely omitting this condition, Erxleben gives the impression that the description holds true for every distance. Although he specifies that the hole for admitting the light should be small, even then the visible image on the screen will have a white center with color at its fringes when the screen is placed close to the prism. Furthermore, the number of colors one sees, their hue, and the proportion of the entire spectrum that each area of color occupies all vary with changing positions of the screen. Nor is it strictly true that the rays of the sun are parallel before refraction. Yet the entire description is predicated on the postulated existence of real rays that can be represented by geometric lines. This supposition is traditional in the theory of geometric optics and was already well established in Newton's day. Although for most purposes the line rays depicted as coming from the sun can be treated as parallel, in the theory strictly construed they are not. The most oblique rays contained within the beam form an angle approximately equal to the apparent angle subtended by the disk of the sun, about 31 minutes of arc, slightly more than half a degree. This small deviation from the parallel is not completely insignificant, however, because, given this slight obliquity of the rays, the geometric theory predicts a certain elongation of the spectral image, except for a unique orientation of the prism. Yet in his specifications for the experiment, Erxleben omits mentioning the inclination of the prism to the light.

Erxleben goes on to describe further experiments and the conclusions that are to be drawn from them. A lens placed beyond the prism so that it intercepts all the refracted light will recombine the rays to form a white image; this demonstrates that white light is a mixture of all the colors. If a second prism is placed beyond the first so that it refracts just one of the colored rays that the first prism has already refracted (and thus separated from the other components of white), this single ray will retain its color after the second refraction, which will be least for a red ray, greatest for a violet. This differential refraction holds true not only for sunlight, but for all light, including that reflected by bodies.

Light that comes from other luminous bodies also produces by means of the prism the same seven kinds of colored rays that sunlight produces; even the light by means of which we see opaque bodies; as truly opaque bodies in the presence of luminous ones are also, as it were, luminous bodies. (Erxleben 1787, par. 365)

Interestingly, this passage no longer emphasizes the requirement that the rays of light be (nearly) parallel and that the beam passed through the prism be sufficiently narrow; rather, it can be taken to suggest that when one looks through a prism at objects of any kind, even a white wall, one will see the light separated into its component parts. From the context it cannot be reasonably expected that someone unfamiliar with the details of the theory and looking to Erxleben for enlightenment would have recognized that the outcomes of these different experiments vary with circumstances, especially with the distance of the object from the prism. Erxleben's omissions and vagueness, understandable as they may be, are misleading, and his statements are not sufficiently qualified.

In paragraph 366 Erxleben attributes these basic phenomena and the theory he has presented to Newton:

Newton concludes herefrom that not only sunlight but other light as well is an unhomogeneous light mixed and compounded out of seven kinds of simple and homogeneous lights. Each kind of this simple and homogeneous light has its own degree of refrangibility, and that is the reason that these simple kinds of light are separated from one another by the prism and that the ordinary ray of light is, as it were, split into its seven simple rays of light.

Thus, according to Erxleben, Newton concluded his theory directly from the phenomena of the preceding paragraphs; he performed the experiments described and drew the conclusions stated. Whether or not Newton did exactly or essentially what Erxleben says he did, the reader is left with the impression that Newton's theory and argument are what Erxleben says they are. Three imprecise experiments – one with a single prism, another with a lens and a prism, the third with two prisms – are alleged sufficient to establish the theory.

Up to this point Erxleben's condensed account is fairly typical of the German compendia from this period. A reader of other, nearly contemporary works[5] would have found the same basic theory and repertory of experiments, occasional encomia to Newton, and more or less categorical assertions of the theory's validity.[6] The texts generally agreed that the result was the surest that had yet been obtained in optics, indeed in all of experimental philosophy; they also distinguished, at least in the way their sections on optics or color were organized, this true and certain theory of differential refrangibility and color from the less secure attempts by natural philosophers (including Newton) to account for the phenomena of light and color by means of corpuscles, vibrations, or other hypotheses. In this they adhered, perhaps not knowingly, to Newton's caveat that his theory of differential refrangibility was not to be confused with speculations about the nature of light, because it presupposed nothing and arrived at the truth directly from the phenomena (*Corresp.*, 1: 164, 169, 177).

Because the Newtonian theory of white light and color was regarded as one of the premier accomplishments in all natural philosophy and as an exemplar of the proper method of experimental investigation (see Cohen 1956, ix–x, 17–19, 118–25; Westfall 1980, 640; and Guerlac 1977), it is not at all surprising that it should have figured so prominently in late eighteenth-century accounts of light and color. On the other hand, this prominence of the theory tended to make the science of color appear to be little more than a corollary or even an appendage of the physics of light. Color phenomena that did not fit into the presentation were relegated to secondary status, with the tacit implication that they were inessential or mere consequences of the theory. In particular, phenomena like contrast colors, which are due to the lawful workings of the process of vision, were often categorized (when they were remarked at all) as imaginary, accidental, or defective, caused by some failing or fatigue of the eye. By dint of Newton's achievement, color was considered to be a branch of the mathematicophysical science of light, and these other phenomena did not really fit into the theoretical structure that was supposed to explain color.

In the historical part of *Zur Farbenlehre* Goethe complained, with justification, that the textbook accounts of color repeated the same monotonous melody. Virtually all compendia gave unnecessarily incomplete and inexact accounts of the experiments that Newton had performed, their circumstances, and the course of his argument. Because of the unavoidable condensation of compendia, such deficiency in itself would not be a reproach. Yet sometimes the textbooks were guilty of errors or were unduly misleading. For instance, details were often given erratically or idiosyncratically. Gren describes Newton's experiments at considerable length, but in discussing the appearance of the spectrum he states without qualification that it is five times as long as it is broad and goes on to specify the "exact" proportion of the whole taken up by each individual color (Gren 1793, par. 575). These numbers, taken from Newton (*Corresp.*, 1: 92), are valid only under particular circumstances, virtually none of which Gren mentions. Although he specifies how large the aperture in the windowshut should be, he neglects to include other essential information, like the size of the prism's refracting angle and the distance of the screen from the prism. Nor does he mention the material out of which his prism was made, although physicists had known since the middle of the eighteenth century that different kinds of glass produce different proportions and different degrees of color dispersion in the

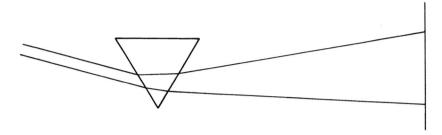

Figure 2.4   Another commonly used illustration exemplifying Newton's theory.

spectrum, so that no universally applicable proportions for the different colors in the spectrum can be given. From reading Gren one would expect that the spectrum is always and everywhere the same.

Furthermore, illustrations in the compendia often are unsatisfactory (cf. Lohne 1967). One of the most popular shows a line segment, which represents an incident ray of white light intersecting another line segment, which is supposed to be the interface of two different transparent media such as air and glass; on the other side of the interface, there radiate from the point of intersection a number of line segments, each of which is meant to stand for one of the refracted color rays (Fig. 2.1). Erxleben used another common diagram showing two parallel lines, supposed to be the outer edges of a beam of white light, that enter at one face of a prism; after leaving the other face, the beam's edges diverge and are intercepted by a screen (Fig. 2.4). This illustration does not exclude, and may even suggest, the possibility that the spectrum will appear in its classic form as soon as the beam leaves the prism; the accompanying text did not discourage this impression. On the other hand, this illustration is more realistic than the preceding one because it depicts the ray of light as having dimensions. The line segment that is "split" into several other line segments is a fiction, a purely heuristic device that corresponds to no demonstrable thing, not even to the phenomenon of the spectrum derived from sunlight, which is a continuum of colors, not a finite set of discrete points of color. Especially in the representation of colors, line drawings are inadequate and often misleading. Even apart from these shortcomings, the compendia provided too few diagrams to give the uninitiated a clear idea of what actually happens and how the theory explains the experimental results. For example, Gehler is one of the few authors who mention that objects seen through the prism – as opposed to images formed on a screen – may not appear completely dissolved into colors but instead display partial spectra at their edges, yet he does

Figure 2.5   Erxleben's erroneous diagram.

not provide an illustration to supplement his text. A diagram would have made this notion almost immediately comprehensible; without it, his description is vague and confusing (Gehler 1787–96, 2: 136–37). Thus if Goethe consulted some work other than Erxleben, it is not likely that he found a materially better exposition.

In addition to being misleading or confusing, the compendia could sometimes be wrong. In fact, an astonishing error appears in Erxleben's account. In paragraph 370 Erxleben explains how one can separate the colors of the spectrum: If one puts a lens between the hole in the window shut and the prism, "then each simple light will be displayed individually in the form of small round disks, each one over the next in a row," and the accompanying figure (which Goethe cited in the "Polemic," *FL-P*, par. 246) shows seven tiny circles completely separated from one another (Fig. 2.5). But this alleged phenomenon does not and will not occur in practice, nor does Newton's theory predict it. Erxleben's assertion seems to rest on a misunderstanding of an argument Newton presented in the *Opticks* (*Opticks*, 64–67) about how to achieve a better unmixing of the potentially infinite variety of kinds and colors of light in white sunlight. Because each kind of color-producing ray has associated with it a specific index of refraction different from the indexes of refraction for every other kind of ray, when the prism is placed in the so-called position of minimum deviation that Newton specifies, all the rays of the same kind (i.e., all rays that have the same index of refraction) would, if they could be isolated from all the other kinds of rays in white light, produce a circular image of the sun when intercepted by an appropriately placed screen (see Fig. 2.6). Consequently, the entire spectrum can be conceived as the sum of all these circles produced by rays of differing refrangibility. Because the number of circles that make up the spectrum is extremely large, if not infinite, there will always be some

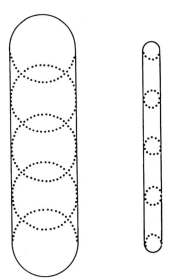

Figure 2.6   An illustration from the Opticks *showing Newton's conception of how the color circles can be separated from one another. These are but five of innumerable overlapping circles that cannot be displayed discretely.*

overlapping; consequently, separating the different kinds of light perfectly is impossible, even under the best of circumstances. Nevertheless, Newton prescribes a method by which the degree of overlap may be reduced so that the spectrum might approach perfect separation of the rays. If the aperture is made smaller or if a focusing lens is used to concentrate the rays, the proportion of the width of the spectrum to its length will be reduced; thus, the diameters of the overlapping circles will be smaller, so that some of the rays that overlapped in the wider spectrum no longer overlap in the narrower one. As long as the windowshut aperture has any dimension larger than zero and the rays of light are not all exactly parallel, there will inevitably be some overlapping of the rays and their corresponding circles. Neither in practice nor in theory, however, are the rays ever separated into discrete circles; the spectrum remains continuous.

Newton's explanation is accompanied by a diagram showing a wider spectrum next to a narrower one; dotted or dashed circles are used to depict how the circles that overlap in the former no longer do in the latter (Fig. 2.6). Apparently, Erxleben was misled by the diagram into thinking that the narrower spectrum was actually separated into discrete circles. This kind of error is not unprecedented, however. For example, the first edition of Gren's *Grundriss der Naturlehre* (1788) contains the same misinterpretation, as does a work from 1768 by one of Erxleben's predecessors at the University of Göttingen, Albrecht von Haller (Hargreave 1973, 493–94). Interestingly, the third and succeeding editions of Erxleben, prepared by the eminent physicist and scholar Georg Christoph Lichtenberg and an unnamed assistant, never corrected the error of the seven discrete circles, although many other additions and emendations were made. However, Gren, who may have been misled by Erxleben's book, corrected the error in the second edition of the *Grundriss*, published in 1793. This correction may not have been incidental, for between publication of the two editions, Gren had reviewed Goethe's *Beiträge zur Optik* for his *Journal der Physik*, which suggests that Goethe's work may have forced him to examine more carefully both the theory and the phenomena.

In his study of the development and reception of Thomas Young's theory of color vision, David Hargreave points out how unreliable most eighteenth-century accounts of Newton's theory were, and that one of the principal sources of error was the nearly unanimous belief of the commentators that there were exactly seven fundamental colors and rays (Erxleben states this in paragraph 369), the so-called *ROYGBIV* colors (Hargreave 1973, 477–95). In his writings, Newton frequently refers to precisely these colors as the components of the spectrum (sometimes orange and indigo are excepted); in principle, however, he argued for the existence of an indefinitely large number of intermediate colors as well. Nevertheless, it is important to recognize the genuine ambiguity that Newton introduced into the terminology of color and the conception of how many colors there are, an ambiguity that suggests the inevitable tension between the physical interpretation and the observed colors. An empirically produced spectrum displays not an infinite but a relatively small finite number of distinguishable colors; these colors do not gradually shade off one into another but appear to have relatively conspicuous boundaries. This difference between theory and phenomenon is irreducible so long as the theory gives no explanation of why, beyond the infinite gradation corresponding to indexes of refraction, there exists a finite number of color categories.

What did Goethe hope to find in these scientific compendia, and why, even if they had given an accurate account of Newton's theory, might he still have been disappointed? Goethe's attention had been attracted first to color in art, then to color in nature. A theory of color relevant to art would have to account for such matters as color mixing, permanency, temperature, harmony, neutralization, and enhancement. A theory of color in nature would have to account for the colors of bodies, whether animal, vegetable, or mineral; of atmospheric phenomena, including the changing colors of the sun and sky during the day, halos around the sun and the moon, and rainbows; of colored shadows; and of any other kinds of color phenomena that appear in nature. Goethe's disappointment in the conventional textbook chapter is understandable. The science of his day had little to offer that would have been of any use to artists, craftsmen, dyers, chemists, or other technicians and, for the most part, did not even attempt to describe or explain phenomena like the harmony and temperature of colors. Nor could science give more than vague explanations for the most commonplace natural color phenomena, apart from the scientific account of the rainbow.

A theory like Newton's that asserts the existence of an infinite number of different colors in white light does not in itself explain very much about color, nor is it always clear how the general theory is to be applied to individual cases. Of course, no theory is perfectly exhaustive in its coverage, so that the inability of a theory to explain a few phenomena does not justify the conclusion that the theory is useless. For example, although no one was sure why the sky appears blue, the Newtonian theory suggested that for some reason the rays coming from the sky were predominantly blue-producing rays. But no one had any idea of how this predominance of blue came about in the first place. More to the point, perhaps, is that the blue of the sky is one of the most commonplace and universal experiences imaginable, yet the theory had nothing definite to say about it. There was a similar difficulty in accounting for colors of bodies; only explanations in principle could be made. Insofar as physics is conceived as the systematic understanding of nature – the predominant (essentially Aristotelian) conception prior to the nineteenth century – any theory that cannot explain what occurs regularly and frequently in nature has at best dubious title to the name physics and is of questionable utility, both theoretically and practically. Furthermore, Newton's theory had had, at least before the second and third decades of the nineteenth century when Fraunhofer investigated the differences between spectra, few practical applications and hardly any theoretical elaboration. It is unlikely that the compendium Goethe consulted supplied answers to many of his questions. Nevertheless, he did suspect that the spectrum contained the key to understanding colors, and this suspicion induced him to examine the phenomena of the prism. This is confirmed by an early outline draft of the "Konfession": "Conviction that one must turn to the physicist. Consideration of what is to be concluded from the spectrum. And what can be concluded from its step-scale. Desire to see the experiments myself. Büttner's prisms" (*LA* I, 3: 362–63).

This glimpse of relevant passages from the German compendia and these reflections on the kinds of questions Goethe had in mind allow some provisional conclusions to be drawn about the result of the hasty experiment in his newly painted room. The theory he had in mind as he raised the prism to his eye was more or less Newtonian; although he did not have it direct from Newton, what he had heard or read was un-ambiguously attributed to him. Most compendia, and in particular the one he is most likely to have consulted, would not have prepared him well for phenomena seen through a prism, as opposed to the results of experiments performed in a dark chamber where the rays are cast onto a wall or screen (although even in the latter case he might well have gotten misimpressions if not astoundingly false information). Moreover, what he read may have suggested that the results would not be essentially different whether the experiments were objective (using the screen) or subjective (viewing directly through the prism).[7] Thus he might have not unreasonably expected to see a single, full, seven-colored spectrum as he gazed through the prism at the wall, rather than the undifferentiated white and the incomplete spectra with a smaller number of colors that he actually saw at the boundaries between light and dark. In the spirit of a rigorous inductivist who knows that a single black swan destroys the validity of the claim "All swans are white," Goethe, having encoun-tered a phenomenon that contradicted the predicted result, declared that the theory was wrong.

This solution is only partial, however, because nowhere in the "Konfes-sion" does Goethe expressly repent his initial reaction as not truly ap-plying to Newton himself. Did he ever discover the differences between Newton and his epigones? In describing the occasion of his first reading of Newton, Goethe remarks that he was pleased "to have already made the captiousness, the falsity of his first experiment [in the *Opticks*] evident by means of my displays [of the kind used in the *Beiträge*] and to be able to unravel comfortably for myself the whole puzzle" (*HA*, 14: 263). He goes on to say that, as he penetrated further into the *Opticks*, he reper-formed all the experiments and found that "the whole mistake rests on the fact that a complicated phenomenon was supposed to be laid as the foundation and the simpler to be explained from out of the composite" (ibid.).

This labor took much time and care, however. It might be reasonable to conclude, then, that Goethe learned eventually that the aperçu in his newly painted room had not genuinely refuted Newton; nevertheless, even by itself it was sufficient to cast doubt on Newton's version of the theory. Goethe apparently expected the reader to be able to see this connection. We recall that only four paragraphs before describing his initial aperçu Goethe mentioned consulting a typical textbook account; and also that the "Konfession" comes at the end of *Zur Farbenlehre*, which suggests that Goethe presumed that the reader was already familiar with the whole work, including the critical analyses, in the polemical and the historical parts, of Newton's theory and its eighteenth-century suc-cessors. We may surmise that Goethe felt no need to apologize for his initial outburst because, despite its limitations, it expressed a basic truth that the rest of the work had made clear: that there was an essential connection between the deficiencies of the original and the errors of the successors, even if the latter were often pale images of the former. We have already remarked that the widespread notion that there were exactly seven colors in the spectrum derived from an ambiguity in Newton's usage; it turns out that other problems with Newtonian accounts also have their origin in Newton's (see esp. Chapter 3).

Goethe and method

Goethe was not a neophyte to natural science when he first took up the physical study of color.[8] Soon after the Duke of Sachsen-Weimar, Carl August, had invited the poet to join his court in Weimar (in 1775, when Goethe was 26), Goethe began assuming official and unofficial duties that required technical knowledge, particularly in botany, geology, and mineralogy. Because of his interest in drawing and painting, he also took up the study of human and animal anatomy. It would be misleading to suggest that these scientific and technical acquisitions were merely enforced or accidental, however. In his university years (1765–71), he had shown an intense interest in the sciences of nature. He had devoted as much time and energy to anatomy and chemistry as to the juristic curriculum he was ostensibly following; he also attended lectures in physics and even pursued alchemical studies for a time. This early learning was unsystematic, however, more the work of an enthusiast than of a student doing programmatic research. Although he had gained some scientific knowledge before coming to Weimar, he had acquired neither a specialization nor a rigorous method of investigation.

Even in the years of *Sturm und Drang*, however, nature was at the center of Goethe's conception of the world. It is hardly an exaggeration to say that nature was the mysterious, omnipresent, and vivifying source of all that is for the younger Goethe; he longed to have immediate and even intoxicating access to its mysteries and tried to express them directly through his poetry. He conceived nature as mighty, all-encompassing, and turbulent: "What we see of nature is force [*Kraft*], force devours, nothing present everything passing, crushing a thousand seedlings each moment a thousand born, great and meaningful, manifold unto endlessness; beautiful and ugly, good and evil, everything with equal right existing side by side" (Fairley 1947, 45). His responsibilities in Weimar gave him a soberer, if not less intense, attitude; indeed, his turn, out of practical concerns, to empirical investigation in depth and to theoretical matters seems to mark a realization that he had been given over too much to enthusiasm and arbitrariness and thus had fallen short of the requirements of nature, which, he now believed, works slowly, lawfully, never arbitrarily (cf. *HA*, 13: 45–47, 48–49).

In learning the sciences, Goethe typically sought instruction at first hand as well as from texts; for example, he learned botany from Friedrich Gottlieb Dietrich, whose family was in the business of providing botanical specimens for instructional use, and August Carl Batsch, professor of botany at the University of Jena; his chief texts were Linnaeus's *Philosophia botanica* and *Fundamenta botanices* and Johann Gessner's dissertation on the elements of Linnaeus (*HA*, 13: 153–56). Whenever possible, he studied nature in the field rather than abstractly, and he acquired the habit of taking careful notes of his observations. In this manner Goethe began to study the phenomena of nature in painstaking detail, became well-versed in several disciplines, and even conducted original research. Already in the mid-1780s he was in pursuit of a principle that would account for the order and unity of plant species, and he was performing dissections in search of the premaxillary (or intermaxillary) bone that was reputed to differentiate human beings from other mammals because it was not present in the human species. Not surprisingly, when setting out for Italy in 1786, Goethe considered himself as much a researcher into nature as a poet-artist; and the journals from this trip are filled with notes on the atmosphere and weather, geological formations and terrain, and, above all, plant life.

Thus, if the poetry of his early period overflows with the sense of nature's all-encompassing, originative power, which the young man longed to penetrate and share, and if the first years in Weimar were marked by the practical and theoretical acquisition of vast amounts of concrete detail, Goethe's Italian experience represents a reconciliation of the two approaches and an overcoming of their inherent limitations. In Italy he discovered in concreto the universality of nature through the incredible variety of its particular manifestations. Whereas he had once understood nature in opposition to society, with the human spirit caught between the two, in Italy he had come to recognize that even society grows lawfully out of nature and that art and its truth are also rooted therein.

Since Goethe's earliest scientific work was in botany and anatomy, which require practice and skill in description (and which some might therefore call pretheoretical), and since like any student he needed first to become acquainted with the rich variety of specimens the sciences had as objects of study, it is not at all surprising that Goethe should have considered as the first aim of science to give a carefully detailed account of the things and phenomena of nature. Yet Goethe was never a mere compiler of facts. For one thing, the task of organizing and classifying, whether of rocks, plants, or animals, already presupposes some (if perhaps minimal) theoretical point of view; for another, Goethe in his approach to nature was always in search of principles of natural unity.

In searching for the principles of the unity of nature by way of particulars, Goethe was part of a tradition of experimental science that flourished in the eighteenth century. To natural philosophers of that century, physics signified not so much a specialized natural-scientific discipline that studied matter, motion, and forces, but rather the knowledge of all nature, including the realm of the animate as well as the inanimate. Physics in German-speaking lands was often called "*Naturlehre*" (doctrine of nature) and in English-speaking countries "natural philosophy." As the Cartesian physicist Jacques Rohault had written in the 1690s, physics is "the science that teaches us the reasons and causes of all the effects that Nature produces" (quoted by Heilbron 1979, 11). One hundred years later one can find similar definitions. Gehler defined physics as "the doctrine of nature, natural philosophy, natural science. This name is borne by the entire doctrine of nature or corpuscular world, or of the properties, powers, and effects of bodies. To natural science belongs, in the broadest sense of the word, everything about bodies that has ever been experienced or thought" (Gehler 1787–96, 3: 488). Gren in his *Grundriss* first defined *Naturlehre* in a broad sense, as the science of properties and effects of created things, whether material or immaterial, then gave a more restricted meaning that still implied a more than ample physics: "We limit ourselves to the rational knowledge of the objects of the world of the senses, which constitutes physics or *Naturlehre* (*Physica*) in the narrower sense and has as its purpose the changes of material things according to their causes" (Gren 1793, par. 6). Physics conceived along these lines was, not surprisingly, organized rather differently than the science that we know by the same name; it tended, in Aristotelian fashion, to coalesce around the various genera of natural things: light, magnetism, plants, animals, and so on.

Natural philosophy, *Physik*, *physique*, or *physica* of the eighteenth century, of course, included matters that had already achieved a high degree of theoretical elaboration (some already in Greek antiquity) and that we would include in the modern sense of physics. Astronomy, geometric optics, statics, kinematics, dynamics, and mechanics were all sciences whose chief phenomena were well understood and fairly simple to mathematize. Beginning from certain familiar phenomena like those of the balance or the rectilinear propagation of light, they had abstracted mathematical principles that provided the basis for a complex theoretical elaboration without any insistence on the need to control theory by frequent experiment. In these sciences, a few basic principles reflected the behavior of real physical systems sufficiently well so that any divergence of the phenomena from the theory was for the most part explicable or at least negligible (see T. Kuhn 1977, 31–65).

However, eighteenth-century natural philosophy also included a type of nonmathematical empirical and experimental science that had no clear precedent before the seventeenth century and that died out after the middle of the nineteenth (ibid., 42), a science that even in the seventeenth century was already called Baconian after its greatest propagandist, Francis Bacon. The kind of science that Bacon recommended placed the experiment at its focus. Looking over the knowledge that human beings had acquired through the ages, Bacon lamented the scantiness of what had been secured, the human proclivity for fruitless disputation, and the virtual nullity of what could be achieved through ordinary human efforts. His counsel was to set aside vain speculations and imaginings, to restrain the urge to generalization, and to proceed "to the particulars themselves, and their series and order; while men on their side must force themselves for a while to lay their notions by and begin to familiarize themselves with the facts." Bacon noted that "the best demonstration by far is experience, if it go not beyond the actual experiment. For if it be transferred to other cases which are deemed similar, unless such transfer be made by a just and orderly process, it is a fallacious thing" (Bacon 1960, bk. 1, par. 36, 70). The major part of the *New Organon* was thus devoted to sketching out a just and orderly process by which one could cautiously move first from particulars to a modest level of generality and then by stages to ever higher levels, until finally one reached the most comprehensive generalizations of all.

The Baconian tradition emphasized induction through observation, which was directed toward naturally occurring phenomena; however, an even higher premium was placed on the contrivance of experiments, for "the secrets of nature reveal themselves more readily under the vexations of art than when they go their own way" (Bacon 1960, bk. 1, par. 98). The chief vehicles of this type of science were so-called natural and experimental histories, which in the first instance aimed at comprehensively assembling the material upon which induction must work, and in the second at achieving comprehensive generalizations about the relevant facts.

If Bacon provided a rationale for the experimental sciences and their method, he did not produce a successful specimen of such work. Robert Boyle, one of the best of the Baconian natural philosophers, did compose several relative successes, including a work on color that Goethe regarded as one of the two forerunners of *Zur Farbenlehre*,[9] but Boyle also availed himself of the theoretical advantages of corpuscularism in focusing his experiments. Strict adherence to rigorous induction, on the other hand, tended to result in little more than collections of curiosities.

On the continent, of course, Cartesianism, which provided seventeenth- and eighteenth-century science with a more speculative turn on the basis of rational, mechanical hypotheses, offered an alternative; but the use of mechanical hypotheses naturally raised the question of whether they were true, especially when they took the form of crude or far-fetched analogies (e.g., a tennis racket's striking a corpuscle of light, and thus changing the corpuscle's direction as it entered a refracting medium). The Baconian experimental sciences, however, needed some supplement that did not betray their inductive method. By producing a more rigorously focused method, Newton gave the tradition of empirical induction new life.

Newton hoped to reform the science of his day by uniting the tradition of the more ancient, mathematized sciences like statics and geometric optics with the way of careful experiment. The mathematical structure was not to be artificially imposed by means of artificial hypotheses but was to be found, through experiments, as inhering in the very properties of the things of nature. In this way induction would aim for and be enriched by the powerful techniques of mathematics (see Mamiani 1976).[10] The problem in each experimental science, then, was to find as quickly and efficiently as possible those properties that availed themselves of accurate mathematization. In optics the phenomenon of differential refraction according to color proved to be precisely what was needed to fulfill this hope; by prudently designing experiments and using accurate measurements, one could compel nature to make visible the mathematics of the phenomena – one could, as it were, read the mathematical theory off the experiments.

In contrast to the *Philosophiae naturalis principia mathematica*, however, and even in contrast to the *Lectiones opticae* delivered at Cambridge University in the early 1670s, Newton's major writings on light and color published during his lifetime (correspondence with the Royal Society of London and the *Opticks*) considerably muted the mathematical character of his theory. They did not, for the most part, require much more than arithmetic and elementary plane geometry and occasionally plane trigonometry. Instead, they experimentally isolated and then verified the presence of arithmetical and geometrical characteristics like the correlation between refrangibility and color. These characteristics were not always subjected to a truly exacting mathematical analysis, but for the sake of merely establishing their existence such analysis did not seem necessary. By the very fact that the optical writings were less complicated mathematically than the *Principia*, they were able to appeal as much to a popular audience as to experts in optics; and in this guise the *Opticks* in particular spurred the eighteenth-century flowering of a new generation of Baconian experimental science, which ranged from the study of electricity, heat, and magnetism to the inner functionings of plants and animals, from the invention of new machines for demonstrating natural phenomena to the invention of a new language in which to express the findings of Lavoisier's modern chemistry.

The historian I. B. Cohen has characterized this science at its best as "the advance of scientific knowledge by simple, ingenious experiments that led to concepts closely allied to laboratory operations. The theories that rose from these experiments were tested by new experiments, producing a continual stream of new phenomena which broadened man's view and understanding of nature" (Cohen 1956, 18). This kind of experimental science was often nonquantitative; its chief focus was the elaboration of experiments that might give rise to the fundamental concepts and structures of a theory. The proliferation of experimental phenomena, techniques, and theories that it fostered can be seen as a prelude to the new wave of mathematization and the redefinition of physics that occurred at the end of the eighteenth and the beginning of the nineteenth centuries (Heilbron 1979, 13). In the earlier part of the eighteenth century, these sciences helped bring about a vogue for scientific compendia and encyclopedias (ibid.), which tried to keep pace with the expanding base of physical knowledge; at the same time the cultural prominence of experimental philosophy made a deep impression on the popular and even the expert conception of proper scientific method.

Although the period of Goethe's initiation into natural science more or less coincided with the emergence of the new wave of specialized, mathematized physics (in France), he clearly understood his own work as part of the tradition of inductive science. The unities he sought in nature were to be arrived at through a careful study of the particulars in a certain class, with the aim of bringing out the full range of relevant observations and phenomena. Careful measurement and mathematical formulation might be possible, but they were not to be cultivated for their own sake (indeed, insofar as Goethe's earliest scientific studies concerned living beings, he thought that measurement was likely to be superficial and extrinsic; see *HA*, 13: 7–8). The purpose of experimentation was to allow the phenomena to show themselves as eminently as possible without the intervention of hypotheses, for hypotheses are more likely to correspond to our preferred way of thinking than to the things themselves (*HA*, 13: 8–9). Moreover, his goal, like Bacon's and Newton's, was not to discover just any unities or correlations in things but the essential and natural properties of the object under investigation.

This last-mentioned goal put Goethe clearly on one side of a leading debate in eighteenth-century natural science (especially natural history), whether the things of nature ought to be studied and understood "naturally" or "artificially." Linnaeus's taxonomy of plants provides an example of what was at issue. In his taxonomy he hoped to achieve a natural system of classification that included the wide range and variety of the many characteristics of plants; but in practice he had to be satisfied with a classification on the basis of just one characteristic, their reproductive organs. Prima facie, the latter seems comparatively artificial in contrast with the ideal of a system that takes into account the whole plant. However, natural methods tend to exact the high price of complexity and inconsistency; what an artificial system loses in richness, it gains in simplicity and comprehensibility (see Mason 1962, ch. 28, and von Engelhardt 1972, 299).

Although Goethe had the highest regard for Linnaeus and had acquired facility in using his taxonomic system, he became aware of the one-sided and static nature of its method of classification, especially in view of the variability of plant forms and the dynamics of their growth and development, and thus he came to desire a higher kind of *Anschauung*, a grasp of the ideal unity underlying the manifold phenomena (*HA*, 13: 161). Similarly, in his anatomical studies Goethe's interest lay in development and unity, not in mere division and classification. In his controversial discovery of the intermaxillary bone in human beings,[11] his work was spurred by the question of whether its absence in human beings distinguished them from other animals (e.g., apes) in a way that might help support claims of the uniqueness of human beings in the plan of nature. Goethe believed, however, that nature is continuous with itself, that it operates according to the lawful variation of form. Goethe agreed that the intermaxillary is not identifiable as separate in most human beings; it is, however, visible in embryo and in some infant skulls, and one of its typifying sutures can be seen in nearly all adult human skulls. The intermaxillary is thus ontogenetically present, and the human intermaxillary represents one of the determinate forms that the bone can assume in the economy of the mammalian skeleton, indeed a limiting or extreme form. The way of determining the presence or absence of this bone is not merely taking a human skull and saying, "Yes, it is here," or "No, it is not." Rather, the process involves defining the place that the bone typically fills in mammals; noting the limited variety of shapes, its fusion, function, and development; and then, within this context of dynamic mammalian form, determining in what sense one may legitimately assert its presence or absence. Thus, although it may be correct to say that the intermaxillary does not appear in the normal adult human being, it is nevertheless also correct to say that the genesis of the bones in which human incisors are seated is immediately continuous with the phenomenon as it occurs in related animals.

One might easily make a similar argument for the scientific work that immediately preceded the *Beiträge zur Optik*, *The Metamorphosis of Plants*. There the object was to recognize a morphological type and its economy. Drawing upon a great variety of typifying (but also atypical) examples of cotyledons in process of growth, Goethe attempted to draw botanists away from an overconcern with classification to a consideration of the lawful development of plants – namely, the metamorphosis of an *Urorgan*, the so-called primal leaf, which in its development is the source of the "inner identity" of the parts of the plant (*HA*, 13: 84). (Goethe did not mean to imply that the leaf had any ontological priority. Because of this inner identity, he might easily have chosen to designate another part as primal; see *HA*, 13: 101.)

We may sum up the rationale of Goethe's method on the eve of his optical studies as follows: Our theories have a tendency to atomize phenomena; it is thus necessary to follow a method that explores laws, relationships, similarities, and homologies in the course of natural development – a genetic, even a dynamic method (insofar as it identifies forces at work). There is, accordingly, such a thing as a natural method, which brings out the intrinsic interrelatedness of things natural. Natural things must be studied not in isolation but within a larger context; and this context is always capable of further enlargement, in the direction of the totality of phenomenal nature. At the level of the object one needs to give a full account of the relevant phenomena and conditions. As far as possible one ought to let things speak for themselves; one must first labor to find the appropriate kind of *Anschauung*, onlooking, so that one might develop an adequate terminology and method of presentation that expresses tolerably well the full gamut of the phenomena.

The Beiträge zur Optik

The *Beiträge zur Optik* is an experimental history of a certain class of prismatic color phenomena. Although it may appear to be just a collection of well-known phenomena, it is actually an example of inductive generalization through the judicious concatenation of phenomena, an attempt at exhaustive analysis of a class of phenomena, an effort to see the phenomena in their emergence and passing away, a critique of prevailing doctrine and pedagogy, and the reopening of the scientific investigation of color. Before we can appreciate these dimensions, however, we must become acquainted with the work itself, the *Beiträge zur Optik*, part 1 and part 2.

The central portion of part 1 of the *Beiträge* (par. 33–71) is devoted to observations and experiments, followed by a recapitulation and an account of the apparatus needed for the experiments. Preceding the central portion is a brief overview of colors in nature; the state of optics and color science; Goethe's intention in performing the work; and general considerations about light, darkness, and color. Because the heart of the *Beiträge*, its method and theoretical viewpoint, begins with paragraph 33, we shall commence there.[12]

Beiträge zur Optik: *the experiments*

Let us pretend that we have never heard of Isaac Newton and his ideas about light and color, and that we know very little about the prism and its workings. This is easier said than done, for almost everyone has heard of and perhaps even seen what is referred to as the decomposition of white light into colors, though precisely what this decomposition amounts to may be less familiar. However, because no human being possesses an innate knowledge of Newton's theory, making this pretense is not altogether idle.[13]

The easiest and most natural way for someone to begin investigating the prism is not to reproduce Newton's experiments exactly but rather to pick up the prism and look through it. (There is strong evidence that this is how even Newton began; see Hall 1948.) What does someone see by looking through a prism? Even a person fully conversant with Newton's theory may not be able to say with certainty what the outcome will be. At any rate, the outcome depends on the circumstances. For the moment, let us assume that the observer has a prism made of common glass (spectacle crown glass) with three 60-degree refracting angles – an equilateral prism.

What the observer sees through the prism of course depends on the field of view. Even if the observer looks at a "normal" scene – for example, the interior of a well-lit living room or a daytime landscape with houses, grass, trees, flowers – we leave open a virtually infinite number of possibilities. Nevertheless, it is possible to give a general characterization of what the observer sees. First of all, the scene will appear to be displaced from its original position; second, colors other than those of the original objects will be visible and will tend to blur the distinctness of those objects; third, despite this blurring, the scene and most of the objects in it will still be easily identifiable, and they will not be entirely "decomposed" into the colors of the spectrum. The observer may be surprised to see that much of the scene retains its natural appearance, including its "natural" color. The spectral colors appear as fringes of the objects in the scene, and a closer examination reveals that they are not at all random. For example, if the observer rotates the prism about his line of sight, he will continue to see the same basic phenomenon, the scene displaced and its objects fringed with spectral color, but the direction of the displacement and the orientation of the fringes change. The observer probably will soon discover a close relationship between the boundaries of objects, the fringes of color, and the orientation of the prism. The boundaries seem to be the source of the fringes; the colors appear to originate and stream out from the boundaries of objects, and the degree to which they stream out from the boundary depends on the orientation of the boundary to the prism. Smaller objects (those subtending a small angle with vertex at the eye) may be completely dissolved into spectral colors so that they appear as variegated blurs, but larger objects display spectral colors only at their edges and retain their natural or characteristic colors elsewhere. These edge spectra seem to emerge from the boundaries, so that red, yellow, green, blue, violet, and purple appear in a certain order and harmony, although the exact nature of this orderliness is not immediately evident (par. 33–38).

If by good fortune the observer looks upon something that greatly simplifies the phenomenon, for instance a white wall with some few contrasting features (dark spots, a window frame, nails, brackets, holes), he can focus his attention upon isolated instances of edge spectra rather than on the bewildering variety presented in most everyday scenes. By isolating events and by simplifying the circumstances, an observer may often much more easily recognize characteristics of the phenomena that are hidden or confused in a more complicated situation. Simplification also facilitates the description of phenomena and can even aid the observer in arriving at preliminary conclusions and explanations. In the case at hand, simplification of the field of view helps confirm the initial impressions that the colored fringes conform to the borders of objects and that the width of the fringes depends on the mutual orientation of the prism and the borders. Those boundaries that are parallel to the refracting edge of the prism have the broadest bands of color; those that are perpendicular have no special fringes at all; and those in between these orientations have spectral fringes of intermediate widths that are greater the more closely the border approaches the parallel position and less the closer it comes to the perpendicular. Furthermore, these edge spectra are not complete spectra: Each displays but a few of the colors familiar from the spectrum made famous by Newton. If the observer simplifies the scene even further by eliminating all boundaries – for instance by viewing a white wall free of blemish or a cloudless blue sky – the edge spectra disappear; the only color visible will be the white of the wall or the blue of the sky. But wherever there is a dark speck on the wall or a cloud in the sky – that is, wherever there is a boundary of some sort that deviates from a perpendicular orientation to the refracting edge of the prism – the observer will once again notice the colors of edge spectra (par. 38–42).

Our preliminary observations, then, lead us to associate colors that appear through the prism with the boundaries of objects. Rather than use real objects, suppose that we draw simple pictures on posters or cards and, to reduce complications, use only black and white. By drawing many squiggly lines on a card, we can obtain a picture that corresponds in a rough way to a field of vision containing many different black-and-white objects. The variations on squiggly lines are endless, of course, but by consistently pursuing the simplification of the experimental circumstances we can try to avoid losing our way among insignificant modifications. Thus we might test what happens when we substitute regular patterns for random squiggles by using straight lines, rectangles, and squares on our displays. Indeed, the colors do begin to appear with greater regularity and less confusion.

Let us simplify even more by trying a single white rectangle on a black background. For the sake of easier description, let us suppose that we always hold the prism with its refracting angle downward; this means that the objects observed through it will appear to be displaced in a downward direction (they also seem to come nearer to us). With the long sides of the rectangle parallel to the refracting edge, and at a sufficiently large distance from the display card – using a crown-glass prism with a 60-degree angle and a rectangle one-half inch wide, about two and one-half to three feet will be sufficient – the rectangle will no longer exhibit even a trace of white; in place of the original white rectangle, we will see an even broader multicolored rectangle, a spectrum of, from top to bottom, red, yellow, green, blue, and violet (Fig. 2.7). Each color occupies a band running parallel to the refracting edge of the prism; yellow and violet will occupy broader bands than red and green. The blue band, narrow and dusky, is relatively hard to distinguish between the green and the violet. Just five distinct chromatic hues will be visible; there is no infinitely fine gradation of color in this spectrum. Yellow, for instance, appears in essentially a single hue, a lemon color, which occupies a distinctive rectangular area between red and green; the same holds true of the other bands as well, mutatis mutandis. The boundaries dividing them are for the most part quite distinct.[14] Perhaps most striking of all is the division between blue and violet. It looks almost as if it coincides with the boundary between the white rectangle and the black background that, as it were, is seen through the colors. Against the apparent background of black we see the violet band; against the apparent background of the original white rectangle we see blue (par. 43–45).

When we reverse the colors black and white, taking a narrow black strip on a white background, we see more or less the inverse of the preceding case (Fig. 2.8). The colors will now be brighter, however, and in place of green there will appear at the center of the spectrum a color not seen in the previous example, purple or magenta (*Purpur*). The exact

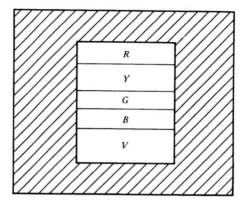

Figure 2.7   A white rectangle, with its long axis horizontal and displayed against a black ground, seems to be vertically elongated when it is viewed through a prism with the refracting angle downward. R = red, Y = yellow, G = green, B = blue (cyan), V = violet. (This and the following diagrams are schematic. It is recommended that readers obtain a prism and view appropriate black-and-white displays for themselves.)

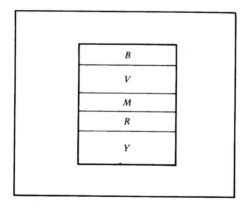

Figure 2.8   As in Figure 2.7, but with white and black reversed. The central color (M) is magenta or purple, what Goethe ultimately called (pure) red.

order, once again from top to bottom, is blue, violet, magenta, red, and yellow, although it should be noted that the violet easily disappears into the magenta, so that it may hardly be visible (par. 46).

In both these experiments, there are two boundaries parallel to the refracting angle of the prism – one with white over black, the other with black over white. This suggests the next and last simplification, to reduce the display to a single boundary. We paint half of a display card black,

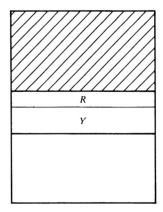

Figure 2.9   A display that is half black (top), half white (bottom), with a straight-line boundary, viewed through a prism.

the other half white, with the boundary between them a straight line. Keeping this line parallel to the refracting edge, which is still turned downward as usual, and the black field above the white, we will see from top to bottom the black field, then red and yellow (with perhaps a bit of orange discernible between them),[15] and finally white (Fig. 2.9). By turning the display upside down so that the white half is on top, we see white, blue, violet, and black (Fig. 2.10). When we turn the card so that the boundary line is perpendicular to the refracting edge, we see no chromatic hues at all: The white and the black fields will be divided by a very sharp and completely colorless straight boundary. By slowly inclining this boundary or the prism to one side or the other, colors appear again, at first in very narrow bands, then ever widening until they reach their maximum width at the point where the boundary line is once more parallel to the refracting edge. Which colors are seen depends on the direction of rotation: If the black gets even slightly "above" the white, we see red and yellow; if white gets above the black, blue and violet. At every position of the prism the bands of color are parallel to the boundary line (par. 47–49).

An especially instructive experiment is one in which two such single-boundary display cards are placed side by side so that the resulting display resembles four squares of a black-and-white checkerboard. If the white squares are at the upper left and the lower right, viewing the display through a prism will yield blue and violet on the left and red and yellow on the right (Fig. 2.11). The blue and red will appear to have the same width and be located almost exactly side by side, as will the violet and yellow, which are, however, considerably broader than the blue and the

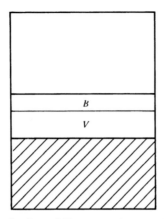

Figure 2.10   The display of Figure 2.9 is rotated 180 degrees and viewed through a prism.

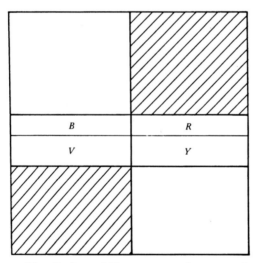

Figure 2.11   The displays of Figures 2.9 and 2.10 are juxtaposed checkerboard-fashion and viewed through a prism.

red. Thus, there seems to be an interesting symmetry between the two different kinds of edge spectra (par. 50).

Let us once again resort to the single white rectangle on a black ground and the black rectangle on white, only this time we will turn them 90 degrees so that their long sides are perpendicular to the refracting edge and their short sides parallel to it. Instead of seeing the continuous spec-

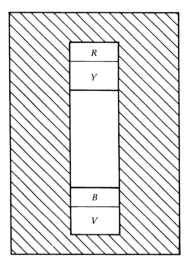

Figure 2.12   The white rectangle of Figure 2.7 is rotated 90 degrees and viewed through a prism. The central area is white.

trum that appeared when the two boundaries of the rectangle were close together, now that they are far apart we find that each kind of edge spectrum appears separated from the other. With a white rectangle on a black ground we will see, from top to bottom, black, red, yellow, white, blue, violet, black (Fig. 2.12); with black on white the sequence is white, blue, violet, black, red, yellow, white (Fig. 2.13). Where green appeared when the figure was turned 90 degrees there is now white; where magenta appeared, there is now black (par. 51–52). With both the white rectangle and the black rectangle, the edge spectra appear exactly where the single-boundary experiments would lead us to expect. In the case of the white rectangle, there are two boundaries parallel to the refracting edge: At the top of the rectangle the black field surmounts the white, and there the colors red and yellow appear, just as happened in the corresponding single-boundary case; at the bottom of the rectangle the white is above the black, so that blue and violet appear. The sides of the rectangle that run perpendicular to the refracting edge display no color at all. In an analogous way, the black rectangle on white confirms the one-boundary results: Blue and violet appear at the top, where white is above black, and red and yellow appear at the bottom, where black is above white.

We can summarize our experience in the form of a rule: At boundaries where black is above white, we get the colors red and yellow (the warm colors); where white is above black, we get blue and violet (the cool colors). Red and violet always appear nearer the black field, yellow and blue nearer the white. Of course, these rules hold only when the refracting

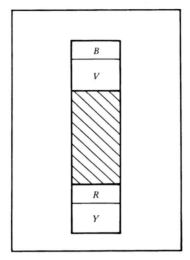

Figure 2.13   The black rectangle of Figure 2.8 is rotated 90 degrees and viewed through a prism. The central area is black.

edge of the prism is pointed downward, but it would not be difficult to define rules of transformation so that these two basic principles might be adapted to other orientations of the prism (Goethe in fact provides such rules in paragraph 88). We can also state generalizations that conform to our experimental results, for instance that the width of the edge spectrum varies according to the mutual orientation of the refracting angle and the boundary. These rules and generalizations are not only summaries of previous experiences but also leading principles for future research and testing; they have genuine predictive power, perhaps not enough to impress devotees of the Newtonian theory, but nevertheless real.

On the other hand, these rules do not explain of themselves where the green and the magenta that formerly occupied the centers of the white and the black rectangles, respectively, come from, because there is no trace of either with a single boundary or with two boundaries far apart. What we need is a way to demonstrate a connection between these events. Earlier we performed an experiment that involved continuously varying one of the conditions: We rotated a single-boundary display to observe the appearance, disappearance, and changes of the edge colors. Let us now perform another experiment that involves a somewhat different kind of continuous variation.

Using the white rectangle on a black background, oriented just as in the last pair of experiments with the length perpendicular to the refracting edge (so that the boundaries where colors appear are far apart), let us take a position close to the display and view it through the prism. The two edge spectra will be separated by a large central rectangle of white. Very gradually now we will move backward, away from the display, and watch what happens. When we are close to the display, it appears that the image is very little displaced from its actual position; as we back away, the displacement of the image increases. The colors at both the top and the bottom, which are narrow at first, grow ever broader. The part of the red band that adjoins the black field forms the trailing edge of the displaced image of the rectangle; it is displaced at the same rate as the entire field of view. The other edge of the red band, however, seems to expand in the direction of the yellow faster than the field as a whole is displaced; and in its turn the yellow band, at an even faster rate, virtually streams out across the white center toward the blue. Like the part of the red next to the black, the part of the blue next to the white center moves very little with respect to the displacement of the entire field, while its opposite edge moves at a faster rate toward the violet, which, like the yellow, streams outward into the black ground. (By using the checkerboard display, we could confirm that the slow advance of the red keeps in step with the slow advance of the blue, and likewise that the rapid advances of yellow and violet proceed at the same rate.) As we continue to back away from the white rectangle, the yellow gets closer and closer to the blue, until finally the formerly white center is completely tinted with color (Fig. 2.14). At the point when the yellow begins to touch the blue there quite suddenly appears green; continuing to move farther away, we discover that the area occupied by this central green grows broader and ultimately swallows up the adjoining blue and yellow, so that at a large distance from the display we are able to discriminate only three hues in the spectrum, red, green, and violet (Fig. 2.15).

In the case of a black rectangle on a white ground the progression is similar, except that in the center violet encounters red to produce purple-magenta, with the final result the three-color spectrum of blue, magenta, and yellow. We can obtain analogous results by varying other circumstances as well – for example, by contriving so that we can alter at will the dimensions of the rectangle or change the refracting angle by using (as Goethe did) a hinged water prism, while holding all the other factors constant. The witness of the eye in all these cases suggests that both green and magenta are produced by the mixture of colors from opposite edges (par. 53–62; cf. par. 89–92).

Having instructed ourselves in the phenomena of one and two boundaries and having derived certain rules and expectations therefrom, we can now explore what happens when we draw curved figures on the display cards. What we have learned from straight lines can be applied as well to curves. The same basic principles still hold: By determining

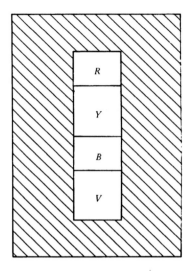

Figure 2.14   The white rectangle of Figure 2.12 viewed from a greater distance, just before the blue and yellow overlap to produce green.

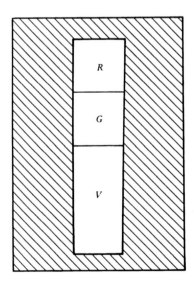

Figure 2.15   The white rectangle of Figure 2.14 viewed at an even greater distance: the yellow and blue have disappeared, leaving a trichromatic spectrum.

whether white is above black or vice versa and by taking into account the precise orientation of the boundary (or rather of the tangent to the boundary) with respect to the refracting edge of the prism, we can predict which colors will appear and how broad they will be. For instance, a small white circle on a black background will, when observed through the prism at a sufficiently large distance, produce a spectrum very much like the one that appears in optics textbooks as the spectrum of Newton, a long narrow rectangle of colors terminated by semicircles at both ends; from top to bottom some or all of the colors red, orange, yellow, green, blue, and violet will be visible, and the blue may show some traces of differentiation into bright blue and dark blue. If a black circle is observed against a white background, the elongated spectrum will consist of some or all of the colors blue, violet, magenta, red, orange, and yellow. Because of the curvature of the boundaries, the colors will not be so distinctly separated as in the experiments with straight boundaries. But just as in those latter experiments, by moving closer to the display, by using a smaller refracting angle, or by substituting large circles for small, we can make the central green or magenta disappear so that the edge spectra will be separated by white or black. Having grasped the essential characteristics of the phenomena with straight lines, we are able to understand the phenomena with curved figures. The only complication is that, whereas the orientation of a straight line to the prism is the same at all points of the line, for curves there is a continuous variation in this condition from point to point (par. 63–71).

A natural extension of these experiments would involve examining what happens when we introduce grays and chromatic hues into the diagrams. With grays the edge colors still appear, but they are dusky, even dingy, as though the luminous colors of the experiments with black and white were mixed with darkness. The edge colors are still as broad as they were with black and white, however, and on the whole the phenomena with grays do not seem to require any changes in the rules and principles governing the prismatic phenomena already considered. They rather emphasize that the contrast between the lighter and the darker is at the root of spectral colors, for one can predict the kind and the intensity of colors one will see according to the contrast between the shades of gray in the diagrams. The lighter gray takes the place of white and the darker the place of black in determining whether one will see red and yellow or blue and violet at a boundary, and as the contrast becomes greater (that is, as it approaches the stark contrast of black and white), so do the intensity and purity of the spectral colors increase (par. 93–100).

A new twist is added when we begin experimenting with colored rectangles on black and white backgrounds. On the one hand we would hope to find additional confirmation of what we have already uncovered, that the kind and the intensity of the colors seen through the prism depend on and can be predicted according to differences in brightness and darkness and in the orientation of the boundaries; after all, every color is lighter than black and darker than white. To some extent, the phenomena bear out this hope. On the other hand, there is an important new phenomenon: The colored fringes are affected in hue, breadth, and intensity by the color of the rectangle. The various possibilities are far too numerous to be recounted here, but the results can be summarized briefly without seriously distorting the actual events.

When the rectangle is of the same basic hue as one of the fringe colors expected according to the contrast of lighter and darker, the colors enhance or intensify one another, so that the rectangle would appear elongated at that edge (e.g., a red rectangle would appear elongated on the side where the red and yellow fringe ought to appear; both the red and the yellow of the expected fringe "mix" with the red of the rectangle to yield shades of red and reddish yellow). When the color of the rectangle, however, is of a kind opposite to the expected fringe colors – the red rectangle is "opposed," to varying degrees, to both the blue and the violet of the blue and violet fringe – the hues combine in a way that tends to neutralize them; the result can be a dingy hue or sometimes a virtually undetectable hue approaching brown or gray, so that on this side the colored rectangle appears truncated when compared with an achromatic rectangle of the same size likewise observed through the prism. Under most circumstances, however, the fringes, albeit inconspicuous, are visible to an eye trained to expect them. To put the results with colored rectangles even more briefly: Every refracted image has the tendency to produce red-yellow and blue-violet fringes; when the original image is colored, some kind of mixture of the original colors and the fringes occurs, and there results either an enhancement of the original color, a color intermediate between the original color and the fringe hue, or a neutralization of both, depending on whether the original color and the fringe hue are akin, somewhat similar, or quite dissimilar; consequently the refracted image may not produce a complete spectrum of color, and the hues visible may be different from those of the "regular" spectrum (par. 101–122).[16]

Beiträge zur Optik: *the way to a context for science*

In the previous section, we have followed the basic experimental sequence and argument of the first and the second *Beiträge zur Optik*. A remarkably thorough presentation of what Goethe called the subjective prismatic colors, the *Beiträge* have an astonishingly natural "feel" in their way of going about the investigation. Beginning with an almost casual experience with the prism, they gradually build up to a comprehensive familiarity with certain classes of prismatic colors by way of a detailed analysis of the manifold conditions under which the phenomena appear. While avoiding causal explanations and hasty generalizations and hypotheses, Goethe concentrates on the phenomena as events that occur under variable circumstances. Rather than formulate explicit propositions that are to be confirmed or rejected by phenomenal tests, Goethe prefers to elaborate the phenomena by ascertaining significant correlations between the conditions of the experiments and the events that occur.

That scientists like Helmholtz considered the *Beiträge* a pleasantly arranged and lucid account of the phenomena in question is understandable. But what are we to conclude from it? In its utter simplicity and matter-of-factness it hardly seems to make an argument at all. As for the dispute with Newton, Goethe seems to think that the experiment in which the black rectangle or circle on a white ground is dissolved into colors is sufficient evidence to confound the traditional theory, and that the evolution of the complete spectrum out of the two edge spectra presents a serious obstacle to those who defend Newton (*BzO*, par. 56). The few reviewers of part 1 of the *Beiträge* did not agree; they interpreted Goethe's scruples about explicit theorizing as a sign that he did not grasp the working principles of the theory and took it upon themselves to explain in detail how it should be applied in a ray-by-ray analysis. Although they admired the lovely and well-ordered demonstration, they said that it added nothing substantially new to the science of color, much less refute Newton (see *LA* I, 3: 54–58, 453–58).

This criticism misses an essential dimension of the *Beiträge*, however, which is to reopen the science of color to new lines of investigation and to reform the method of theorizing implicit in the Newtonian doctrine. The first thirty-two paragraphs of the *Beiträge* in fact signaled these intentions but did not make them explicit. As we shall see, a greater unreserve on Goethe's part might have forestalled some of the misunderstandings of his object in publishing the *Beiträge*, if not all the disagreements. In particular, we shall see in "Der Versuch als Vermittler von Objekt und Subjekt" an essay that, if it had been published as a companion piece, might have set off a productive debate on the method of experimental science. Instead, the *Beiträge* met with misunderstandings that have marked the reception of Goethe's chromatics ever since.

The introductory part of the *Beiträge* establishes a context for the experimental account that follows; yet because it is so "charmingly" written and subtle, it is easy to overlook its bearing on the questions of the place of science in the economy of things, the problematic influence of Newtonianism, the proper experimental method, the importance of scientific controversy to progress, and the basic principles that Goethe brought with him to his investigations. Once we have examined these matters, we shall be in a better position to judge the meaning of the experimental part.

Goethe begins the *Beiträge* with an evocation of color in its broadest and most familiar setting, phenomenal nature. Color is virtually everywhere; it is seen throughout visible nature, and few human beings are insensitive to its stimulation. This stimulation can occur as a general impression, as in the green of fields and forests, or a particular one, in flowers and blossoms, animals, insects, and birds. In an evocation of his recent journeys to Italy, he contrasts the vivid hues of the Italian landscape and sky (with their intense purity and bright harmonies) with the dull and somber colors of northern climes. In Italy the harmony of atmosphere unifies the colors of water, sun, sky, and shadow as if they were composed in a painting. The colors and their accords are so striking that one sometimes forgets that both light and shadow are present (*BzO*, par. 1–4).

This introduction may seem like so many beautiful words meant to entice a curious reader onward; it certainly recalls that Goethe's scientific interest in color arose from his Italian studies of art and nature and that he was inclined to think of color as a product of light and darkness. These aesthetic and biographical matters are of little interest to the color scientist. Nevertheless, they hold a threefold implication for any science of color. First, the contrast between dusky Germany and shining Italy corresponds to the difference between color phenomena occurring in obscure isolation and the eminent appearance of the full range and variety of color in a harmonic totality. The geographical difference is not merely an accident of climates but symbolizes the distinction between occasional or random observations of nature, such as those that are possible in Germany, and the pure, orderly evidence that is the result of favorable conditions, whether the Mediterranean climate of southern Europe, the deliberate selection of art, or the painstaking analysis of experimental science. There is an important analogy between science and art: Both strive to rescue phenomena from the obscurity of accident by raising them to significant eminence and clarity. Still, no single portrayal of phenomena embraces the whole truth, not simply because of its singularity but also because where some evidence and relationships are enhanced and clarified others often withdraw from view. Not only the connoisseur of art, marveling at the luminosity of a painting's colors, forgets the cooperation of light and shadow; so also does the scientist of color whose ray theory neglects the different degrees of brightness and darkness in colors. Goethe's experiments with black-and-white figures seem to confirm that the different colors have different degrees of affinity to bright white and dark black – for example, in each of the edge spectra, the darker of the two colors adjoins the black – and perhaps as well that a contrast between light and dark is essential to the production of color. These possibilities deserve continued study.

Second, art and science both take their lead from nature. The inquiring mind finds direction and purpose through and among the *res naturae*. Anyone who pays attention to color will notice that it is both universal and particular. The meadow is green, but the variety of individual shades present in the meadow is almost bewildering. Mere cataloging of all the instances does as little justice to universality as sweeping generalization does to the particularized instances. Both a primitive empirical isolation of the individual phenomena and a pale abstraction must be avoided. Here the Italian experience hints at an idea that promises to overcome the dilemma: There appear to be intrinsic harmonic and disharmonic relationships among the various colors (these relationships subsequently became the principal subject matter of the concluding section of the didactic part of *Zur Farbenlehre* more than a decade later). The artist follows this lead by studying nature in order to learn how to accommodate colors to one another in his compositions; perhaps the scientist as well ought to seek a similarly natural path to enlightenment. Third, the practical uses of color – for example, by the artist, the chemist, or the dyer – may bear important implications for the science of color, and the science of color in turn may help bring about a more intelligent and rational practice.

After his introduction of the subject, Goethe broaches the question of laws in nature. Colors arise, disappear, and change in ways that observe a certain regularity, and so men try to explain them according to constant laws and correlations. He gives as an example the blue of the sky, which many observers had attributed to a blue quality of the atmosphere. This seems to account in turn for the bluish color of distant mountains. A closer examination leads us to reflect that if there is a blue quality to air it should increase the intensity of the color the farther away the mountains are; but this hypothesis conflicts with the evidence of the senses, for the more distant the mountains are, the more their color approaches white (*BzO*, par. 5–6). Rainbows, halos, and other phenomena also seem to be subject to a simple, constant law, although the exact character of this law is not immediately evident. These phenomena have always been familiar, and different peoples, even the same person at different stages of his life, experience them in various ways that lead, and have led, to myths, diversion, entertainment, and invention. Despite these differences, however, the history of optics reveals a common theme: For ages people have observed and contemplated colors, reproduced them by means of artifice, and tried to find out their causes and relationships (*BzO*, · par. 7–9).

Once again, the implications of Goethe's words must be considered. Science begins not merely with phenomena but with the perception, however unclear, of some law or unity that needs to be elaborated. Sometimes a plausible explanation is easily found, but plausibility is not sufficient, for any proposal occasions consequences that must be tested against experience. The attempt to come to terms with the lawfulness of phenomena is further complicated by the diversity of ways in which human beings experience the phenomena. One might expect that some of these ways are more productive of understanding than others, perhaps that one alone is truly scientific. Goethe does not here try to answer this question, because his purpose is not to exclude certain approaches as illegitimate and approve others as correct but rather to sketch out the territory, to describe the boundaries and conditions that are intrinsically part of the experience of color.

In characterizing the ways in which people young and old experience color, Goethe says that the adult man aims to eliminate colors from his prisms and lenses; color is a nuisance to be gotten rid of for the sake of improving optical instruments more than it is a subject for investigation in its own right. It is no accident that shortly thereafter he mentions the "profound man" (*BzO*, par. 10) who built up an edifice of optics a century earlier; he means, but does not name, Sir Isaac Newton, who at the time of his landmark discovery was trying to eliminate the distortion by color of lens images. Implicit is a criticism that Goethe would voice in later writings: The accepted theory had only a peripheral concern with color. But here in the *Beiträge* Goethe avoids explicit opposition; instead he points out that in the course of the next century important objections were raised against the theory and, though some were left unanswered, the powerful Newtonian school had repeatedly suppressed criticism and relegated the critics to oblivion. He declares himself hesitant to venture into an investigation that requires not only that one judge the validity of experiments that are "complicated and hard to reproduce" but also that one enter into an abstract theory whose "application cannot be judged without the most exact insight into higher mathematics" (*BzO*, par. 13). This last demand would have discouraged him from becoming involved but for the reflection

that pure experiences ought to lie at the foundation of all natural science, that one can set up a series of them without considering any further relation; that a theory is estimable only when it comprehends all experiences within itself and aids in its practical application, finally that calculation itself, if, as so often happens, it is not to be effort futilely spent, must work toward secure data....

... Thus my duty was to perform once again as exactly as possible the well-known experiments, to analyze, compare, and order them, through which effort I was able to invent new experiments and to make their sequence more complete. (*BzO*, par. 14–15)

Goethe thereby defends his incursion into optics against anyone who might object that the present theory is already adequate. Different ages, different people, even the same people at different times in their lives can bring to the phenomena new eyes that may not only see things afresh but sometimes also rediscover what has been forgotten. By acting as though there still remains much to be done, Goethe tries to place himself outside whatever theory holds the field and concentrate instead on the phenomena. According to the testimony of even his harshest critics, at least in this respect, in concentrating on the phenomena, he succeeded. Goethe's stated intention is to avoid controversy; rather than attack a theory, he will elucidate phenomena by making the experience of them pure, by analyzing and comparing them, by organizing them into significant groupings. Goethe therefore intended to make the *Beiträge zur Optik* an instance of an intrinsically phenomenal science, which is why it appeals so strongly to the aesthetic sensibility.

It is useful to contrast Goethe's intended procedure with another possible approach, the use of a hypothetical model. Such a model's primary purpose would be more to relate all the phenomena to the terms of the model than to organize, analyze, and compare them in their relations to one another. It would ordinarily take on a mathematical form, although at an early stage almost any representation would do, as long as it allowed a reasonably good accounting of what had been determined to be the salient data and as long as it generated consequences. The model should enable one to explain phenomena without constant resort to new hypotheses and constructs; morover, it ought to have predictive power. The use of a model involves a shuttling between phenomena on the one side and the development of the model on the other. The model implies certain consequences that are referred to experimental testing, and then it is further refined and elaborated, perhaps ultimately even rejected, with the aid of the accumulated data and experience.

This kind of theory making is almost entirely absent from the *Beiträge*. In its stead there is a progression from experiment to experiment seemingly devoid of abstraction and virtually unaccompanied by any theoretical commentary, until a simplest experiment is reached. Then suddenly the direction of motion is reversed. Not surprisingly, many have gotten the impression that Goethe's putative incapacity for genuine physical science was rooted in a fear of the kind of abstraction that is necessary for arriving at a scientific theory, or have described Goethe's method as the attempt to make phenomena explain one another (e.g., Helmholtz 1971).

How much more sophisticated Goethe's understanding of science was, how much more complex his justification of a minimally abstract method was, emerges from paragraphs 16 and 17 of the *Beiträge*.

In these past years we have seen a science grow unbelievably, and it continues to grow, to our joy and profit, virtually every day: I mean chemistry. But what a common effort of the most keen-sighted men has been at work therein! What variety of experiences! What exacting investigation of the bodies upon which they work; what acute examination of the instruments by means of which they perform their operations; what methodological progress [*methodischer Fortschritt*]; what fortunate exploitation of accidental appearances; what boldness in hypotheses; what liveliness in debating them; how many inventions in this conflict forced, as it were, from both parties; what impartial utilization of those things that by virtue of common effort belong not to one but to all!

To many who know the diligence and care with which optics has already been elaborated, it may seem strange should I undertake to wish such an epoch on this science as well. But if one recalls how often plausible hypotheses have fixed themselves in the imagination of men and have asserted themselves there, and have finally been banished only by virtue of an overwhelming preponderance of experiences; if one knows how easily a shallow pictorial representation is taken up by the imagination and how wont man is to persuade himself that he has grasped the true relationships with his intellect [*Verstand*]; if one has noticed how cosily he often believes he comprehends what he only [thinks he] knows; then, especially in our decade, when the most ancient rights are being doubted and attacked, one will find it pardonable should someone investigate the documents on which an important theory has based its tenure.

As noted, in the eighteenth century the theory of differential refrangibility according to color was often presented in a deficient form. Moreover, the relatively little research that was done on color was sporadic and often undertaken within the conceptual framework of Newton. Many commonplace phenomena remained unexplained, yet for the most part color seemed to be a settled issue, settled by the physics of light and color. Chemistry, on the other hand, was undergoing its modern revolution at the hands of Lavoisier and his contemporaries. The phlogiston theory of combustion, which had dominated chemical thought for the major part of the century, was being steadily displaced under the pressure of new experiments and interpretations. Even as Goethe wrote (1791) the outcome was not completely settled: Cavendish and Priestley were still defending a modified version of phlogiston, and in fact Lavoisier had opened the final campaign against phlogiston only six years earlier. In Germany, chemists were still divided; Gren, for instance, wrote of the absurdity of the antiphlogistic system, while Johann Friedrich August Göttling, a professor at the University of Jena and Goethe's chief source of chemical knowledge at the time, was avidly proselytizing for "French chemistry."[17]

Since Goethe was not directly involved in this aspect of the scientific revolution, his opinion does not carry any more weight than that of other intelligent outside observers. Yet the passage from the *Beiträge* does not take sides; it rather expresses admiration for the advantages that chemistry has been able to derive from the increased attention to details and to a variety of hypotheses. The common effort of chemical researchers has uncovered new experiments, reexamined old ones, produced new inventions, brought progress in method, exploited accidental discoveries, and not least of all encouraged bold hypotheses that spurred a spirited debate. Goethe's emphasis is not on right or wrong but on the way in which science is done, on the breadth and depth of scientific activity, on how scientists act and think and debate, and on the amount of life or liveliness there is in the science.

The old chemical theory had indeed been capable of providing reasonably good explanations of a range of phenomena, especially those of combustion, but it had also entrenched itself so that its limitations were often inapparent. Its very success overshadowed its failures, and it impressed in the minds of chemists a terminology that made it difficult to express new phenomena unhypothetically and to reconceive the phenomena it seemed to have explained well. For these reasons Goethe was unsympathetic to the phlogiston theory, and he was struck by the greater ease with which the new oxidation–reduction theory could account for the very phenomena that had been mainstays of the phlogiston theory and by the unexplored vistas that the French chemistry opened. In experiments with chemical colors he often borrowed his terminology from the new chemistry and tried to coordinate his findings with the principles of oxidation and reduction. Goethe's attitude toward chemistry, in 1790 and later, shows by itself that Goethe was not opposed to modern science and its abstractness per se, contrary to the claims of critics like Helmholtz. Goethe praised chemistry not only for its exact experimentalism but for its bold hypotheses as well. Although it might be argued that hypotheses are not conceptually identical to abstraction, they nevertheless depend on the ability to abstract from and generalize what is immediately given in individual phenomena. The abstraction involved in forming hypotheses, however, does not necessarily lead to abstract models, as is evident from the kind of abstraction Goethe employed in the *Beiträge:* For example, his black-and-white figures abstract from the appearance of an ordinary visual field, but because they themselves can be viewed through a prism to produce the same kind of phenomena as a natural visual field, they are *concrete abstractions.* If Goethe feared abstraction, he feared it when it was applied abstractly, rather than concretely.

To Goethe's mind, the scandal of optics was not its abstraction but rather inattention to the concrete application of its tenets to the whole range of color phenomena, as well as its theoretical and practical inertia in the late eighteenth century. Accordingly, Goethe's object in writing the *Beiträge* was not solely or even primarily to effect the triumph of a theory but to stimulate new activity in optics. From his excursus about chemistry we can see that it was not the triumph of Lavoisier over phlogiston that was crucial but the scientific activity and the conflict of hypotheses produced by new discoveries. Goethe thus rose above mere partisanship to arrive at a sophisticated insight into the nature and conditions of scientific progress – an insight that would ripen into the historical part of *Zur Farbenlehre*. Goethe had confidence that science could rectify its mistakes, overcome its limitations, and contribute to the general welfare as long as it remained active and open to debate. The greatest threat to science was the sterile passivity induced by degenerate scientific scholasticism, the mere handing down of a written tradition without substantial criticism.

A lively science is a science in progress, a science progressing experimentally, theoretically, and methodically. In the controversy over the Farbenlehre the question of method has too often been overlooked (especially important exceptions, however, are Weinhandl 1932, Blasius 1979, and, above all, Gögelein 1972). But even Goethe's earliest writings on color make clear that he intended not only to improve on the scientific presentation of the phenomena but also to make an original contribution to scientific method; these were not separable goals but intertwined aspects of a single process. Science depends on phenomena, but on phenomena presented in a particularly illuminating way. Natural events are systematically amplified by methodically contrived experiences.

In paragraph 21 Goethe says that "this first installment will contain the simplest prismatic experiments: few but notable experiments, which indeed are not all new, yet not as familiar as they deserve to be." The criticism that these phenomena had already been treated in the Newtonian theory misconstrues Goethe's intention. Is an experiment that was performed in the past "old" in the sense that it is exhausted? Does familiarity imply that nothing more can be learned from it? These questions can be answered only by explicating the proper way of approaching and comprehending experiments, that is, by methodological considerations. Goethe proposes to examine the simplest experiments, experiments that are notable. What makes them simple and notable? Once again, this can be answered only by reflecting on scientific method. Our present concern, then, is to ascertain in what relationship the method that Goethe follows stands to the method of the traditional theory.[18]

The methodological background in "Der Versuch als Vermittler"

In an essay Goethe wrote upon completing the second installment of the *Beiträge,* titled "Der Versuch als Vermittler von Objekt und Subjekt" (the experiment as mediator between object and subject), he discussed what lies behind the apparently uncomplicated *Beiträge*. The leading question of "Der Versuch als Vermittler" is whether there can be any way of ensuring that the subject, the researcher, can discover what is intrinsic to the object of study – whether the researcher can help the object provide its own meaning rather than simply reinforce the opinion of the researcher, despite the bewildering diversity of the empirical world and the difficulty if not the impossibility of drawing one's standards from the things of nature rather than from the limited standpoint of a single human being, who often resorts, wittingly or not, to ad hoc hypotheses, theories, systems, terminologies, and conceptions not inherent in the things of nature.

Nevertheless, Goethe believes that the human being is able to pose the question of what and how things are in themselves, independent of the particularities of the point of view. This approach requires the greatest vigor in directing attention both outward and inward; the researcher must be perfectly aware of the extraordinary demands this method entails. Yet the capacity for shrewd observation is widespread, and one can expect here as elsewhere "that the interest of many directed to a single point is capable of bringing forth something excellent" (*HA*, 13: 12). By cooperating, observers can complement one another's efforts and correct one another's errors. Indeed, "a science is in and for itself such a great mass that it can support many human beings even if no one human being can support it" (*HA*, 13: 13). Once knowledge reaches a certain niveau, it is as much the age as the individual that makes discoveries. One can hardly realize "how necessary communication, assistance, reminders, and contradiction are in keeping us on the right path and in moving us forward" (ibid.). Science is unlike the arts, in which one is better advised to conceal one's work until it is completed; in the sciences it is useful to report publicly every experience and even every conjecture and to refrain from erecting a scientific doctrine until the plans and materials have been publicized, assessed, and selected.

Goethe proposed that the experimental method was the best way of meeting these demands for rigor and publicity, of mediating between the subject's desire for comprehension and the rights of the object to justice and truth. The peculiar value of the experiment, Goethe emphasized, is that under certain specified conditions, using a familiar apparatus operated with requisite skill, one can produce the phenomenon in question as often as the specified conditions are met. This definition highlights the repeatability of the experiment, without which it would be useless for establishing anything dependable. It does not exactly correspond to our notion of the experiment, however. In modern science an experiment is used to test or extend a theory or theoretical proposition, to gather data, or simply to see what will happen under certain circumstances; the phenomena are merely the given, the data, and it is theory that makes sense of them, gives them order, and relates them to one another. For Goethe, on the other hand, the experiment qua phenomenon has an intrinsic importance and bears certain natural affinities and relationships to other phenomena. Something of this difference between the two notions emerges from the passage that immediately follows the definition:

> No matter how valuable any single experiment may be considered by itself, it nevertheless receives its value only through association and connection with others. But to associate and to connect even two experiments that have some similarity to one another demands more rigor and attention than even keen observers often have required of themselves. It can happen that two phenomena are related to one another, yet not by any means so closely as we believe. Two experiments can seem to follow from one another when there in fact would have to be a long series between them in order to bring them into a genuinely natural connection. (*HA*, 13: 14)˙

Goethe names no names, but this passage is surely directed, at least in part, against the traditional method of teaching the theory of light and color, which resorted to but a handful of experiments in proving the differential refrangibility and coloration of light. Each one was adduced to settle a point or to substantiate a proposition, without any explicit attempt to explore their exact relationship to one another. In this basic Newtonian theory, one tries to find out the hidden common denominator of the phenomena – that is, their cause, the different rays; once this cause is discovered, all the individual phenomena can receive an explanation by reference to the cause. For Goethe, on the other hand, the first duty of a scientist is to explore the associations and connections of one phenomenon to another, without the intervention of a theory or hypothesis, rather than try from the outset to give proof to a theory. The initial quest must adhere as closely as possible to the phenomena. This is not to say, however, that one phenomenon explains another, or that every idea must have sensuous immediacy. Although the phenomenon often does yield something that can be expressed only as immediately given, for instance the peculiar quality of each color, Goethe's object is less to preserve sensuous immediacy than to restrain the human urge to generalize on too narrow a basis.

> Therefore one cannot take too many precautions against concluding too swiftly from experiments, wanting to prove something immediately from experiments or to confirm some theory through experiments; for it is here at this pass, at the crossing from experience to judgment, from cognition to application, that all the inner enemies of the human being lurk: the power of imagination that with its wings lifts him on high when he thinks he is still touching the earth, impatience, temerity, self-satisfaction, inflexibility, form of thought, preconceived opinion, indolence, frivolity, changeableness, and the rest of this troop with all their followers, however they may be named; all lie in ambush and unexpectedly

overpower the active observer as well as the calm and quiet one who seems secured against all passions.

In order to arouse a more vigorous alertness I should like here to raise a kind of paradox as a warning against this danger, which is greater and closer at hand than one thinks. I venture namely to assert: that a single experiment, indeed even several experiments in combination prove nothing; in fact nothing is more dangerous than to want to prove a proposition immediately through experiments, and the greatest errors have arisen precisely because people did not recognize the danger and the inadequacy of this method. (*HA*, 13: 14–15)

Goethe remained suspicious of proof by means of experiments to the end of his days; a similar but even more skeptical warning against such proofs stands at the beginning of the polemical part of *Zur Farbenlehre*. The problem is not that we can be certain about nothing; on the contrary, this essay and the Farbenlehre as a whole are predicated on the notion that we can achieve an extraordinarily high degree of certainty – about the experiments, not about propositions. There is a difference, nay a gulf, between the certainty of phenomena and the certainty of a theory: The former are part of experience, whereas the latter comes from a particular way of conceiving that experience. The dangers attend not only the attempt to advance a theory, however, but even the attempt to associate just two phenomena.

Each experience that we make, each experiment through which we repeat the experience, is really an isolated part of our knowledge; through frequent repetition we can raise this bit of knowledge to certainty. Two experiences in the same subject can be known to us, they can be nearly related but appear even more closely related, and usually we are inclined to consider them more closely related than they are....

This mistake is closely related to another, from which it also for the most part arises. Namely, human beings take more pleasure in their representation than in the thing, or rather we must say: Human beings take pleasure in a thing only insofar as they conceive it, it must suit their turn of mind, and try as they may to raise their way of conceiving things ever so high above the common run, try as they may to purify it ever so much, it nevertheless commonly remains but one way of conceiving things: that is, an attempt to bring many objects into a certain comprehensible relation that, strictly speaking, they do not have, and hence the inclination to hypotheses, theories, terminologies, and systems, which we cannot condemn, since they must necessarily spring from the organization of our being. (*HA*, 13: 15–16).

What comes first for Goethe is the experience – for example, his initial experience with the borrowed prism. The experiment is the subsequent attempt to duplicate or reproduce the experience. By performing the experiment repeatedly, one can become sure of the experience, but this certain bit of knowledge stands in problematic relationship to others. The human spirit does not and cannot leave these bits in isolation; it attempts to comprehend and unify them in whatever way it can. This is the point where the Goethe of the *Beiträge* recognizes possible mischief for science; for although there exist nearer and remoter relationships among the various experiences and experiments, the exact nature and degree of affinity can be determined only with the greatest difficulty, not least because the intellect strives to discover a more perfect congruence than really exists.

This argument can obviously be used against the theory of differential refrangibility, which seems to need no more than three experiments in the course of the proof: the formation of the full spectrum with a small aperture and a single prism; the second refraction of colored light already refracted once, using a second aperture and a second prism; and the recombination of once-refracted light by means of a lens or a second prism. The proof seemed so nearly unexceptionable, in particular because of its geometrical aspects, that hardly anyone questioned its self-evidentiality or actively sought an alternative.

Of course, one has to be careful to distinguish between the dependability of mathematics and the completeness, accuracy, and naturalness of a physical theory in mathematical form as it is applied to natural events. From his earliest studies of mathematical physics, Goethe insisted upon this distinction, which underlies all his pronouncements on the relationship between physical science and mathematics. In principle, at least, most of Goethe's immediate contemporaries in the German scientific world were still aware of a gap between mathematics and physics (see von Engelhardt 1979, 63–64, and Caneva 1975, 104–16; cf. Heilbron 1979, 17–18). Not mathematics itself, but the false or misleading application of mathematics to physics is what Goethe wished to ban. Far from wanting to abandon mathematics, Goethe went so far as to call his own method mathematical. To understand what he meant by this, we must look to the end of "Der Versuch als Vermittler," where he explains how his own method circumvents the problems he diagnosed.

His discussion starts from what may be taken as a major premise: "In living nature nothing happens that does not stand in a relationship to the whole, and if experiences appear to us only in isolation, if we are to look upon experiments solely as isolated facts, that is not to say that they are isolated; the question is, how are we to find the relationship of these phenomena, of these givens" (HA, 13: 17). Although the notion of an intrinsic relationship of every natural event to the whole may seem merely speculative and thus problematic, Goethe is thinking of these relationships as determinately differentiated and mediated, and if it is not perfectly evident how one might characterize the relation to *the* whole, it is nevertheless possible to give concrete and exact content to the idea by considering ways in which the *Beiträge* elaborate natural phenomenal wholes. For instance, each isolated experience of looking at objects or displays through the prism gives a single "fact" to be reckoned with. But by means of constant comparison, contrast, simplification, and recomplication, Goethe is able to represent these many apparently isolated facts as different moments of a single dynamic phenomenon, moments that correspond to the varying conditions of the basic experiment. If one first observes a display card at a distance of two feet, then at four feet, one is not performing two different experiments but variants of one. All the variants of a single experiment can thus be comprehended in a kind of superexperiment that consists in changing distances, sizes of apertures and images, and other variables. In some cases the conditions can be varied continuously (e.g., the distance of the screen from the prism); in others this must be done in stages (e.g., the angle of refraction, by substituting different prisms made of the same kind of glass). The resulting superexperiment and superphenomenon represent a natural whole that has been discovered by prudent experimentation.

This process is what Goethe is referring to when he says that the sequence of experiments in the *Beiträge* "constitutes as it were just one experiment, presents just one experience from the most manifold perspectives. Such an experience, which consists of several others, is obviously of a higher kind. It represents the formula under which countless single examples [*Rechnungsexempel*] are expressed" (*HA*, 13: 18). This higher kind of unity is sought by the very best investigators, who according to Goethe proceed from a single experience or experiment to what is immediately adjacent, to what follows directly, and "therefore the manifolding [*Vermannigfaltigung*] of every single experiment is the real duty of the naturalist" (ibid.).

It is *Vermannigfaltigung*, manifolding by variation and augmentation, that constitutes the essential methodological principle of the *Beiträge zur Optik*. The series of prismatic experiments is intended to constitute a single ramified experience/experiment. It proceeds from an initial empirical experience to a systematic amplification, simplification, and finally recomplication of the relevant experiments – that is, experiments that surround the central phenomenon. Each step, each discovery suggests new possibilities that are in turn tested circumstantially. The method depends above all on utter familiarity with the phenomena and on the exhaustive enumeration of all contributing conditions and their variations. The experiments continue until a limit is reached, the point beyond which the phenomenon itself (in this case, color) disappears. If the phenomenon persists when a circumstance is omitted, or if varying the circumstances has no effect, then it is not essential to the appearance of the phenomenon. Once the elemental level has been reached – when all the essential conditions for the appearance of the phenomenon have been discovered, elaborated, and simplified – then the analytical stage has been completed, and a resynthesis can be undertaken to reconstruct the original event and the original experience of the phenomenon and to view it again with comprehension.

This comprehension is not, however, an end result that leaves all the individual cases behind for the sake of a formula, in the way that one can ignore all the individual addends once one has taken their sum. Comprehension does not take the form of a theory abstracted from the phenomena but rather the form of a seeing embedded in the fullness of phenomena. The proximate goal of Goethe's method is to achieve what he called a *naturgemässe Darstellung*, a presentation in accordance with nature, which implies that the presentation has to correspond to the fundamental elements of the phenomenon in question, such as the continuities, associations, contrasts, and wholes that give it structure. Goethe's physical science of color is thus morphological in much the same way that his other sciences are: It studies the manifold forms that the phenomenon (which is in itself a significant entity like color, a plant, an animal) assumes in its emergence, development, and disappearance. Goethe studied the phenomenon in its phenomenality. His method seeks to provide a simple and complete overview of the phenomenon by following the course of the experienced phenomenal event and its articulations.

The presentation according to nature ultimately cannot rest content with the analysis and resynthesis of an isolated phenomenon, however; the phenomenon must be assigned its appropriate place in the larger context of all nature, or at least within a significant part of nature. The color phenomena of the prism need to be analyzed, to be sure, but qua color they must not be cut off from other appearances of color. The subject of color as a whole must in turn be brought into concrete relationships with other subjects and phenomena, indeed with the whole of phenomenal nature. The implication, then, seems to be that until we have reached an understanding of the whole we have not truly understood its individual elements − color, for example. Consequently, the task of science is endless. But can science offer nothing useful or dependable while investigations are in progress? On the contrary, there are many events and phenomena, like colors of the prism, that can be produced and reproduced at will and that can be linked to one another and to other events and phenomena by the study of their conditions. Logically, such study of particular objects leads to and reflects upon the whole, which in its turn redounds upon the particular, because the scientific study of any topic cannot even begin without some provisional knowledge and experience that already implies a tacit understanding of what it is, the forms it takes, and its place in the economy of the whole. The analysis of the prismatic phenomena must necessarily be preceded by general reflections on color and its nature; and following every analysis there must be a recomposition of the elements into the phenomenal wholes to which research always and everywhere must return.

The logic of the *Beiträge* is thus the logic of a phenomenal, experiential science of nature. We have already seen that the opening paragraphs are not merely poetically evocative but also suggestive of themes for scientific research; now we see in addition that the context in which they discuss the subject of color, phenomenal nature, is for Goethe the appropriate, indeed the inevitable context from which all serious research must proceed and within which it must be conducted. Furthermore, Goethe's ensuing discussion of the human desire for explanation and of the variety of human experience analogously sets the stage for a particular kind of experience and explanation, science, and then for a particular science, optics. Explanation has a history; in the case of optics, the history shows that the science has been dominated by a particular interpretation, whose proponents are less than generous to its controverters. Since there are phenomena on the one hand and interpretations of phenomena on the other, Goethe hoped to evade the labyrinths of theory by concentrating his efforts on evolving the phenomena apart from theory.

The *Beiträge zur Optik* survey one demesne of the realm of color, the subjective prismatic phenomena, in order to demonstrate that they have an intrinsic coherence that can be experimentally articulated. From what remains of Goethe's project for a continuing series of *Beiträge*, it is evident that he planned to carry out similar analyses and resyntheses for the other phenomena of color as well, until he had traversed the entire circle of color (see *LA* I, 3: 64–81, 190–209). Although he ended the series after publication of the second part, he did not abandon the overall plan, which, recast and revised several times, culminated in the schema for *Zur Farbenlehre*. Nor did he turn his back on the fundamental method: to begin with a question about a natural phenomenon, something that appears as a part of a whole; to discover through systematic experimentation the prerequisite conditions for this appearance; and to vary and recomplicate the elemental conditions so that the research leads back toward the original standpoint, from which, when it is regained, the observer will see with a sharper and better-trained eye and with a better grasp of the whole and its parts. The empirical phenomena will then be surveyed and embraced in their entirety as a unified and comprehensive scientific phenomenon.

By way of contrast, explanation by means of the ray concept is both more complex and less phenomenal. The ray is a theoretical construct; it is geometrical rather than phenomenal. The ray concept is motivated by various considerations – for example, that light is some kind of matter or the motion of matter; that the rectilinear propagation of light and the nonzero breadth of the physical beam imply the existence of a smallest part of light, either a line ray or the very small particle or disturbance that follows the rectilinear path; and that this ray is in some way decomposed by refraction. Furthermore, all actually observed phenomena are to be explained as the sum of microphenomena – that is, as the result of the overlapping of all the spectra, perhaps an infinite number of them, produced separately by each line ray. All of these suppositions may be true and may form the basis for scientific investigation, but it is hardly credible that anyone could argue that investigation founded upon them is no more theory laden than Goethe's *Beiträge*. Those wishing to do color research outside of these suppositions – for example, physiologists or psychologists for whom the minute structure of radiation was a matter of indifference – might well find these ray investigations irrelevant or even an impediment to their own work. On the other hand, people conceiving color as a strict function of wavelength and intensity and radiation might dismiss studies of the colors of afterimages as insignificant. But Goethe's work can be of some use to anyone interested in prismatic phenomena. Goethe would have been delighted by the words of the eminent colorimetrist Deane B. Judd: "The advantage of trying to follow Goethe's explanations of color phenomena is that, by the time you have succeeded in doing so, your thoughts have become so divorced from the wavelength explanation of colors, that you can begin to think about color theory relatively unhampered by prejudice, either ancient or modern" (Judd 1970, xv). This remark does not prove that the Farbenlehre is theory free – indeed Goethe himself would have denied it – but it suggests that the Farbenlehre may have at least partly succeeded in its intention to free its readers from an excessively theory-bound way of seeing, if they had known how to read it.

We have already mentioned that the object of Goethe's phenomenal demonstration is not to reach a level of generalization that leaves the empirical basis behind, but rather to work through the empirical givens toward the discovery of a unifying appearance or event that can be recognized in all the individual instances. In part 1 of the *Beiträge* the experiments with black-and-white figures led to the case of the single, straight-line boundary, from which we were able to determine that the phenomenon depends on the orientation of the boundary with respect to the prism. This discovery made it possible to look at more complicated prismatic phenomena as combinations and variations of the single-boundary phenomenon. A square or rectangle has four straight-line boundaries at various angles to the prism; a curved figure has boundaries deformed from the straight, but consideration of the orientation of the boundaries to the prism at any point of the curve permits one to predict how wide the band of colors will be and what hues will be visible. Through all these complications we can still recognize a basic phenom-

enon that appears according to constant rules. Moreover, it is not merely
the last step to the elementary single-boundary phenomenon that gives
us scientific insight, but the entire chain of observation, experimentation,
and critical thinking, from the casual event that arouses our curiosity to
the realization that we can unravel an Urphenomenon from all the individual instances.

Each of the prismatic experiments is constructed out of the synthesis of
basic elements or conditions; each can thus be analyzed into these elements, which are understood in light of what our ramified experimentation reveals about them. This construction of phenomena out of elements
that need to be present for the phenomenon to appear suggests that there
are simple as well as complicated phenomena, and even a simplest one (or
rather, in this case, two simplest ones: the two single-boundary experiments, black above white and white above black, both of which confirm
Goethe's initial aperçu that the fundamental condition for the appearance
of color in prismatic experiments is the presence of a boundary between
lighter and darker). The Urphenomenon, the phenomenon that arises from
the simplest synthesis of conditions necessary to the appearance of that
phenomenon, can therefore be considered as literally phenomenal, as
something that appears; what makes it an Ur-phenomenon is that it allows
a truly unifying vision and understanding to someone who conscientiously
pursues the ramifications of the phenomena.[19] Consequently, seeing and
understanding are correlative and inseparable in this method. The initial
aperçu is already the beginning of understanding, for it includes the moment of recognition of the larger and detailed significance of events, and
understanding aids and ultimately perfects seeing so that the individual
cases no longer appear in isolation. What unites the two is the mediator between object and subject, progressive and manifold experimentation.
Thus, as long as innovations and new discoveries are possible, the process
cannot be finally closed. Goethe quite consistently realized that this condition applied to his work as well as the work of others (see LA I, 3: 364
and 8: 180). The discovery of new factors, for instance, would at the very
least require a revised presentation of the phenomena or some modification of the basic concepts employed.

One intriguing aspect of Goethe's exposition of the phenomena is that
it incorporates a fundamental concept of modern mathematics and mathematical physics, the limit of a series, potentially if not actually infinite.
The superexperiment, whether continuously or discretely varied, allows
one to approach phenomenally a limit that may not be reachable in fact
– for instance, an aperture with the breadth of a mathematical point.
The limit of an infinite series is often used in modern science as an abstract
aid to calculation that is justified by theory but not always by exhaustive
experimentation; in Goethe's demonstrations the notion assumes a phe-

nomenal character. Actually seeing what happens to the phenomenon as the experimental conditions are varied to approach an unreachable limit can provide invaluable information about the "phenomenon" at the limit, information that might aid in formulating hypotheses and higher levels of theory. For example, if the aperture in the classic prismatic experiment in camera obscura is made smaller while all the other conditions are kept constant, the spectrum tends to display fewer rather than more colors (see Raman 1968, 22–28). Because the Newtonian theory predicts a more perfect separation of the kinds of light with a smaller aperture, one ought on the contrary to expect a greater variety of colors. Although this limiting phenomenon might not induce one to discard the idea of differential refrangibility, it should at least prompt reconsideration of the notion that there is a perfect correspondence between refrangibility and color and perhaps even raise intriguing questions about the entire process of perceiving colors.

Other mathematical characteristics can be found in Goethe's method in the *Beiträge*. Heisenberg suggested that there are resemblances between modern theories of symmetry and number and Goethe's elaboration of the morphology of color phenomena (Heisenberg 1952, 65). In some of the posthumously published manuscripts, there are other startling similarities to modern mathematics. In one that may have been intended as another installment of the *Beiträge*, Goethe derives straight-line boundaries from a curved boundary by performing what amounts to a continuous topological deformation of space: A flat black disk on which the observer with a prism stands is gradually deformed into the shape of a bowl, so that when the boundary reaches eye level it appears as a straight line (*LA* I, 3: 176 and corresponding figure).

The earliest critics of Goethe's color science thought it was unmathematical because it lacked exact measurements and ignored the sine law governing refractions. This criticism may be misdirected, however, and not merely because Goethe encouraged others to apply measurement to his results. The superexperiment by its nature provides an intrinsic ordering of all the isolable instances of the phenomena with respect to one another. Although for lack of a prism with a refracting angle of, say, 37 degrees, we may not be able to demonstrate that, all other things being equal, the spectra and edge spectra it produces are intermediate between those produced by prisms with refracting angles of 35 and 40 degrees, we will nevertheless have a clear, even an exact notion of where this particular case should fit into the entire sequence. Goethe's "theory" predicts the result in undemonstrated cases relative to other, known results. The more and the less, the earlier and the later are landmarks that make possible relative measurements; after all, measurement has a purpose only when something can be intelligently compared with other similar or related things.[20] Goethe explicitly stated in part 1 of the *Bei-träge* that measurement and calculation could be applied "to a certain degree" (*BzO*, par. 69), and in the didactic part of *Zur Farbenlehre* he encouraged the mathematically inclined to seek out ways in which they could further the science of color (*FL-D*, par. 727). Goethe's immediate object was to provide a nearly exhaustive presentation of phenomena in a naturally significant order, on the basis of which other researchers, including mathematicians, might add their own contributions in complete awareness of what needed to be done. It cannot be emphasized too much that to Goethe's mind direct experience in a proper order of the full range of color phenomena was the absolute prerequisite for any genuine, much less comprehensive, progress in color science.

Goethe once said of mathematical symbolization that it has the potential to become nearly identical in the highest sense with the phenomena that it represents (*LA* I, 11: 57); still he was wary of the human inclination to search prematurely behind, beneath, and beyond the phenomena. A mathematical theory, though it be concisely and accurately founded and erected on exact data, ordinarily cannot simply displace or trivialize the data when they are immediately given phenomena. Even when a mathematical theory is based on purely numerical data, the numbers are almost always derived by means of concrete operations and instruments that ultimately refer to some phenomenon, to some visible or at least detectable event; and mathematical formulas must always be qualified by the conditions and limitations of their applicability to real events.

Goethe's presentation in the *Beiträge* therefore highlights a number of phenomena that are neglected by the mathematical theory. For example, the magenta that appears at the center of the black rectangle on a white ground when viewed through the prism was overlooked because it did not appear in Newton's solar spectrum; yet in modern color theory it is as fundamentally important as the *ROYGBIV* colors, and takes up nearly one-third of the standard *CIE* color triangle. Although the indexes of refraction are continuous and thus suggest that the transition from hue to hue is likewise smoothly continuous, the spectra that Goethe described have few colors, which quite suddenly give way to one another. Goethe also demonstrated systematic polarities in the prismatic phenomena, none of which can be articulated in the language of refractive indexes.[21]

No matter how good the fit, the observed phenomena ought not to be supplanted by an abstract theory, for, at the very least, knowledge about how one is to apply the theory is itself metatheoretical and therefore metamathematical. Goethe's method, to demonstrate through judicious experimentation phenomenal wholes that unify the appearances – to elucidate the form and structure of the phenomena – is a prerequisite for the scientific application of mathematics. Such a method is to be recommended all the more in cases like color where mathematical theories almost inevitably overlook the intrinsic character or quality of the phenomena. The ray theory of light and color translates the phenomena into constructs that seem to reveal what is behind the phenomena. Color is merely a product of the ray, an epiphenomenon as it were, and is treated as an indicator of the presence of the construct, the kind of ray, rather than as the true object of investigation. The conditions of the experiment and the instruments used are correspondingly devalued: They are simply means to the end of gathering information about the theoretical construct and so have no intrinsic interest. For example, the aperture selects a larger or smaller bundle of rays out of the mass of those coming from the sun; the prism merely changes their direction. The phenomenal event is thereby reduced to the behavior of the ray, and the phenomena are rendered in the language of ray analysis. But then is it the phenomena that vouch for the theory, or the translation of the phenomena? This is a restatement of the problem with which Goethe began "Der Versuch als Vermittler."

We are now in a better position to understand that Goethe's attempted contribution in the *Beiträge* was more methodological than theoretical and that the method could not have been other than phenomenal/experimental.

In the first two installments of my optical contributions I have sought to erect such a sequence of experiments [i.e., ramified through *Vermannigfaltigung*] that first and foremost border on one another and touch one another without mediation; indeed, when one knows and surveys them all exactly they constitute as it were a single experiment, they represent a single experience under the most manifold perspectives.

Such an experience, which consists of several others, is evidently of a higher kind. It presents the formula under which countless individual examples are expressed [*Rechnungsexempel*]. To work toward such experiences of the higher kind I consider the duty of whoever does research into nature; the example of the most excellent men who have worked in this field points us this way, and the conscientiousness in placing the closest next to the closest or rather in deducing the closest from the closest we must learn from the mathematicians, and even where we attempt no calculations we must always go to work as though we owed an account to the most rigorous geometer. (*HA*, 13: 18)

That is, the method must be so consequent that any gap in the demonstration will be immediately obvious; and the method's "proofs are really just circumstantial expositions that that which is brought forward in combination was there already in its simple parts and in its entire consequence, was surveyed in its entire compass and devised so as to be correct and irrefutable under all circumstances. And so this method's demonstrations are always more expositions, recapitulations than arguments" (*HA*, 13: 19).

The "experiences of a higher kind" are Goethe's answer to the propositions proved by more or less isolated experiments. They are the result not of an attempt at proof but of a long series of phenomena that are shown by experiments to be intrinsically connected. Whereas scientific propositions that are to be proved are ordinarily expressed in the artificial terminology of abstractly theoretical constructs, the utterance of experiences of the higher kind will conform to and summarize the experimental sequences; they will achieve a higher level of generality. They will be

enunciated through short and comprehensive propositions, placed one next to another, and, when more of them have been worked out, organized and brought into a relation such that they stand, just like mathematical propositions, unshakable, either singly or taken together. The elements of these experiences of a higher kind, which are many individual experiments, can then be investigated and tested by everyone, and it is not hard to judge whether the many individual parts can be expressed by a general proposition, for there is no arbitrariness here. (ibid.)

Once such a proposition has been secured, reason, imagination, and wit may do with it as they please: "This will not do harm, indeed it will be beneficial." Nevertheless, the initial work – the collection, examination, and organization of the phenomena – must be done with the greatest care, industry, rigor, and even pedantry, so that when wit and imagination are set loose they do not distort the phenomena at will. In this way one assures both that important phenomena are not neglected and that the subsequent theories and hypotheses remain bound to the full evidence.

Scientific method and scientific evidence are thus inextricably bound together at every stage of research. Goethe's method is distinguished from the optical science prevalent in his day by its concern for the conditions and interrelationships of the phenomena and its attempt to avoid descriptive terms that are actually theoretical constructs. Where the Newtonian sees evidence for rays, Goethe sees colors, or rather the event or occurrence of color, and is first and foremost concerned with what is apparent, including all the conditions of the event. The event of the phenomenon constitutes the real subject of inquiry, and thus may not be immediately adduced to "reveal" something about the nature of light or to determine whether some theory is right or wrong, as though the phenomenon had no importance apart from theory verification. Before the scientist attempts to elaborate hypothetical explanations of the phenomena, he is duty bound to secure the phenomena by placing them into a comprehensive and significant relationship to one another; only thereafter is he free to speculate about possible causes and abstract theories. One of the chief advantages to be gained from putting this systematic experimental account at the beginning of scientific work is that it provides a common ground for the community of researchers, a sense of the complete range of the relevant phenomena and its order in the natural domain, and a demonstration of some of the basic and controlling characteristics that need to be borne in mind as the researchers work out their hypotheses.

The positive and negative doctrines of the Beiträge

Given Goethe's methodological caveat against premature theorizing – that is, theorizing before an adequate experimental history has been established – it is not surprising that the Beiträge do not offer a theory as elaborate as Newton's and seem like an assemblage of already well-known phenomena. Yet, from the method outlined in "Der Versuch als Vermittler," it is perfectly clear that they are no mere assemblages, but the elaboration of fundamental unities that are to serve as the foundation for further research. With his typical early Baconian reserve, however, Goethe gave at the end of part 1 of the Beiträge only a hint of what was to come.

Perhaps before I close I ought to propose some general observations and point to the distant place whither I intend to lead my readers. But probably this can well occur only at the end of the next installment, since what I could possibly say here would still necessarily appear as undocumented and unproved. But I can say this much to those who would like to press forward: In the few experiences that I have brought forth the ground is already laid for everything to come, and it will be almost mere elaboration, when in what succeeds we shall discover the law revealed by means of ground glasses, in water drops and vapors, even finally with the naked eye under certain given conditions. (BzO, par. 73)

As much as possible the theory must wait upon the phenomena, although theory is always ready to leap beyond what has been achieved. As we shall see shortly, Goethe eventually reassessed the place and contribution of theory so that he could no longer agree with what he had asserted at the end of part 2 of the Beiträge, that a simple law would be "found, made clear, and applied in a thousand different ways, without one's having chosen or ventured a theoretical way of explanation" (BzO, "Nacherinnerung," LA I, 3: 51). This tension is already present in the Beiträge. In several places Goethe finds himself anticipating what is to come; and in the advertisement he wrote to announce part 1 of the Beiträge he remarked that because he was writing for amateurs as well as experts he had been unable to completely avoid binding the experiences to be presented by theory and hypothesis (LA I, 3: 4). This statement probably refers in part to the views about light, darkness, and color expressed in paragraphs 22–32, which Goethe called "the more general things." The more specific reference, however, must be to a notion he found himself anticipating (and that was implied already in par. 55); as he noted toward the end of part 2 of the *Beiträge*, "we must of necessity place two opposed edges before us, if we want to see all the prismatic colors at once, and we must bring these edges relatively closer to one another if the appearances, separated from and opposed to one another, are to be joined and to present a series of colors by way of a mixed transition" (*BzO*, "Nacherinnerung," *LA* I, 3: 50).

This is the experience of a higher kind that is to be derived from the sequence of experiments; it is, as it were, the "formula, under which countless singular examples are expressed," examples like the phenomena of the *Beiträge*, especially as they are formulated in "short and comprehensible propositions" in paragraph 72, "Rekapitulation" (e.g., no. 1: "Black, white, and pure, uniformly colored surfaces show no colors through the prism"), which in turn are correlated to the experimental demonstrations. In 1792 Goethe believed he had achieved the desideratum of organizing, elaborating, and ordering the basic propositions without admixture of theory; later he changed his mind. But it is clear, in contrast to the Newtonian method, that Goethe is rather less interested in proving a theory than in demonstrating phenomena and striving to formulate them adequately in words. The results of his work are a beginning rather than a perfection, a new articulation of phenomena rather than an investigation of their underlying causes. Keeping in mind these differences, that we are contrasting an emerging theory with one that was more or less complete, let us summarize the results of the *Beiträge* that are immediately relevant for criticizing the accepted theory of color.

In order for prismatic colors to appear there must be some kind of alternation of brightness and darkness in the image that is seen through the prism. Colors do not appear all at once; they first emerge from the boundaries where dark and bright areas adjoin. The complete spectrum does not become visible unless there are two boundaries, where the blue from one boundary begins to overlap yellow from the other. As an observer holding a prism close to his eye moves farther from the object viewed – or, in an objective camera obscura experiment, as the screen is moved farther from the prism – the spectrum changes in both color and proportion. First there is a white center; as blue and yellow overlap to produce green the colors attain the greatest variety; finally, as the distance becomes ever greater, the variety of colors is reduced until only three distinct hues, red, green, and violet, are visible. Similarly, with a dark image on a light background a central magenta appears only when the red and violet outstreamings meet, and the corresponding spectrum tends toward three hues, yellow, magenta, and blue.

Now we may consider some of the criticisms that can be inferred:

1. The traditional theory asserts that the prism separates or decomposes

white light into its component colors. Yet a uniform surface viewed through a prism does not manifest any prismatic colors at all, and a white figure on a black ground (or, alternatively, an isolated beam of white light) remains white at its center for some distance from the prism; that is, white light can be refracted without (immediately) becoming colored (cf. *LA* I, 3: 166–69). Let the size of the white rectangle (or the white circle) on the black ground be reduced at will, so that it resembles a small aperture of the kind used in the objective experiments: One will still be able to find a position where the center is uncolored when observed through the prism. The bald assertion that white light is decomposed by refraction thus needs qualification.

The Newtonian protest that the visible image is merely the sum of the myriad spectra produced from the individual rays begs the question. First of all, if the experiments adduced in evidence actually used individual rays, the proof might be valid, but every experiment that is even conceivable employs a beam, not a line ray, so that one never sees what happens to an individual ray. Second, how does one justify saying that a ray of white light is decomposed? If the image produced by refraction were colorless, one might say that it had been spread or diffused but certainly not decomposed. Why must we presume that the color rays are already present in the white light? Perhaps the encounter with the prism does more than just separate previously existent color rays; perhaps it creates the colors in the first place. Although there is no denying that colors appear after refraction, it is not clear, on the basis of the standard presentations, why we should take the colors as uniquely identifying a single kind of ray, whether before or after refraction. Indeed, the alteration of colors in the spectrum as the circumstances of the experiment are varied leads to uncomfortable consequences. For example, it would have to be demonstrated why the particular circumstances cited in the standard accounts (size of aperture, position of screen, and other variables) should be taken as authoritative. If you put the screen close enough to the prism, the center of the spectrum is white; ergo, a white-producing ray falls thereupon. Saying that it is necessary to place the screen farther away so that the rays may be better separated does not help because if you go far enough the spectrum is reduced to the three colors, red, green, and violet (see *BzO*, par. 59, 61; cf. *LA* I, 3: 180). Does this imply that the yellow-, orange-, and blue-producing rays have disappeared? How could this happen? And if they are still present, why do they not produce yellow, orange, and blue? Apparently, the experimental argument for the theory is neither sufficient as proof nor self-evidently true.

Furthermore, diagrams that suggest that a full spectrum is visible from the moment of refraction and, even worse, those that show a multitude of color rays in the central portion of the refracted beam as it emerges from the surface of the prism are misleading, if not false, because they prompt one to imagine as present a thing hypothesized, not really visible. Such diagrams illustrate a theory, not the phenomenon. Goethe would contend that a theory ought to help one observe the phenomena rather than replace them with constructs and symbols that induce one to look at the phenomena abstractly (cf. *LA* I, 3: 302). If the presentation of a theory is to have genuine pedagogic value it must enlighten uninitiates about what has been, and what can be, demonstrated with certainty before passing on to what can only be inferred. Putting just a single experiment or a small number of experiments at the threshold of the doctrine of color is working backward; the proper method is first to present an experimental history of the subject and only then, when a student is thoroughly familiar with the phenomena and thus prepared to make an intelligent and comprehensive judgment, to advance a hypothetical or theoretical point of view.

2. The traditional theory asserts that violet is refracted more than any other color. Yet if one observes the developing phenomenon, for instance by walking further away from the white rectangle on a black background (in the subjective case) or by moving the screen farther from the prism (in the objective case), one notices that the yellow band advances in the same direction and increases at the same rate as the violet band (*BzO*, par. 50, 92). Because the yellow and violet emerge not from the same edge of the image but from different edges, one ought to measure the degree of displacement or refraction from the respective edges, not from some presumed common central origin. To put this conclusion in terms of refrangibility, the refracted image has a leading edge and a trailing edge, from both of which colors stream out. The yellow or the yellow-producing rays seem to be as much refracted relative to the trailing edge of the image, from which red and yellow issue, as the violet-producing rays are relative to the leading edge, from which come blue and violet. The yellow advances until it blends with the blue, after which it is no longer visible because these two colors combine into green (*BzO*, par. 56, 59).

On purely phenomenal grounds, then, it appears that the violet and the yellow are equally refrangible. The violet only seems more refrangible in the full spectrum because the yellow has been absorbed in the green mixture. A corresponding experiment with a black rectangle on a white background would lead to a similar conclusion, with roles reversed: Yellow streams out ahead of all the other colors, but violet advances just as rapidly across the black center until it mixes with red to form purple-magenta (*BzO*, par. 56, 59). In paragraph 67 of the *Beiträge* Goethe goes so far as to say that this latter experiment might tempt someone to conclude that a "beam of darkness" is decomposed into its colored components, that yellow is the most refrangible color, blue the least, and the other colors intermediately refrangible. He immediately repudiates the idea because it would almost certainly bring about hopeless confusion. The point, however, seems to be that a beam of darkness being dissolved into its components makes as much sense as the decomposition of light, given the phenomenal criteria (the appearance and the location of color) applied in the accepted theory. But a beam of light is "something" and darkness is "nothing," according to the traditional response, justified by long practice. Yet phenomenally, even a beam of light is defined by both brightness and darkness. A beam of light is bounded by darkness just as a "beam of darkness" is bounded by light; and darkness cannot be nothing, because it is visible. Indeed, brightness and darkness and thus light and dark seem to be correlative terms, definable only with respect to one another. The phenomena of the prism reinforce the symmetry of light and dark; therefore, one should hesitate before dismissing darkness as a nothing that leads to nothing.[22]

3. Although both green and purple-magenta can be produced under circumstances that are identical except for the reversal of black and white, according to the accepted theory green is one of the fundamental colors while magenta is not. But magenta, qua color, is no less chromatic and no less distinctive than green. The accepted theory justifies the distinction on the grounds that magenta is a mixture of red and violet, whereas green is simple. But it is precisely this distinction that Goethe's phenomena call into question, for they seem to demonstrate that both are mixtures (BzO, par. 58). This conclusion is further reinforced by what one sees when looking at green figures through a prism: They appear fringed with blue and yellow.[23] The point here is not, as a Newtonian would say, that Goethe fails to understand the accepted theory, but that Goethe is calling into question virtually all the phenomenal criteria by which the Newtonian draws his conclusions and showing that the very descriptions of the phenomena offered by the Newtonians are already saturated with theory.

4. All colors are darker than white and brighter than black (BzO, par. 102); that is, in comparison to white they are shadowed or dimmed, in comparison to black they are like sources of light. Colors are, as it were, a blend of light and dark – something one can appreciate more distinctly by considering the results of viewing through the prism gray rectangles on both lighter and darker achromatic backgrounds: The colors of the edge spectra are dusky, darkened in comparison with the edge spectra produced by black-and-white figures. Moreover, some spectral colors when mixed enhance one another, brighten one another; others seem to have a canceling effect, to muddy or darken one another. What these results imply is that color cannot be understood merely by taking the

sum of rays, for rays are pure light, yet the light that comes to the eye conveys the impression of duskiness (darkness) as well as of lightness. For example, if the rays add up to objective white, why do they sometimes yield the impression of dark gray? Ray theory itself does not exhaustively explain the colors one sees; color science, therefore, is in need of other principles in order to account for the appearances.

5. The accepted theory hardly treats of the relationships of the individual colors to one another. Newton did invent a color circle to account for the results of mixing colors, but he and his followers took no particular interest in other relations that this circle might have revealed.[24] Furthermore, Newton formed this circle by bending the linear spectrum into a curve and merely joining the ends; consequently it omits the purples that are intermediate between spectral red and spectral violet. Newton also expended much ingenuity trying to establish a correspondence between the numerical proportions of the tones in the musical octave and the positions of the colors in the spectrum; but Goethe's demonstration reveals that Newton's proportions are based on an arbitrary selection of the experimental circumstances, which, if chosen differently, give quite different results.

Goethe on the contrary sought to determine the relationships that subsist between colors by studying not isolated phenomena but phenomena placed within the context of phenomenal events, particularly as revealed in an experimental sequence. The Beiträge show that there is an initial separation of red and yellow from blue and violet; that within each pair the brighter color adjoins the brighter part of the field, while the darker color adjoins the darker part; that blue occupies the same area as red, and violet the same as yellow; that green and magenta emerge in analogous circumstances with the poles white–black reversed; and so on and so forth. These various symmetries suggest natural affinities and contrasts; although their exact nature and extent need further elucidation, it is highly unlikely that they are insignificant for understanding color (e.g., see LA I, 3: 190–209). The discovered relationships sometimes also augment the understanding of qualities and characteristics previously encountered. The artist's distinction of warm and cool colors, for instance, is naturally related to the polarity of the two kinds of edge spectrum, and prismatic phenomena substantiate the subjective feeling that green and magenta form transitions between pairs of colors, blue and yellow on the one hand, red and violet on the other. In the Beiträge Goethe does not insist on a universal polarity or assert that these phenomena prove the validity or exhaust the content of the artist's notions of warm and cool (but see BzO, par. 20); yet the phenomena as presented do exhibit a remarkable polarity that supports the artist's distinction, and this correspondence ought not to be dismissed lightly as of no scientific interest. Even if neither polarity nor the contrast of warm and cool can be shown to have a more profound physical sense, these notions can and probably should form the basis of further color studies.

6. The accepted theory was ambiguous about the number of fundamental colors. The spectrum as traditionally represented was variously said to display five or seven or an indefinitely large number of colors. As we have already seen, even serious natural philosophers like Erxleben and Lichtenberg could be confused about the exact number. Strictly construed, the theory of different kinds of rays requires a potentially infinite number of fundamental colors; but the theory, strictly construed, badly misrepresents what is seen. The visible colors are far more homogeneous than the theory implies, no matter what the exact circumstances under which the spectrum is produced; the visible colors depend in part on how and where one focuses one's attention; and the transitions between discriminable colors are not gradual but so rapid that often they seem to be clearly demarcated boundaries.

7. Last of all, the theory of diverse refrangibility was, practically speaking, useless (see *LA* I, 3: 158–59, 181–83). As of the late eighteenth century it had generated few if any practical applications; and with respect to questions about reasons for colors in specific circumstances, the theory could give answers only in principle. (Why is a vase blue? Because it reflects predominantly blue-producing rays. But this explanation is tautologous.) Moreover, the theory had been of no assistance to those who worked with dyes, pigments, and the like, and gave neither the theoretician nor the technician or artist a better understanding of his craft.[25]

The foregoing criticisms derived from the *Beiträge* give a clear sense of what Goethe thought was at issue. Most are based on phenomenal grounds, which cannot easily be separated from methodological questions. Perhaps the core of Goethe's methodological differences with Newton has to do with the question of what provides the context for understanding the significance of an experimental phenomenon. Goethe rejected the idea of isolated crucial experiments because they left the phenomenon in its primitive singularity without consulting similar phenomena for comparison and elucidation. As an alternative, he proposed a point of view from which natural wholes and affinities, comprehensible only within the frame of the entire phenomenal demonstration, become conspicuous. Consequently, although both Goethe and his critics agreed that certain fundamental facts about color were evident from the prismatic experiments, these facts and the very manner in which they were to be established were quite different.

Goethe's critics, accepting the technique of Newtonian ray analysis as self-evident, accepted essentially ostensive proofs of the theory. Ray analysis provided the unquestioned context in which the "facts" were described and their theoretical consequences deduced, a context that made color seem a branch of pure geometry. Goethe did not dispute the merits and successes of geometric optics, but he did question its accuracy and sufficiency when it was applied to the phenomena of color (*HA*, 13: 328). Rather than appeal to a crucial experiment that was supposed to refute independently the accepted theory, Goethe offered a nexus of experimental phenomena meant to articulate their intrinsic characteristics and also to point up shortcomings and omissions in the Newtonian hypothesis. His motive was not a poetic or metaphysical whim, but fidelity to what appears when one observes prismatic colors and the sober belief that no theory, whatever its merits, ought to be substituted for the phenomena.

A month after part 1 of the *Beiträge* appeared, Goethe openly declared to friends and acquaintances his outright opposition to Newton's theory, because, as a contemporary witness of the incident wrote, "it has been completely overthrown through [Goethe's] experiments" (*LA* II, 3: 49). Whatever reserve the *Beiträge* may have displayed, Goethe clearly had a polemical intention, the intention of proving Newton's theory wrong. We must not, however, overemphasize the polemical intent of the *Beiträge*. Goethe's earliest writings can hardly be called polemical, at least not in the sense of the polemic of *Zur Farbenlehre*. No scorn or ridicule is directed toward Newton and his followers, and despite Goethe's willingness to pronounce the theory overthrown in private he appears to have tried to avoid public antagonism. It can hardly be argued that Goethe's primary interest was polemical, that he developed his own theory because he wanted to overthrow Newton. Instead, he undertook a project that was meant to develop his insight that color in prismatic experiments depends on the adjacency of brighter and darker fields. In the course of this work he tried to point to flaws in the accepted doctrine as it was taught in the late eighteenth century, flaws that ultimately derived from the theory taught by Newton.

Goethe's aperçu was twofold: In realizing the inadequacy of an existing theory, he glimpsed the elements of a new teaching. Although to Goethe's critics the negative aspect is most conspicuous and the positive seems to be nugatory, for Goethe the negative aspect was subsidiary. Only in 1793 did he start work on a number of essays that would culminate seventeen years later in the polemical part of *Zur Farbenlehre*. Not until late 1796 did he actually publish overt criticisms of Newton, and then only in verse epigrams. The necessary inference seems to be that during the first years of his optical and chromatic studies Goethe did not plan to take the field against Newton and the Newtonians except indirectly. Insofar as the old theory obstructed his new approach, it had to be opposed, but there was no animosity, open or covert, toward its proponents. He was far more concerned to enlist the aid of others in combing through the scientific literature on color in physics, chemistry, botany, anatomy, and any other disciplines that might produce relevant phenomena, information, and interpretations; in inventing, performing, analyzing, and resynthesizing the necessary experiments; and in studying and criticizing the classic works on optics and color to ascertain what was still of service and what was in need of revision (see, e.g., *LA* I, 3: 130–36; cf. 64, 81–89).

Goethe himself says in the "Konfession" that he would have preferred to turn his chromatic studies over to others, because he found himself "in a new, unbounded field, the measure of which I did not feel qualified to take." Through his conversations and publications he hoped "to rouse in some other mind the aperçu that had worked so vigorously in my own." He wanted to set the science of optics on a new course without having to do all the exploration himself. But his criticism of the accepted theory had just the opposite effect. It isolated him from his contemporaries and forced him to carry out all the work by himself (see *HA*, 14: 261–62.). He apparently had anticipated little resistance to the *Beiträge* and expected that a discrepancy between the phenomena and the accepted theory would be immediately apparent and that the cardinal tenets of his own doctrine would be clear to all who took the trouble to view the experiments. If this is a sign of Goethe's naiveté, it is a Baconian naiveté – the expert will recognize the truth through simple induction from experiments and observations (which was indeed the professed method of most natural philosophers). Goethe swiftly overcame his naive Baconianism. The failure of his attempt to let the phenomena speak for themselves helped him outgrow the narrowness of strict inductivism and impelled him in the direction of viewing science as intrinsically historical and dominated by implicit theoretical imperatives, even in initial approaches to the subject matter. More than most of his contemporaries he strove to make his stated method accord with what he actually did.

Goethe's methodological purpose completely escaped his contemporaries. Perhaps this result is not so surprising when we consider that he did not publish "Der Versuch als Vermittler" or any other explicit statement on method until much later. Moreover, even if they had grasped his purpose, his contemporaries might still have argued that the accepted color theory met the stringent test of accounting satisfactorily for the most important phenomena of color. They might further have pointed out that even Bacon had written that "inquiries into nature have the best result when they begin with physics and end in mathematics." Newton's optics was thus an example of the perfection of Baconian method – a physical investigation that arrived at a mathematical doctrine by induction from experiments.

Unfortunately for Goethe and for other participants in the subsequent controversies, the discussion of what amounts to satisfactory proof and in what ways mathematics is essential to the founding of a science never got even this far. As we shall see in Chapter 4, the failure to establish common ground with contemporary physicists in the 1790s may have been decisive, for the changing climate of physics between 1790 and 1810 made it ever less probable that he would be able to win an audience. Although soon he changed his mind about being able to prove Newton wrong, to the end of his days Goethe insisted that the *Beiträge* had brought up difficulties sufficient to necessitate a reexamination of Newton's theory. To some small degree, he perhaps succeeded. As has already been mentioned, Gren revised his erroneous account of 1788 in the edition of 1793 (he also included a critique of the *Beiträge*), and Gehler gave a detailed explanation of Newton's theory in direct response to Goethe. Lichtenberg's successive editions of Erxleben, however, went uncorrected.

Toward Zur Farbenlehre

Between the publication of the first two installments of the *Beiträge* (1791–92) and 1798, the year in which he drafted the first outlines for what became *Zur Farbenlehre*, Goethe discovered that his initial plan for a continuing series of *Beiträge* could not be accomplished. The problem developed in the projected third installment on colored shadows. When an object is illuminated by two differently colored lights, the shadows they cast can take on colors that are not explicable solely on the assumption that the composition of the radiation coming from the shaded areas completely determines the perceived color. Goethe's experiments with sunlight, skylight, moonlight, and candlelight (see *LA* I, 3: 64–81) showed that the two shadows cast by an object illuminated from two different light sources tend to appear in colors diametrically opposite on the color circle that he was developing, a phenomenon that we call complementary hues. At first he believed that the critical factor was the difference in the intensities of the two illuminants, and he was inclined to interpret the phenomenon of colored shadows as an interaction of relative light and darkness. Some years later (1798), he described this early approach of his as a rigid realism and stumbling objectivity (*LA* I, 3: 305; cf. 363); he had been searching for a univocal objective correlate of color, much as Newton had sought an object corresponding to color and found it in the ray.[26]

For a while Goethe corresponded with Lichtenberg about these shadows (*LA* I, 3: 81–89). Lichtenberg admitted that he did not have an explanation, but he believed that part of the solution lay in the human proclivity for allowing judgment to confuse sensation. White, for instance, is the disposition of the surface of a body to reflect all kinds of colored light equally well in all directions; but such an object appears truly white only under very rare conditions. Perhaps the only person to see a real white is someone who observes snow in the high mountains when the sun is shining brilliantly. Although Goethe was himself interested in the problem of giving colors an objective definition, he could not sympathize with this Newtonian attempt to define color that turned the experience of white into an unrealizable ideal, and he began to see that Lichtenberg would not or could not allow the extraordinary difficulties that colored shadows created for the Newtonian theory of color – in that the hues seen may not correspond at all to the composition of the light coming from the shadow – to shake his theoretical convictions.

Suppose an opaque object (e.g., an obelisk) sitting erect on a white surface is illuminated by two lights, one tinted with some color and the other white, so that two distinct shadows are cast on the white surface. The shadow cast by the colored light will then be illuminated by the white source, the other will be cast by the white light and illuminated by the colored. Not surprisingly, the shadow illuminated by the colored light will appear in that same color. What occurs with the other shadow, however, is astonishing. The light coming from it is "objectively" white; the white surface reflects all the different kinds of rays in the white light equally well. The shadow should, theoretically, appear white or gray. But the shadow will ordinarily display a chromatic hue complementary to the color of the chromatic illuminant. This means that by varying the hue of the colored light source, one can make this shadow, from which in every instance "objectively white" light is being reflected, appear variously as red, orange, yellow, green, blue, violet, and magenta. This kind of discrepancy between the theoretical color and the perceived color led Benjamin Thompson, Count Rumford, to conclude that colored shadows are optical illusions; to which Goethe thundered in reply: "It is blasphemy to say there is such a thing as an *optical illusion*" (*LA* I, 3: 93). Far from being a subjectivist revolt against science, this outburst was a reasoned consequence of Goethe's deepening realization that to seek a purely external and objective definition of color is to misunderstand what it is. His study of colored shadows soon led to a heightened interest in other color phenomena that do not manifest a strict correspondence between the so-called external stimulus and the sensation. These are Goethe's physiological colors; they comprise not only colored shadows but also afterimages, visual adaptation to light and color, colors seen when the eye suffers a blow or pressure, and other phenomena. He enlisted the aid of physiologist Samuel Thomas Sömmerring and conducted experimental investigations of these colors; eventually he also studied (1798 and after) cases of color blindness that were brought to his attention.

The discovery[27] of the physiological colors led to revisions and modifications of both Goethe's doctrine and his method. First of all, it was no longer appropriate to look for a purely objective correlate of color, for example a dynamic interaction of light and dark. All color is seen, and thus any comprehensive science of color must reflect this fact by incorporating as a fundamental condition the activity of seeing and the lawful contributions of the eye. Yet there remain significant homologies between the laws governing the physiological colors and those pertinent to physical and chemical colors; and these Goethe attempted to embody in his circle of color, which he used to summarize essential relationships such as what we call complementarity between chromatic hues. For example, one of the most striking characteristics of the perception of color is the eye's tendency to see the complementary of the color with which it is directly presented, as in the case of colored shadows. This phenomenon suggested the idea that the eye strives for totality by way of polar opposites, that what one sees in one part of the visual field affects what one will see in the rest, and that what one sees at one moment conditions what one sees at the next. Goethe increasingly regarded this kind of polarity, which had already been intimated in the experimental demonstrations of the *Beiträge*, as fundamental to the experience, and thus to the understanding, of color (see, e.g., *BzO*, par. 55; cf. *LA* I, 3: 97). Polarity does not imply a rigorous calculus, however, so that given color A one will always and everywhere see color B as well; it instead expresses a tendency or potential that may, under particular conditions, be actualized, modified, or suppressed.[28]

Just before publishing part 1 of the *Beiträge*, Goethe announced that he had managed to reduce the phenomena of color to their fundamental principle and that he was able to encompass the entirety of color (*LA* I, 3: 100). But even in this most optimistic mood, when it seemed possible to reduce all color to a single, unified, objective principle, he exercised methodological caution; the *Beiträge*, following the prescriptions of "Der Versuch als Vermittler," investigated the conditions under which the phenomena appear rather than their causes. Later, by introducing the process of vision as a condition sine qua non, he was forced not only to doubt whether color could be studied apart from the observer but also to question the kind of unity that would be possible in the science. If *n* number of conditions have to be met in order to produce a phenomenon, what sense does it make to isolate just one and call it the cause? What of the other $n-1$ conditions? When many years later the young Arthur Schopenhauer, after receiving instruction in the Farbenlehre, proceeded to regard it as a mere prolegomenon to his own theory that color is due to the activity of the perceiving eye, Goethe had to disagree despite the theory's affinities to aspects of his own position; for although this activity is a fundamental condition of all color perception, it is not the sole condition. Therefore, the only reliable unifier of all the conditions is the phenomenon itself, in the form of the *Urphänomen*. It is within the experience of the phenomenon that one can carry out the analysis of conditions and, if one wishes, the pursuit of causality. Goethe ultimately worked out a tripartite division that he hoped would elucidate the most basic conditional categories, within which further subdivisions could be carried out. The three main categories comprised the contribution of the eye, the contribution of the medium through which the image-bearing light passes, and the contribution of the illuminated and perceived object – which Goethe named, respectively, the physiological, physical, and chemical aspects of color.

In 1794 Goethe wrote to Sömmerring that the physiological component was far more important than people realized, which made the difficulty of distinguishing what was objective from what was subjective greater than ever (*LA* I, 3: 91). Although in late 1796 a series of verse epigrams directed against Newton and the Newtonians appeared (*LA* I, 3: 232– 33), there is little evidence of Goethe's work in color research during these years. It appears that physiological colors posed a dilemma he could not immediately resolve. Not until late 1797 did he resume research in earnest and begin work toward the magnum opus on color that evolved into *Zur Farbenlehre*. But now there was an important difference in his approach to the accepted theory. In "Der Versuch als Vermittler" he wrote as though he had discovered a technique for methodically distinguishing between various levels of certainty. Most certain of all were the basic phenomenal demonstrations and descriptions; next the experiences of the higher kind; and finally, as a kind of superstructure erected on these, hypotheses, theories, and jargons. Among the latter he included the *Vorstellungsarten*, the ways of conceiving things, which he had characterized as the attempt to bring many objects into a relationship that, strictly speaking, they did not have with one another. Goethe's avowed intention in developing the method of "Der Versuch als Vermittler" was to give the researcher some defense against the human tendency to prefer the conception of phenomena to the phenomena themselves. By late 1794, however, Goethe began to take a greater interest in the possibility that there are manifold legitimate ways of conceiving things. In a letter to Jacobi he said that his optical studies included not only discovering phenomena, fixing them in the form of experiments, and organizing the experiences, but also getting to know the various *Vorstellungsarten*, with the object of remaining as many-sided as possible (*LA* II, 3: 83). By 1798 he had begun to categorize the ways in which human beings conceive of the phenomena of light and color as he became engrossed in the history of science and tried to outline the plan of his major work on color.

Goethe's idea of what constituted a *Vorstellungsart* had changed since 1792, as is evident from two letters he wrote late in 1798. On 26 November he referred to the "Vorstellungs Art" of a young man who was color-blind (*LA* II, 3: 120); and on the next day he made a request for Schiller's assistance in sorting out his conception of color.

Everyone holds that the separation of hypothesis from fact is extremely difficult, but it is even more difficult than one usually thinks, because every presentation itself, every method is already hypothetical.

Since from now on you as a third party will listen bit by bit to my presentation, you will better divide the hypothetical from the factual than I henceforth will be able to, because certain ways of conceiving things have indeed become inveterate with me and, as it were, facticized. (*LA* I, 3: 331)

Whereas before the *Vorstellungsart* was something to be excluded from the basic presentation and description of the phenomena, now it was understood as inseparable from presentation and implicit in the very act of seeing. But this means that the theoretical faculty exerts its power at a far earlier point than Goethe had formerly suspected, and although its influence may be reduced it cannot be eliminated. In the foreword to *Zur Farbenlehre* he took this insight to its ultimate consequence for the relationship between theory and phenomena.

It is certainly an extremely strange demand, which often is made but also not fulfilled even by those who make it, that one should present experiences without any theoretical bond and leave it to the reader or student to construct some conviction for himself as he pleases. For the mere glancing at [*Anblicken*] a thing cannot advance us. Every [directed] looking [*Ansehen*] leads to consideration [*Betrachten*], every consideration to reflection [*Sinnen*], every reflection to connection [*Verknüpfen*], and thus we can say that with every attentive look [*Blick*] at the world we are already theorizing. (*HA*, 13: 317)

And in a passage concerning proof by experiments in the "Polemic," Goethe seems to approach complete subjectivism: "Everything that is an opinion about things belongs to the individual, and we know only too well that conviction depends not on insight but on will, that no one grasps anything but what is conformable to him and what, consequently, he is willing to concede" (*FL-P*, par. 30).

Having determined that there was a lawful subjective contribution to color, Goethe could not refrain from investigating the forms that it took. His study of color blindness in particular must have convinced him that not everyone perceives colors in the same way, that there is an irreducible individual factor in color perception. Yet just as it was possible to ascertain characteristic phenomenal groupings despite the bewildering variety of appearances, it might also be possible to find out characteristic types of *Vorstellungsarten*. The historical part of *Zur Farbenlehre* accordingly surveys the various ways of conceiving color as revealed by the history of the investigation of the phenomena. These *Vorstellungsarten* rarely appear in pure form; the *Vorstellungsart* of any particular individual is most often a blend or mixture of many. They are not necessarily mutually exclusive; consequently, just because some particular *Vorstellungsart* is successful in accounting for certain phenomena, it is not permissible to exclude all others a priori. No single *Vorstellungsart* is capable of embracing the entire truth about nature or the world. In the practice of science the devotees of one type usually incorporate others into their work as well. The only way that one can judge the appropriateness or merits of a *Vorstellungsart* applied to a subject is by its results.

In the case of color, Goethe believed that the atomistic and mathematical ways of conceiving things had introduced systematic distortions in the presentation of the phenomena and obscured important problems, such as the contribution of the eye's functioning to the perception of color and the appearances of color in natural surroundings (rather than in the laboratory camera obscura). This *Vorstellungsart* was due not only to Newton, whom Goethe saw as atomistic, mechanical, and above all mathematical, but as well to the age in which Newton lived and worked. Goethe thought of himself as more inclined to the genetic, the dynamic, and the concrete (*LA* I, 3: 334). In Plato and Aristotle, he saw two distinct approaches to nature, the one ideal and intuitive, the other empirical and architectonic (*HA*, 14: 53–54). Among the Greeks in general, he found a concrete sensuous immediacy and a quick and subtle intelligence, features that contrast with the plodding narrowness and abstractness of the Romans (*HA*, 14: 32–46). In different languages he identified different kinds of expressivity; ancient Greek, for example, is a dynamic language because of its abundance of verb forms and verbal nouns and adjectives, whereas the nominative Latin reifies and abstracts so that its overall effect is static and monumental (*HA*, 14: 75). As we read through the historical part we see the continual emergence, ebb, and reemergence of the genetic and the atomistic, the dynamic and the mechanical, the concrete and the abstract, the mathematical and the physical, the material and the spiritual ways of thinking and conceiving.[29]

The world as experienced is plural. The most fatal epoch that can befall science, then, is one in which a single *Vorstellungsart* predominates nearly to the exclusion of all others. Nevertheless, the plurality of the world does not imply pure relativism or subjectivism, for several reasons. First, it is not so much that the individual's consciousness generates a *Vor-*

stellungsart as that the individual consciousness reflects and is shaped by *Vorstellungsarten*. Rarely if ever can one find a person whose thinking is a pure *Vorstellungsart*, who is, for example, a pure mechanist. In accounting for the variety of phenomena in the universe, he will have to reject some of them (e.g., he may discount consciousness as an epiphenomenon, or perhaps simply ignore the question of how mechanism is compatible with consciousness) or borrow notions from other *Vorstellungsarten* (he may introduce forces to account for gravitation and chemical bonding or simply mathematize what does not easily lend itself to pure mechanism). Second, the *Vorstellungsarten* reveal themselves not in the abstract but in the concrete effort to unify phenomena, and thus they are bound to a determinate, and one may say objective, discipline. Third, each *Vorstellungsart* is directed toward conceiving the whole of things (accordingly, one might alternately designate them as intentionalities); that is, the ambition of each *Vorstellungsart* is total, it seeks to achieve ever more comprehensive unities, and therefore at least implicitly it represents the interest in the whole. This implies that although Goethe may be described as an empiricist, he takes issue with the empiricist's ideological presupposition that the scientist can and does proceed by a kind of mechanical comparison of bits of data and constructs abstractions by a kind of piecing them together. It is in light of this significant difference that we can understand Schiller's coinage for the type of Goethean science, rational empiricism (*LA* I, 3: 310).

The *Vorstellungsarten* in pure form are ideal types; however, they may also be characterized as permanent possibilities of unifying human experience. It is not surprising that this permanent plurality implies important consequences for the critique of Newton. If there are many legitimate ways of conceiving a thing, then there may be no single, authoritative way of presenting scientific "truth"; on the other hand, it may become impossible to establish that a certain *Vorstellungsart*, such as Newton's about color, is wrong or fruitless. Indeed, in the "Polemic" Goethe portrays Newton and himself as champions of different types of theory and admits that an atomistic intelligence will find nothing at all wrong with Newton (*FL-P*, par. 31). Yet the *Vorstellungsarten* also provided an implicit theoretical justification for the polemic against Newton. Science cannot tolerate the authoritarianism of sects and schools, because a sect holds tenaciously to what is only a part, which is presented, nevertheless, as if it were the whole. To use an image that Goethe employed in "Der Versuch als Vermittler," science ought to resemble a free republic (*HA*, 13: 16). One might infer from this the right of the citizen to try to overthrow a tyrant.

At the time of the first *Beiträge* Goethe hoped to produce virtually self-evident demonstrations of the contrafactuality of Newton's theory.

An unpublished essay on Newton's hypothesis of diverse refrangibility from 1793, while broadly sketching the defects in Newton's argument, promised a more detailed and compelling analysis in the main work that was supposed to follow (*LA* I, 3: 155, 160–61). However, the discovery of the physiological colors, his interest in *Vorstellungsarten*, and his experience of the practical and theoretical interrelationships between hypotheses, phenomenal observation, and description intervened. Although these perhaps ruled out the possibility of proving Newton perfectly wrong, Goethe nevertheless held on to the conviction that an evaluation of Newton's descriptions and arguments could still identify inaccuracies and errors and thereby encourage a republican rather than a despotic science of chromatics.

Goethe did not waver in his commitment to a comprehensive experimental science that aimed at a direct and immediate comparison of what is seen by the eye with what is seen through theory. Scientists had to be compelled, constantly, to face the difficult task of unraveling facts from hypotheses; for even if this attempt turned out to be impossible in the ultimate sense, it could still bear practical fruits, not the least of which would be the systematic comparison of different ways of conceiving things. As long as a scientist remained entirely wrapped up in a single dominant *Vorstellungsart*, he would be unable to criticize his work adequately, unable perhaps even to conceive that there might be something lacking from his understanding of nature. Thus these critical and historical undertakings were not inessential appendages of science but rather an intrinsic and fundamental activity of science itself – fundamental in the sense of establishing a foundation on which all can build, in the sense of being concerned with the totality of the subject in question rather than just a part. As an essay on morphology from the 1790s stated, it is a "necessity to put together all the *Vorstellungsarten*, not at all to get to the bottom of things and their essences, but to give to just some degree an account of the phenomenon and to communicate to others what one has recognized and seen" (*HA*, 13: 120). The *Vorstellungsarten* were thus the very foundation on which the scientific community was built.

If the major problem faced in "Der Versuch als Vermittler" was the danger and necessity of relating phenomenon to phenomenon and the goal an authoritative presentation of all relevant phenomena, Goethe's discovery of *Vorstellungsarten* led to an extension of the same unifying impulse, although in turn it implied a qualification on the authoritativeness of any single presentation. The scientist whose concern transcends the particular phenomenon or the boundaries of his discipline is interested in ever larger and more comprehensive wholes; to grasp more fully the object of his study he ought at least to recognize alternative conceptions of the object. Thus, by schematizing (which is not to say systematizing) the *Vorstellungsarten*, Goethe expanded the dimensions of science, and wherever the history of a science does not present a concrete example of a given *Vorstellungsart*, the possibility always exists that this particular way of conceiving things may nevertheless bear the seed of an alternative program of research.

To point to a possibility is not to guarantee success. The proof is in putting the possibility to the test – only actualization can demonstrate its specific virtues and demerits. No researcher is going to undertake work simply because someone points out a mere possibility; in this sense, the schema of *Vorstellungsarten* is an abstract ideal. But in the course of human life what turns possibility into actuality is the aperçu, the moment of insight in which we glimpse what the future may bring and which spurs us to invest the necessary labor. Through the aperçu we recognize a totality, the context in which the particular takes its place; and thus the aperçu is by its nature the anticipation of a whole, if not *the* whole. But the aperçu is problematic. "A decisive aperçu is to be regarded as an inoculated disease: One does not get rid of it till one has fought the disease through" (*HA*, 14: 263). The aperçu can be true, false, or both. What is crucial to the development of the aperçu is the strength of character of the person who experiences it and the person's willingness to submit to the discipline of the phenomena, but it is precisely the strongest spirits who are likely to slight the phenomena. Goethe believed that Newton was just such a person – one of those productive geniuses who

bring forth from themselves a world without much asking whether it agrees with the real one. If it happens that what has developed in them agrees with the ideas of the world-spirit there become known truths at which men marvel and for which they have reason to be thankful for centuries. But if there emerges in such an able, genial nature some illusion that has no counterpart in the common world then such an error may no less powerfully spread, and overpower and impose upon human beings. (*HA*, 14: 143)

The evolution of Goethe's understanding of the *Vorstellungsarten* apparently has escaped notice.[30] In at least one sense it can be argued that the later development of the idea is adumbrated in "Der Versuch als Vermittler," where Goethe mentions "the powers of the soul in which these experiences are conceived, collected, ordered, and developed" (*HA*, 13: 12); but there the negative side of *Vorstellung* is emphasized, and his method promises to overcome the limitations of one's conception of things by resorting to secure experimental phenomena and equally secure propositions based on them. Without appreciating this shift in Goethe's thinking, it is difficult to make his earlier tendency to infallibilist inductivism consistent with his later thoroughgoing pluralism. Although from the beginning he advocated the collaboration of many disciplines, at first he thought they would supplement one another in a single truth; later it is not a pluralism of disciplines converging on one truth, but a plurality of experience unified by the object that may not admit of such a thing as demonstrated certainty.

Goethe originally conceived of the science of color as a communal effort calling not only on physicists and chemists but also on physiologists, technicians, craftsmen, mathematicians, philosophers, historians, and representatives of any other vocations and disciplines that might have something to offer (see *LA* I, 13: 130–36, from 1793). His discovery of the typology of *Vorstellungsarten* only confirmed that this plan was well conceived and indeed essential to the welfare of science. It would conduce to a many-sided effort to comprehend a common object and necessarily involve the cooperation of various points of view. His plan would compel the participants to recognize that truth is a much more subtle, elusive, and wide-ranging creature than any single human being or *Vorstellungsart* can comprehend unassisted. Whereas the first duty of the individual researcher is to display the phenomena and organize them into a comprehensive whole, the continuing responsibility of the community of researchers is to acknowledge that science itself is a historical activity, a phenomenon with its peculiar characteristics and conditions, rather than an assemblage of eternal verities. Truth is active and is comprehensible only through the cooperation of all. As Goethe emphasized in the foreword to *Zur Farbenlehre*, the theory implicit in every attentive look at the world obliges the researchers to cultivate the most demanding of virtues. "To do this [theorize], to undertake this, with consciousness, with knowledge of oneself, with freedom, and, to use a daring word, with irony: Just this kind of versatility is needed if the abstraction we are afraid of is to be rendered harmless and the resulting experience we hope for is to become genuinely vital and useful" (*HA*, 13: 317). Irony, toward oneself and one's achievements, is a severe demand, but it is necessary if investigators are not to remain imprisoned in their particular conceptions of things and thus do those things grave injustice.

How, then, did someone who believed this come to *polemicize?* Criticism can occur in a spirit of friendship and tolerance; but polemic is war, which is usually settled by capitulation or death. Polemic is an instrument dangerous even to its wielder. The kill is rarely as quick and clean as the polemist hopes, and rapier wit soon gets exchanged for blunter weapons. Those who follow the master often lose sight of the original goal; blinded by blood lust, they rush to the battle lines, wherever they may be drawn, and fight as much for the pleasure in bludgeoning the enemy as for the sake of truth. Waging war hardly seems an appropriate method in science, though it is probably more common than one suspects.

We should not be misled by the title "polemic," however; nor by the tedious name calling in the *Farbenlehre* controversy once the epigones picked up Goethe's banner; nor even by the occasional insults and aggressiveness of the polemical part of *Zur Farbenlehre*. At an early stage of his work Goethe started using metaphors of faith, heresy, churchdom, and sectarianism to describe the rise, triumph, and persistence of the Newtonian doctrine (e.g., *LA* I, 3: 154). His late insight into *Vorstellungsarten* confirmed the appropriateness of comparing scientific with religious doctrine when believers claim to possess an unvarying truth handed down from generation to generation in canonical writings. In joining a polemic to the didactic part of *Zur Farbenlehre*, Goethe was elaborating the metaphor systematically. The Newtonian teaching represented a belief about what cannot be directly apprehended and was expressed in tenets that could be disputed in opposition to other doctrines. Religious polemists attack a heretical doctrine as public witnesses to truth and in an attempt to prevent susceptible souls from adopting falsehoods as their creed. For them the hallmark of truth is its totality, though obviously they must attack untruth in its particular instances as well as en masse. Their task is all the harder because some of the heretical theses may embody at least part of the truth. "Human beings were created to be happy" is true for Christians when happiness is measured by conformity to the will of God, but damnably false when it is used to justify hedonism. The truth of the individual proposition depends on the perspective from which it is understood and its range of application.

Similarly, Goethe in the "Polemic" sets out to compare the doctrine of Newton with the phenomena in their totality from the perspective of a *Vorstellungsart* he calls dynamic and genetic. The propositions of Newton's optics are judged not as intrinsically isolable statements applied to inherently isolated experiments, but as particular instances of a way of conceiving things that is methodically employed to describe and circumscribe phenomena that have their own specifically ramified relationships to one another and thus are not infinitely adaptable to any and every *Vorstellungsart*. Newton's work is therefore examined as an experimental argument to see how faithful it is to the phenomena it is meant to explain and to compare it with another perspective, another presentation. Given the plurality of *Vorstellungsarten*, direct comparisons of theory with phenomena and theory with theory are not merely a desideratum but actually a necessity. The "Polemic" is meant to be constructively destructive: The old theory's distortion of experience and its false pretensions to mathematical accuracy and completeness are to be cleared away so that the view may be freed and the ground prepared for something new. What makes it far more than Goethe's self-interested campaign is the profit that can be derived from examining the phenomena with different sources of illumination – that is, conflicting theories and *Vorstellungs-arten* – and with an eye to the ramifications of the phenomena of color in their totality. All science proceeds from and must return to the phenomena: This assures that a comparison of this kind will not be valueless. The "Polemic" sets out to introduce a new era in the study of color, an era that does not shrink from the conflict of theories. Just as the struggle between phlogiston and the chemistry of oxidation and reduction brought advances to practical and theoretical chemistry, the debate between Goethe and Newton was to usher in a renaissance of its own from which similar progress might be expected, a renaissance to which both expert and amateur might contribute.

But the "Polemic" failed, and so too the entire *Zur Farbenlehre*, as did the *Beiträge* nearly twenty years before. Goethe's hope for a science that would secure its phenomenal basis and cultivate a variety of perspectives was disappointed. The world had learned to see with Newton, to see color from the perspective that his optics had established; *Zur Farbenlehre* could not prevail where seeing was preempted by theoretical constructs. What precisely was Newton's perspective, and how was it established? These are the questions to which we now must turn.

3

The problematics of Newton's theory of white light and colors

It was not hard to discover his error, for many others before me had noticed it; but it is hard to elaborate, for none of his opponents have yet managed it, and perhaps I shall not either; I shall do my best all the same, so that even if I too am damned as a heretic, at least a more fortunate successor may find a usable preliminary work.

– Goethe (*LA*, I, 3: 160–61).

Goethe's critique of Newton: a preliminary orientation

In an essay on Newton's hypothesis of diverse refrangibility, which dates from about 1793 and apparently was intended as the introduction to a major didactic, historical, and critical work on the theory of light and colors, Goethe discussed some of the deficiencies he had discovered in Newton's theory, particularly the version presented in Newton's first genuinely public statement of it, the letter to the Royal Society of London of 6 February 1671/72.[1]

Above all I must emphasize most strongly that diverse refrangibility is not a fact [*keine Tatsache, kein Faktum*]. Newton himself narrates for us the course of his observations and his conclusions; the attentive critic is therefore able to follow close on his heels. Here I will only sketch in the outlines of the detailed presentation, which will be contained in the work itself [that was to follow]. Newton finds, while passing a ray of sunlight through a prism under specified circumstances, that after refraction the projected image of this ray is much longer than it is wide and, what is more, that it is colored with various colors.

Next he takes pains to explore the cause of this elongation of the image, by modification of the experiments as well as by mathematical trial; and as he finds it always longer than it should be according to all the *external* circumstances and influences that he can notice, he concludes: The cause of this elongation must lie *within* the light; the distension of the image in length arises from a division of the light, this division is possible by means of refraction, because the various rays of which the compound light consists are refracted not according to a single universal law but each according to its peculiar law, since subsequently one can recognize them quite easily by their different colors.

This opinion immediately takes hold in him; he performs various experiments that only confirm him in this all the more, and although at first he presents his conviction merely as theory, gradually it becomes so fixed in his spirit that he enunciates diverse refrangibility as really a fact (Opusc. II, p. 371 [i.e., Newton 1744, 2: 371, to be found at *Corresp.*, 1: 293]).

In just the same way his disciples continue to portray diverse refrangibility sometimes as a firmly grounded and irrefutable theory, sometimes as a fact.

This first and greatest mistake must be noted above all. For how can one hope for advances in science if that which is merely concluded, opined, or believed is allowed to be forced upon us as a fact?

It is a fact that under *those circumstances* that Newton exactly specifies the image of the sun is five times as long as it is wide, and that this elongated image appears entirely in colors. Every observer can repeatedly witness this phenomenon without any great effort.

Newton himself tells us how he went to work in order to convince himself that no *external cause* can bring about this elongation and coloration of the image. This treatment of his will, as already was mentioned above, be subjected to criticism: For we can raise many questions and investigate with exactness, whether he went to work properly and to what extent his proof is in every sense complete.

If one analyzes his reasons, they have the following form:

When the ray is refracted the image is longer than it should be according to the laws of refraction.

Now I have tried everything and thereby convinced myself that no external cause is responsible for this elongation.

Therefore it is an inner cause, and this we find in the divisibility of light. For since it takes up a larger space than before, it must be divided, thrown asunder; and since we see the sundered light in colors, the different parts of it must be colored.

How much there is to object to immediately in this rationale!

Apropos of the first proposition, let us permit ourselves to ask: How were the laws of refraction ascertained? – from experience. Good! And, whoever may have had the experience by which the laws were ascertained, did he or did he not observe the exception which is at issue here? – We do not know whether or not he observed it; but he did not take it into consideration. – So we are entitled to doubt the generality of this law of nature and to ask: May it not be possible to enunciate this law more generally, indeed in a way that would include this exception?

It is clear what objections should be raised against this conviction from the standpoint of a complete experience. Here the questions to be asked are: Whether everything has been observed that must be observed? Who can prove that an experience is complete? And does not every presentation of new experiences that belong in this domain bear upon it?

But even granted that there is nothing to object to in the first two propositions and that the conclusion that *an inner cause is at work here* is accepted as valid, nevertheless the conclusion that the cause lies in some property of the light is still premature: For in this case we of course have both refracted *light* and a refracting *medium*, and why shouldn't the medium be able to produce double images through some cause unknown to us or be capable of extending the image in length through an unexplained power, perhaps only *related* to refraction and reflection? Is there really some exclusive and ultimate necessity [forcing us] to attribute to light the mysterious property of letting itself be split and divided into elements by a medium through which it passes?

But let all this not be introduced as if to confirm something or to lay the ground for disputation, but only in order to show how little *diverse refrangibility* can be regarded *as fact*.

Let future revisionists therefore be requested to see to it that no one, whoever he may be, be allowed to pass off an explanation, theory, or hypothesis as a fact. That the stone falls is fact, that it happens through attraction is theory, of which one may be most inwardly convinced, but which one can never experience, never see, never know. (*LA* I, 3: 155–58)

I have quoted this passage in extenso because it outlines at the commencement of Goethe's critical and polemical studies a plan that was carried out over a period of more than fifteen years and that incorporated the demands for completeness of experience and for distinguishing between phenomena and theory that were leitmotifs of his own science of color.

Later in this same essay Goethe argues that the reason Newton's error remained undiscovered for so long was that not enough people performed his experiments and tried to follow the course of his argument. Had this kind of critical work been done sooner, he contends, more genuine practical and theoretical progress in optics might have occurred during the eighteenth century than had under the Newtonian regime.[2] But scientists were more concerned to save Newton's theory than the phenomena. When Newton's prediction that the refracting telescope could not be improved turned out to be false, rather than reexamine the theory to ascertain how he had come to his conclusion and whether his basic theory was truly complete, scientists instead struggled to accommodate the new discovery to the old theory. The authority of Newton was generally considered weightier than the testimony of faithful and attentive observers. The appearance of truth was reinforced by the mathematical cast of Newton's optics; but the mathematics is not so abstruse as is commonly thought, and although it is exact in itself, its application to the phenomena is not. Performing Newton's experiments and testing his conclusions is more important than calculating, and these tasks can be carried out by anyone with sound senses and a clear mind. Because Newton's presentation is not intrinsically mathematical but rather argumentative, it must be read and examined with the utmost care and not treated as necessarily the best, the most complete, or the most accurate presentation possible. Newton's errors are concealed by artifices and illusions, so that they have to be unraveled with the greatest diligence and meticulously analyzed (*LA* I, 3: 159–64).

According to this earliest extant articulation of Goethe's response to

Newton's own work, Newton's theory poses an extraordinary complex of scientific and historical problems, because it fails to account for all the relevant phenomena and to discriminate properly between what is being interpreted and the interpretation. Its astonishing historical success was due more to the negligence of those who followed Newton than to the intrinsic merits of the theory. Scientists had been blinded by the authority of Newton, a sociological factor, and by their own confusion of theory and fact. The very success of the theory had blocked scientific progress. Scientists prided themselves most on the exactness and the objective truth of their work, yet, in the case of Newton's theory, these qualities were more appearance than reality.

In contrast to the *Beiträge zur Optik*, this essay – which was not published during Goethe's lifetime – boldly addressed what Goethe called the *Streitfrage*, the controversial question. Whereas earlier he had simply pointed out certain phenomena or facts that seemed to him to contradict the theory of Newton, he now planned to deconstruct Newton's argument so that all its flaws – logical, phenomenal, methodological, rhetorical, and epistemological – might be exposed to plain view. Moreover, his preliminary remarks on the experimental argument of Newton's letter of 6 February 1672 are unmistakably directed against the theory of differential refrangibility, the foundation and bulwark of the theory of light that is, at least in principle, separable from the doctrine of colors. Ironically, Goethe, the proponent of a new science of color, chose to attack first the aspect of Newton's theory that seems to be most purely physical and mathematical. In what follows, however, we shall see that Goethe was not intrinsically guilty of error or confusion in selecting this aspect as his target, for Newton's theory of differential refrangibility and his doctrine of colors are interdependent and mutually supportive: With Newton, one cannot easily separate the physics of radiation from the psychophysics of color.

Goethe prepared an outline of this essay between mid-May and mid-August 1793, during the French revolutionary army's siege of Mainz; the essay itself appears to have been written later that year, while he was also preparing further installments of the *Beiträge*. It is clear that he had decided that the controversy with Newton could no longer remain implicit, that he had to confront the theory head on in order to shake the public free of Newtonian preconceptions once and for all. The necessary work could not be simple refutation, in which the theory would be proved false and be abandoned on the strength of one or several decisive experiments; rather he had to analyze and even dissect the theory in considerable detail, so that the reader might finally be persuaded that it was not the last word in optical and color science and that its range and validity had been overrated. As he wrote further on in the essay:

I shall spare no pains in going through his experiments in the most exacting way and in showing to what degree they are correct in themselves or to what degree they are open to dispute; whether the observer has seen an undeniable experiment rightly or whether he has let himself be blinded by appearance; whether he notes all attendant circumstances; whether the experiments are complete, whether they are ordered well, and whether the conclusions that he draws from them follow necessarily. (*LA* I, 3: 161)

"Furthermore," he goes on, "we have to apply the greatest attentiveness to his presentation," to determine, for instance, whether it is mathematical or physical, whether it starts from what is simple or from the complicated, whether it is artificial or natural. That is, Goethe intended to explicate not just experiments and logic but also the text and its rhetoric.

Although this essay makes evident that Goethe planned a close reading of Newton's first genuinely public exposition of his theory of white light and colors, no such analysis is extant from the mid-1790s, only a critique of a textbook account of Newton's theory (*LA* I, 3: 210–17; cf. 218–26). Some fifteen years later, in the historical part of *Zur Farbenlehre*, Goethe executed part of that earlier plan by sketching how in the letter of 6 February 1672 Newton had discounted, in some cases rightly, in others not, alternative explanations of the phenomena. At the same time he also prepared an analysis of most of the letter; he apparently at one time planned to use it in the historical part, but it ultimately remained unpublished among his manuscripts (see *WA* II, 4: 441–65).

The polemical part of *Zur Farbenlehre* is an exegesis of the first book of the *Opticks*; therefore, it might seem strange to focus attention on a different and lesser, though still classic, work, of which Goethe never published a detailed critique (there is a section on this letter in the historical part of *Zur Farbenlehre*, however; see *HA*, 14: 145–53). Nevertheless there are strong reasons for working from the letter of 6 February 1672 rather than from the *Opticks*: Newton himself believed that the letter was a convincing statement of his theory, a belief in which many of his eighteenth-century followers concurred; the basic theory of light and colors presented there is not essentially different from the later version; Goethe's various critiques of it are, despite their incompleteness, detailed and the principles according to which they were carried out consistent; and, finally, the literature on Newton's optics has independently treated the letter in considerable detail.[3] Examining the much simpler and shorter letter in the spirit of Goethe still requires a protracted and complicated investigation. Such an investigation, however, is an immensely helpful prolegomenon to reading the "Polemic," a task that would be very nearly futile without a preliminary grasp of Goethe's purpose and of the status and the history of Newton's theory. Consequently, we shall concentrate our attention on this letter.

Newton's Letter on the theory of white light and colors

The letter of 6 February – to be called henceforth simply the Letter – is considered one of the masterpieces of scientific literature. Its argument is both concise and convincing, calling on just a few experiments to establish the theory of differential refrangibility according to color.

Until recently the Letter had been taken at its word; apart from a few isolated dissenters, hardly anyone questioned its cogency. In the past several decades, however, historians of science have made it increasingly clear that the Letter does not really establish everything it sets out to prove and that, despite Newton's claims that the argument is free of hypotheses, the letter contains certain implicit assumptions about the nature of light.[4] Although these studies have considerable merits, very few of them have come to grips with the argument of the Letter taken as a whole. They have been preoccupied primarily with texts and theories and have devoted insufficient attention to the actual phenomena on which the argument rests and the rhetorical structure of the exposition.[5] It was precisely these two aspects that elicited Goethe's polemical and historical interest. He read, and was told, that Newton's theory expressed the very essence of the facts and could explain them as well as one could desire, but when he compared what he read in Newton with what he saw experimentally he decided that the "facts" were expressed in a tendentious theory and that the argument was inexact and sometimes specious.

The Letter falls neatly into two halves: The first deals with the differential refrangibility of light with only an occasional mention of color, the second with the doctrine of color itself. The first half presents a detailed experimental demonstration and argument; the last half then asserts a number of propositions about color that are not actually proved in the Letter. As was mentioned earlier, Goethe, intent on finding out about color, might be expected to have less interest in the first half than in the second. But because Newton's doctrine of color is a natural consequence of the doctrine of differential refrangibility, any critique of the color doctrine must perforce start with a critique of differential refrangibility. This, in fact, is where Goethe began.[6]

The first half of the Letter: differential refrangibility

On 18 January 1671/72 Newton advertised the impending announcement of an important discovery to Henry Oldenburg, secretary to the Royal

Society, in words that indicate Newton's assessment of his own achievement.

> I desire that in your next letter you would inform mee for what time the Society continue their weekly meetings, because if they continue them for any time I am purposing them, to be considered of & examined, an accompt of a Philosophicall discovery wch induced mee to the making of the said Telescope, & wch I doubt not but will prove much more gratefull then the communication of that instrument, being in my Judgment the oddest if not the most considerable detection wch hath hitherto beene made in the operations of Nature. (*Corresp.*, 1: 82–83)

The telescope Newton refers to is the catoptric or reflecting telescope he had invented, which just a few months earlier had been brought to the attention of the Royal Society on his behalf by Isaac Barrow, his mentor and predecessor in the Lucasian Professorship of Mathematics at Trinity College, Cambridge. In attempting to improve the dioptric or refracting telescope by grinding lenses of various sizes and shapes, Newton had noticed some experimental phenomena that persuaded him to work instead on developing a reflector. The purpose of the Letter, then, was to present a story of this discovery to the virtuosos of natural science in the Royal Society.

The Letter itself begins matter-of-factly: "To perform my late promise to you, I shall without further ceremony acquaint you, that in the beginning of the Year 1666 (at which time I applyed my self to the grinding of Optick glasses of other figures than *Spherical*,) I procured me a Triangular glass-Prisme, to try therewith the celebrated *Phaenomena* of *Colours*" (*Corresp.*, 1: 92).

To this end he darkened his chambers, and, having made a small hole in his windowshut "to let in a convenient quantity of the Suns light," he placed the prism at the hole so that the incoming light was refracted to the opposite wall, where it produced a colored spectrum.

> It was at first a very pleasing divertisement, to view the vivid and intense colours produced thereby; but after a while applying my self to consider them more circumspectly, I became surprised to see them in an *oblong* form; which, according to the received laws of Refraction, I expected should have been *circular*.
> They were terminated at the sides with streight lines, but at the ends, the decay of light was so gradual, that it was difficult to determine justly, what was their figure; yet they seemed *semicircular*.
> Comparing the length of this coloured *Spectrum* with its breadth, I found it about five times greater; a disproportion so extravagant, that it excited me to a more then ordinary curiosity of examining, from whence it might proceed. (*Corresp.*, 1: 92)

The received laws of refraction Newton mentions were based on the law of sines first discovered by Willebrord Snel early in the seventeenth century and subsequently made public by Descartes. The law states that for any refraction occurring from one transparent medium into another, the sine

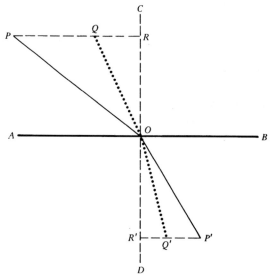

*Figure 3.1   The law of sines illustrated. AB is the refracting surface,
CD a perpendicular (normal) to AB, PO and QO any two incident
rays, OP' and OQ' the corresponding refracted rays; PQR and
P'Q'R' are perpendiculars to CD. Then, according to the law of
sines, for any two such rays there is a constant n such that*

$$\frac{\sin POR}{\sin P'OR'} = \frac{PR / PO}{P'R' / P'O} = \frac{\sin QOR}{\sin Q'OR'} = \frac{QR / QO}{Q'R' / Q'O} = n.$$

of the angle of incidence (*i*) on the refracting surface is in a constant
ratio to the sine of the subsequent angle of refraction (*r*); that is, sin *i*/
sin *r* = *n*, where *n* is a constant depending solely on the kinds of refractive
media involved, for every possible angle of incidence and its corresponding refraction (see Fig. 3.1).

   To understand Newton's surprise at the shape of the image, it is necessary to note one detail that Newton fails to specify until much later in
the Letter, and even then it must be deduced by the reader – the exact
orientation of the prism with respect to the beam of light. Because the
success of Newton's demonstration and description depends on this detail, the historian A. I. Sabra has noted this omission as an oddity that
forces us to become skeptical about the Letter's literal truth as an au-
tobiographical account.

For, in fact, except for one definite position of the prism, namely that of minimum
deviation, a certain elongation of the image should have been expected. As we
go on reading Newton's paper, however, we soon discover that the prism was
fixed at precisely that position. We are therefore here presented with a carefully

planned experiment and not, as the opening sentence of Newton's paper might convey, a chance observation. (Sabra 1967, 235)

Although Newton says that he applied himself "to consider the phenomenon more circumspectly," nowhere in the Letter does he substantiate the reasons for his initial expectation, not even several paragraphs further on when he gives measurements from which it can be inferred that the prism was at the position of minimum deviation.

When the prism is in this position, rays of light refracted by the prism are least diverted from, or turned out of, their original paths – they are minimally deviated. It happens that this position is one of symmetry: The angle the departing ray forms with respect to the second face of the prism is the same as the angle the incident ray makes with respect to the first face. Empirically this position is easy to determine. By rotating the prism about its long axis (with the central axis running parallel to the refracting edge), one can make the image cast on the wall or screen move up and down. As the prism is turned continuously in a single direction, the image moves first one way, stops, then reverses direction. Minimal deviation is achieved at the point where the motion stops.

The received laws of refraction circa 1670 entailed a good deal more than the law of sines, however. Before Newton, white or uncolored light was generally thought to be a simple entity; it might be a compound in the sense that it could be divided into small parts, but these were taken to be essentially alike, all white or uncolored. Even regarding the light beam as a bundle of rays, whether geometric or physical, was not always thought necessary, because in measuring angles of incidence and refraction one could consider the beam as a solid unit and thus take measurements only for the center of the beam (see OL, 50; LO, 38–39; Shap., 314, 315). In practice this approach is reasonable because it means one is always measuring the position of the center of the image produced by the light. Although the colored fringes of the image were noted by many investigators, they did not seem to reveal anything essential about the nature of light or refraction; and because most investigators probably took their measurements fairly close to the refracting surface or after only one rather than two refractions, the fringes would have been negligible and the image basically circular.

Insofar as the beam might be considered the sum of smaller components, each would have been expected to be refracted according to the same sine proportion. In modern terms, for any two given media there was thought to be a unique index of refraction for all rays of light and not, as Newton would teach, a different index for each kind (color) of light. Given such a unique index governing all rays coming from the sun, the light passing through a circular hole in the windowshut and traversing a prism in the position of least deviation ought to be refracted so that the image cast on a wall or screen placed perpendicular to the path of the refracted beam is circular, or very nearly so. Newton gave a long demonstration of this geometrical implication in the *Lectiones opticae* (which were based on lectures Newton had delivered from 1669 to 1671 as Lucasian Professor of Mathematics) but did not refer to this justification of his expectation in the Letter. Apparently he hoped or presumed that the members of the Royal Society would be conversant with the geometrical background to his assertion; but, as Sabra says, "by not providing any explicit geometrical explanation of this assumption he was certainly expecting too much from his readers" (Sabra 1967, 237). Newton's surprise was legitimate, but only someone with acute mathematical intuition would have shared it on so little evidence.

Hoping to learn something from the celebrated phenomena of colors, Newton became preoccupied with a question of geometry suggested by previous optical teachings, chief among which was the law of sines. The optical tradition had handed down a number of possible explanations for color as well, though no single one was universally accepted.[7] In the next paragraph of the letter Newton alludes to some of these, so it will be useful to anticipate these explanations by characterizing them briefly.

Virtually no one before Newton had thought of associating the colors with differential refrangibility, much less with any separation of the original colorless beam into colored components (but see Lohne 1968, 174–76, on Marcus Marci). The predominant theories of prismatic color argued that the refraction effected some physical change in the light that tinged it with colors. In Descartes's interpretation, for instance, light was pictured as consisting of very fine globules that, on refraction, were induced to rotate because of a kind of "friction" at the edges of the beam; the color depended on the direction and the speed of rotation. Because a beam has two sides (when it is pictured in two dimensions), the globules on the one side spin in a sense opposite to those on the other. The rotation is most rapid right at the edge, and at first only affects the edge; but as the beam gets ever farther from the refracting matter the rotation is gradually communicated toward the center of the beam from both sides, so that the colors eventually cover up the entire image. This theory clearly depends on the termination of the beam of light by an adjoining dark medium, the inertia of which helps produce the rotation. Although this interpretation is rife with difficulties and not altogether consistent with other accounts of light Descartes proposed, it does at least describe the phenomena of the spectrum in a qualitative way. Historians of science would categorize it as a modificationist theory of light; the term characterizes all theories that attribute color to some kind of modification or change of simple white light.

Robert Hooke and Ignace Pardies were proponents of two other versions of modificationist theories around the time of Newton's earliest studies in optics (see Sabra 1967, 46–68, 251–68; Blay 1983, 15–60). None of these theories was well enough elaborated to explain all the phenomena of color, but they nevertheless had achieved at least some sophistication and plausibility in accounting for the colors of refraction. The formation of the spectrum in particular was believed to result from the gradual dispersion of the edge colors across the refracted image and from their mixture at the center. The colorless light was thought to be changed by refraction so that the colored light had some characteristic or motion not possessed by white light. In the immediate vicinity of a refracting surface, however, where very little of the refracted image was tinged and where most of the measurements were probably made, the light was still largely unaffected.

These theories of light and colors could separate the geometric from the chromatic problem: The refraction might be calculated according to the sine law, and the colors explained according to some notion of modification. Whether the prism was in the position of minimum deviation was immaterial. With a circular aperture the image produced in camera obscura would appear nearly circular and essentially colorless when the screen was placed near the refracting surface; at greater distances the colors would be more conspicuous and might be expected to produce an elongation of the image – if, for example, there occurred some kind of diffusion of the motion of the globules (or whatever) into the otherwise quiescent medium through which the beam of light passed. Furthermore, even under the assumption of a unique index of refraction for light, the geometry of the sine law would lead one to expect a certain elongation of the image at all positions of the prism other than that of minimum deviation. Thus, the phenomena of the prism seemed explicable in principle according to the unique sine law and the modification of the beam, although no one had actually given such an explanation in a rigorous way.

Newton's theory combined the geometric and chromatic problems to explain both refraction and color according to a single principle, differential refrangibility, executed as rigorously as geometry allowed. Yet in the first half of the Letter Newton turned away from the celebrated color phenomena to focus his attention on the purely geometric problem. Rhetorically, this strategy was quite effective. Aiming to observe the colors of refraction, which were explained by one principle, Newton uncovered a problem with the other principle, the proportion of the sines, which was one of the most notable achievements not only of optics but of all science in the seventeenth century. If he could nevertheless save the law of sines in some form, he would do science a great service. If he could then show that this revised law accounted for color as well, he would unify what seemed like a dual phenomenon and astonish the world of natural philosophy with a discovery that had eluded the best philosophic minds before him.

The first half of the Letter has been interpreted as being concerned solely, or at least preponderantly, with the geometry of refraction by the editors of Newton's correspondence (*Corresp.*, 1: 104, n. 11) and by others (see Lohne 1968, 185). Newton himself was the first to point out that he had organized the Letter so that he might prove without respect to colors that light consists of rays differently refrangible (*Corresp.*, 2: 257). This procedure follows the scheme of the earlier *Lectiones opticae*, in which Newton explicitly postpones the examination of colors upon refraction until he first demonstrates differential refraction both experimentally and theoretically.[8] Yet during the controversy over the Letter Newton stated on several occasions that he had introduced the famous *experimentum crucis* to show that rays of diverse colors are unequally refracted (Lohne 1968, 182–86); and in the *Lectiones* Newton not only speaks of colors where they might just as easily have not been mentioned, but also introduces colors in the course of the first part of the work as an indicator of diverse refrangibility, despite his professed postponement of the examination of colors until the second part (*OL*, 6, 50–51; *LO*, 5, 38–39; Shap., 284, 285, 314, 315).

After expressing surprise at the proportions of the spectrum, Newton continues:

I could scarce think, that the various *Thickness* of the glass, or the termination with shadow or darkness, could have any Influence on light to produce such an effect; yet I thought it not amiss to examine first these circumstances, and so tryed, what would happen by transmitting light through parts of the glass of divers thicknesses, or through holes in the window of divers bignesses, or by setting the Prisme without, so that the light might pass through it, and be refracted before it was terminated by the hole: But I found none of those circumstances material. The fashion of the colours was in all these cases the same. (*Corresp.*, 1: 92)

He began with a curiosity about *color*; now he is inquiring into possible causes for the geometrical *disproportion*. Newton proceeds by conceiving possible explanations, performing experiments, and comparing the expectation with the result. At the moment the investigation proceeds without any explicit mathematics, even though the problem is a geometric one. As he is drawn deeper into the theories and phenomena, however, he starts taking precise measurements and performing exact calculations, so that he might compare an exact prediction with a carefully measured experiment.

The three possibilities Newton mentions here were not without precedent. According to Goethe, the notion that the thickness of the glass had something to do with the appearance of color had been supported by Antonius de Dominis, among others; yellow and red appear nearer the vertex of the prism where it is less massive, blue and violet where the ray has to pass through a greater thickness of glass. Contributions of the size of the aperture and the termination of light by darkness had been emphasized in the theories of Athanasius Kircher and Descartes (*HA*, 14: 147; cf. Shap., 306–307, nn. 4, 5). Without mentioning any of his predecessors, Newton tests a number of proposals only to reject them because they appear insubstantial. So far his method seems to accord with the Baconian principle that it is better to enumerate the possibilities and then begin negating the untenable ones than to rush to a positive conclusion (Bacon 1960, bk. 2, par. 15).

This series of refutations, brief as it is, seems unproblematic until we remark a peculiar ambiguity both in Newton's words and in the object of the refutations. The rejected explanations were primarily intended to account for the colors that appeared, not the geometric elongation, though perhaps they might be adapted for that purpose. Obviously there must be some kind of relationship between the colors and the elongation, but it is not logically necessary that both be reduced to the same principle. Newton's predecessors had not felt the need to unify the two. But then a question arises: Do Newton's refutations apply to the disproportion, the color, or both?

The refutations are accomplished in the course of a single compound-complex sentence, and Newton's casual disparagement of the notions does not encourage the reader to think that there is any genuine merit in them – he "could scarce think" that these factors "could have any influence on light to produce such an effect." But a careful reading reveals a problem. From the immediate context "effect" seems to refer unambiguously to the disproportion that surprised Newton, irrespective of the image's coloring. Yet the conclusion of the paragraph states that when he varied the circumstances as described, "the fashion of colours was in all these cases the same." "The fashion of colors" can mean the figure or shape of the colored image taken as a whole, the geometry of the figure; or it can mean the visible characteristics of the colors themselves (e.g., their hue, disposition, etc.). The conclusion can thus be read to mean that the proposed factors are immaterial either because when they are varied the overall disproportion of length to width remains the same or because in all these cases the characteristics of the colors are unchanged.

It is possible, of course, that Newton intended both, or that he did not think the ambiguity important, or perhaps the ambiguity was unintentional. The entire question might be considered a mere semantic cavil were it not for other evidence in the Letter and also elsewhere in Newton's writings. Consider, for instance, the passage in the *Lectiones* that corresponds to this group of refutations in the Letter. There Newton says that "in every Case the Appearance of the Colours will be alike," ("in quovis casu persimilis erit colorum apparitio"), and that varying the size of the aperture only augments or diminishes the "Light exhibiting the Colours" (*OL*, 40–41; *LO*, 31; Shap., 306, 307). "The appearance of the colours" is perhaps less equivocal than "the fashion of the colours"; although the term can include the geometry of their configuration, it seems to refer primarily to their chromaticity. The phrase is interesting in context as well, for up to the point where it appears in the first section of the first part of the *Lectiones* Newton scrupulously avoided mentioning color or colors in describing the phenomena, except where it was necessary for the sake of avoiding confusion. (It is in the following section that color starts to be used as an index of refraction.) Thus there is an initial small but curious discrepancy between Newton's stated intentions and his execution in both the *Lectiones* and the Letter. In the former it seems more like a lapse or oversight; in the latter it is more subtly ambiguous. Could it be that Newton was simply trying to evolve a more neutral vocabulary in his successive attempts at formulating the theory? A case might be made for this; but this neutrality nevertheless produces an ambiguity that serves to conflate geometry and color.[9]

If turns of phrase in a few paragraphs were the only evidence, our suspicions might be ill founded. As we continue to ask whether separating the issues of geometry and color is indeed possible, however, we shall find out that the ambiguities run deeper than mere phrases and conflicting declarations of intention.

Let us first note the mode of Newton's refutations. From the unchanging fashion of colors Newton dismisses the relevance of the alleged contributory circumstances; hence any theories that rely on these must be false. Only when the variation in a circumstance leads to a change in the phenomenon, in the effect, can the causal relevance continue to be maintained. This kind of argument observes another stricture of Francis Bacon: "For the problem is, upon a review of the instances, all and each, to find such a nature as is always present or absent with the given nature, and always increases and decreases with it; and which is, as I have said, a particular case of a more general nature" (Bacon 1960, bk. 2, par. 15). For example, the idea that a certain thickness of glass (the first nature) is required to produce a given color or a certain elongation (the given nature) can be dismissed by showing that the length of the light ray's path through the prism is immaterial; whether the light enters the prism near the vertex, where the path is short, or near the base, where it is longer, the colors and the proportion of the spectrum remain the same. The refutation appears to succeed in this case.

Although Newton's experiment does dispense with this particular interpretation, it does not completely eliminate the possible relevance of thickness. For if we reformulate the proposition so that the significant correlation is not to the absolute length of the path traversed but rather to the relative difference of the path lengths traversed by the different sides of one and the same beam of light, then all Newton's experiment does is to confirm this correlation of relative length to the appearance of the spectrum. Had Newton gone on to increase and decrease this "first nature" – that is, if he had substituted prisms with larger and with smaller refracting angles, so that the relative difference was made greater and smaller – he would have discovered that the given nature, the length of the spectrum, likewise increases and decreases, and that there appear changes in the hues and the proportion of the colors besides (cf. Goethe's evaluation at *HA*, 14: 147).

This first defect is rather minor. There are more serious defects in the other refutations, however. Although Newton varies the size of the windowshut aperture with no noticeable effect, the event is not conclusive. Once the hole in the windowshut is as large as the face of the prism on which the beam falls, there will be no significant change in the spectrum, because any additional sunlight admitted through an even larger hole would quite simply pass beyond the edges of the prism and thus not be refracted at all. With small prisms this point is soon reached as the aperture is enlarged. With the screen at a distance of twenty-two feet the length and the colors of the spectrum will indeed appear only slightly changed; on the other hand, the proportion of length to width changes noticeably. But if one uses a much larger prism, moves the screen closer to the prism, or reduces the refracting angle, there will be dramatic changes (of the kind described in Chapter 2 in the sections on the experiments and the doctrines of the *Beiträge*) in both proportion and color. A sufficiently large hole will lead to an incomplete spectrum – that is, there will be an uncolored center between the two separate edge spectra – a phenomenon that Goethe tenaciously opposed to the Newtonian conception.

Did Newton include these phenomena among the changes and circumstances that were not "material"; would he have concluded in all these cases that the fashion of the colors was "the same"? If one increases the diameter of the aperture from ¼ inch, the measure Newton cites, to ¾ inch, the proportion of length to width becomes 4.4:1 instead of 5:1; if it is further increased to 1½ inch, the proportion is 3.3:1 (these values are calculated on the basis of data given in the Letter). Are these evident changes also immaterial? After all, Newton says only that the disproportion he found was 5:1. Nowhere in the Letter does he mention that it ever comes out differently, and so if his statement about the fashion of the colors being the same applies to the elongation, then the apparent implication is that the proportion is always 5:1.[10] If, on the other hand, "fashion of the colours" has to do with color as well as with geometry, then one may legitimately question whether the refutation has any but the most limited validity under very restricted conditions.

In his third refutation, Newton states that a prism placed outside the windowshut gives the same effect as one inside, so that light need not first be bounded or determined by an aperture to produce color. However, this refutation also has only a conditional validity. A termination is introduced in both experiments; thus they demonstrate that the sequence of termination and refraction is not crucial, not that termination itself is irrelevant. To ascertain whether termination per se is required, other tests would have to be performed. For instance, one might try to eliminate the small hole altogether by placing the prism in the sun's full light at the open window; although the room will then no longer be a pure camera obscura, the familiar spectrum will still appear on the wall opposite. Yet not even this experiment is conclusive, because the very face of the prism terminates the light and acts as an aperture; moreover, the source of light itself, the sun, is essentially a bright circle (aperture) against the relatively dark background of the sky: Newton's experiment does not eliminate these determinations of the light and therefore cannot prove them to be inessential – something Newton was aware of in the lectures (OL, 40; LO, 31; Shap., 306, 307). Although Newton appears to eliminate possibilities by following Bacon's method, the phenomena conceived more fully from a slightly different perspective actually tend to confirm significant correlations between the experimental conditions and the consequent phenomenal effects that Newton wants to dismiss.

The third refutation has a further defect. In order for the experiment to confirm Newton's conclusion, the prism outside the windowshut must be placed very close to the hole, and the light that falls on the hole must be from the white center of the incomplete spectrum. If the prism is too far away, or if the light falling on the hole comes from the edge, what enters the dark room will be colored light, and then the effect will be quite materially different both in proportion and in color: The elongation will be considerably reduced and only part of the spectrum will be visible.

At this point one might ask again: Are these defects truly serious, or are they merely peccadilloes? The answer depends on what Newton makes of the refutations. What ensues in the Letter is a proof of the theory of differential refrangibility. We are attempting to ascertain whether this proof is truly cogent by acquainting ourselves with what a natural philosopher before Newton might have known or believed about light and color, and in what ways he might have responded to the particulars of Newton's Letter. We may not assume that this hypothetical natural philosopher already accepts all the principles of differential refrangibility or interprets all the experiments in accord with Newton. Newton's refutations make it clear that he is attempting proof, so, whatever the merits of his theory, appealing to the Newtonian conception of color as virtually self-evident would amount to begging the question insofar as the validity of the original demonstration of that theory is at issue.

Although the objections we have raised so far by no means demonstrate that Newton's theory is useless or objectively false, or that any other theory is right, they do tend to limit our confidence in the cogency of the argument. It is nevertheless clear that Newton's aim was to establish his theory beyond suspicion of doubt. In a passage suppressed from the printed version of the Letter in the *Philosophical Transactions*, Newton wrote:

A naturalist would scearce expect to see ye science of those [colors] become mathematicall, & yet I dare affirm that there is as much certainty in it as in any other part of Opticks. For what I shall tell concerning them is not an Hypothesis but most rigid consequence, not conjectured by barely inferring 'tis thus because not otherwise or because it satisfies all phaenomena (the Philosophers universall Topick,) but evinced by ye mediation of experiments concluding directly & wthout any suspicion of doubt. (*Corresp.*, 1: 96–97)

Two months later he wrote to the Jesuit Ignace Pardies, who had referred to the theory as an hypothesis:

I am content that the Reverend Father calls my theory an hypothesis if it has not yet been proved to his satisfaction. But my design was quite different, and it seems to contain nothing else than certain [*quasdem*, "some"] properties of light which, now discovered, I think are not difficult to prove, and which if I did not know to be true, I should prefer to reject as vain and empty speculation, than acknowledge them as my hypothesis. (*Corresp.*, 1: 144)

In his reply to Robert Hooke's critique of the Letter, Newton drew a distinction between the hypothesis of the corporeity of light, which he had argued "without any absolute positivenesse," and his theory of light, which he "had asserted ... with the greatest rigor" (*Corresp.*, 1: 113). To Hooke's objection that Newton's Letter presented only a hypothesis "not soe certain as mathematicall Demonstrations" (*Corresp.*, 1: 113; Hooke had read the original version of the Letter, which contained the offending passage), Newton made an apparent concession.

I said indeed that the *Science of Colors was Mathematicall & as certain as any other part of Optiques*; but who knows not that Optiques & many other Mathematicall Sciences depend as well on Physicall Principles as on Mathematicall

Demonstrations: And the absolute certainty of a Science cannot exceed the certainty of its Principles. Now the evidence by wch I asserted the Propositions of colours is in the next words expressed to be from *Experiments* & so but *Physicall*: Whence the Propositions themselves can be esteemed no more than *Physicall Principles* of a Science. And if those Principles be such that on them a Mathematician may determin all the Phaenomena of colours that can be caused by refractions, & that by computing or demonstrating after what manner & how much those refractions doe separate or mingle the rays in wch severall colours are originally inherent; I suppose the *Science of Colours* will be granted *Mathematicall* & as certain as any part of *Optiques*. (*Corresp.*, 1: 187–88)

Although Newton tried to persuade Hooke that the declaration of his theory's mathematical certainty had been properly qualified and therefore ought not to be offensive to a reasonable person, his explanation certainly does not meet the substance of Hooke's objection and is perhaps disingenuous. After all, he asserted in the Letter that he had gone beyond merely satisfying all the phenomena ("the Philosophers universal Topick"), and his experiments, he said, allowed him to conclude the theory "directly & wthout any suspicion of doubt." His present defense, that his theory was as certain as any part of mixed mathematics (like statics and geometric optics), is in essence a reaffirmation of the claim to certainty to which Hooke had taken exception.

In June 1673, by which time the controversy had been going on for more than a year, Newton restated his theory in the form of five definitions and ten propositions in order to resolve "some misunderstandings" that had occurred between him and Christiaan Huygens. According to the first two propositions,

1. The Sun's light consists of rays differing by indefinite degrees of refrangibility.
2. Rays wch differ in refrangibility, when parted from one another do proportionally differ in the colours wch they exhibit. These two Propositions are matter of fact. (*Corresp.*, 1: 293)

That is, they are not the result of interpretation, they simply are; the propositions are merely statements of what the experiments make apparent. But as we have seen, the Letter has not so far presented an argument that is transparent in meaning and self-evident.

Newton continues the Letter with another refutation.

Then I suspected, whether by any *unevenness* in the glass, or other contingent irregularity, these colours might be thus dilated. And to try this, I took another Prisme like the former, and so placed it, that the light, passing through them both, might be refracted contrary ways, and so by the latter returned into that course, from which the former had diverted it. For, by this means I thought, the *regular* effects of the first Prisme would be destroyed by the second Prisme, but the *irregular* ones more augmented, by the multiplicity of refractions. The event was, that the light, which by the first Prisme was diffused into an *oblong* form, was by the second reduced into an *orbicular* one with as much regularity, as when it did not at all pass through them. So that, what ever was the cause of that length, 'twas not any contingent irregularity. (*Corresp.*, 1: 93)

For the first time Newton explicitly states what he is refuting – that the cause is an unevenness in the glass or some other contingent irregularity. This possibility is disproved by using two prisms positioned so that they cancel one another's effects. If dilation per se is due to some accidental irregularity, then doubling the number of refractions should compound the irregular effect. Since experimentally the resulting image is regular, the phenomenon must not be produced in any irregular way. The argument is simple and straightforward.

Nevertheless, there is something odd about it. For one thing, Newton concludes the preceding paragraph with the remark that the "fashion of colors" was the same in all the cases he had tried; he begins the present one with a question unambiguously about the colors and their dilation; by the end he is once again talking about shape with not a word about colors. Yet one of the striking things about the phenomenon is that the resulting image is colorless as well as circular. Perhaps the word "regularity" implies, among other things, the original colorlessness; however, in context it seems to mean the "regularity of the orbicularity" – that is, the closeness with which it approximates the shape of the sun's image when the light is unrefracted.

This passage contains not only ambiguity but an erroneous description and a subtly false implication as well. The experiment succeeds as Newton describes it only if the second prism is placed very close to the first; at such a point, the image produced after the light is refracted by the first prism is not conspicuously oblong, Newton's statement to the contrary notwithstanding, but rather very nearly circular and tinged with color only at the extreme edges. By claiming that the image is oblong, Newton's argument induces the reader to think and see theoretically. Previously he stated, without specifying the circumstances of the experiment, that the proportion of the spectrum's length to width was 5:1. He then enumerated a few conditions that might be thought germane but dismissed them by saying that when he varied these conditions there was no material change in the effect. In the paragraph at hand he continues to examine how "these colors might be thus dilated," that is, in the disproportionate fashion described earlier; but in trying to eliminate the hypothesis of an irregular cause he gives a false impression about what is actually seen. His description states that the first prism elongated the light's form; nothing discourages the further implication that the elongation is marked (perhaps 5:1?), or that the image is colored in the same manner as the first spectrum that had so diverted him with its colors and surprised him by its elongation. Someone like the German physicist Gren might thus have felt justified in asserting that the proportions of the spectrum are 5:1; and someone like Goethe could legitimately infer that according to Newton's theory the spectrum must be complete immediately upon exiting the prism (see, e.g., *FL-P*, par. 87, 88, 101, 210, and *WA* II, 4: 442–44).

Explaining these distortions and insinuations is not easy. The earlier refutations were highly compressed, so that omissions and equivocations might be pardonable. But here just a single experiment is described, and Newton explains exactly what it is meant to prove. The description is tendentious, yet hardly anyone but a German poet has taken exception to it. Even the equivocation concerning geometry and color appears deliberate (especially in contrast to the *Lectiones opticae*), in that it eases the transition from passages in which it is expedient to have the refutations seem to apply to both geometry and color, to those passages in which rays are to be measured by position alone and differential refrangibility is to be proved irrespective of color.

Although speculating about Newton's intentions is risky, at least one effect of this paragraph is clear. It reinforces in the reader the inclination to conceive of the phenomena of refraction in the image of the first experiment, which produces an elongated, multicolored spectrum from refracted light; and it causes the reader to neglect the distinction between the ideal geometric ray, which has a cross-sectional area of zero, and the actual light, which is refracted under specific and specifiable circumstances that do not always produce exactly the result that Newton describes. That is, the phenomena begin to appear in the image of the theory.

A number of theories, in particular those of Hooke and Pardies, contended that refraction dilated, spread, or diffused light in a way that produced both the gradual emergence of color and the eventual elongation of the image. In the *Lectiones opticae* Newton presented this and several other two-prism experiments as a refutation of dilation theories in general; and in his response to Hooke's critique of the Letter, he stated that the experiment with the inverted prisms by itself decides against dilation as a legitimate explanation. In the *Lectiones* he wrote:

> From the experiments of the two parallel prisms already described [i.e., the one that we have been discussing], it is also manifest, that this dilating of the image does not arise from the spreading or splitting of any the same Ray into diverse diverging rays, for they by another spreading or splitting, in their passage through the second prism, ought then to be resolved into a far greater number and more diverging rays. (*OL*, 41; *LO*, 31; Shap., 306, 307)

Newton reasoned that dilation implies that refraction splits up or spreads the simple original ray into many divergent rays; but then any further refraction would have to have a similar effect on each of these, and so subsequent refractions could only increase, and never eliminate, the elongation of the image.

But if the oblong image made (as has been said) by the refraction of one prism only, did acquire its figure by rays divaricating by no certain law, but refracted scatteringly by chance here and there, when the refractions were doubled by two prisms, the errors also of the rays would become twice as many and also twice as great. (*OL*, 39–40; *LO*, 30; Shap., 306, 307)

Thus is dilation refuted as a possible cause.

Or is it? The question is whether all dilation theories depended on so-called contingent irregularities, in the sense that the event follows "no certain law" but rather amounts to a scattering of individual rays "by chance." For the kind of dilation of the ray advanced by Descartes and Hooke in their modificationist theories the answer is no. Both would of course have denied that there was an inherent, preexisting disposition of the rays to be refracted differently. The dilation or elongation of the light was contingent (i.e., depended) on refraction, which induced an irregularity in a ray or beam that formerly was regular. This irregularity would help bring about the elongation and the appearance of color. It was not, however, an unlawful or a purely chance irregularity. The regularity of colors and their positions in the image vouched for the lawfulness and regularity of the phenomenon produced by the induced differentiation (i.e., the induced "irregularity") of the light.

Descartes and Hooke proposed qualitative hypothetical mechanisms to account for the differentiation, which thus lacked rigorous exactitude. In the *Lectiones* Newton turned this indefiniteness of the theories of dilation and their terminologies against their proponents by translating the event into terms of geometric rays. An infinitesimal ray is "split" or "fans out" at a surface where it is refracted; it is "broken up," "separated," "dilated," "rarefied," and so forth. To Newton all these words meant the same thing: For dilation theories every refraction should increase the degree of splitting or breaking up, but he had found an experiment that manifested no such effect. The dilation theory thus seems helpless in the face of the behavior of the ray. Against this background he introduced differential refrangibility as the one true explanation. In the white light are present all the different kinds of color-producing rays. Because each kind has an index of refraction different from all others, they can be separated by refraction; what is more, the very same cause makes it possible for multiple refractions to reproduce the original white light by recombining the rays that were separated. Newton defies the dilationists to account for this phenomenon. Because dilationists do not believe in the inherent property of differential refraction, all they can say (Newton thinks) is that refraction produces a diffusion or spreading of the original ray into many new rays, perhaps infinitely many. But this is an absurd and contradictory conjecture – absurd because the dilationists give no reason why this happens, contradictory because the two-prism experiment refracts a ray four times without the slightest dilation.

This objection would indeed be serious if the dilationists held to the geometric conception of the ray advanced by Newton, but accounts of the dilation of the ray conceived of it as a visible beam with a cross-sectional area greater than zero. Beams, in contradistinction to geometric rays, have sides and are separated from one another by some greater or lesser distance, and so any differentiation induced by refraction can vary from side to side. "Irregularity" in the beam may simply mean that after refraction the beam is no longer perfectly uniform in the way that a white beam is supposed to be. As we shall see, at least one of the modification–dilation theories current in Newton's day was able to give a satisfactory explanation of the phenomenon of the two inverted prisms.[11]

The Letter, however, is silent about the specific adversaries Newton had in mind and the details and effective range of the refutation. That he actually intended to accomplish the same end in the Letter as in the Lectiones is clear from a response to Hooke's objections. The question whether the ray is not split or otherwise dilated he says is settled by the inverted prisms, which rule out

unevennesse in ye glasse, or any other *contingent irregularity* in ye refractions. Amongst other irregularities I know not what is more obvious to suspect then a fortuitous dilating & spreading of light after some such manner as Des-Cartes hath described in his aethereall refractions for explicating ye Tayle of a Comet, or as Mr Hook now supposeth to be effected by ye splitting & rarefying of his aethereall pulse. (*Corresp.*, 1: 178)

In both the Letter and the Lectiones Newton tried to refute potential adversaries. The refutations are at best only partially successful, however, insofar as Newton refuted not the views of other scholars but rather his interpretation of their work; although his arguments point out some difficulties with existing theories, they are not conclusive.

The strategies of the Letter and the Lectiones are strikingly different, however. In the Lectiones Newton presented his basic geometric notion, demonstrated how it could account for the observed phenomena, and tried to manifest its superiority to all alternatives. But debates over the relative merits of different theories can be endless, and objecting to a theory publicly is bound to offend its proponents, no matter how measured or deserved the criticism may be. It is more effective and politic to fend off adversaries in advance, without naming them, by offering experiments that confute their arguments before proposing one's own theory; and more effective still to make one's own appear as an ineluctable consequence of the phenomena rather than merely as a hypothesis. This approach describes the essential strategy of the Letter. Because no fundamental change occurred in Newton's theory between the *Lectiones* and the Letter, this new strategy was a matter of choice: The Letter's indirection, and especially its rapid sequence of condensed refutations that precede the positive theory, made the argument and its problems all the harder to detect.

Newton's refutations depend in large part on his understanding of the ray, but the word itself does not appear until after the inverted-prism experiment. Up to that point he refers to the visible phenomena by using terms such as "image," "spectrum," "light," "colors," "quantity of light." There is no mention of rays either separated or unseparated. Newton's words treat the visible image as though it were a phenomenal whole, despite his implicit geometric conception of the image and light as consisting of infinitesimal parts. Then, in the fifth paragraph of the Letter, he unhesitatingly takes the image and the light as the sum of infinitesimal parts, geometric points and lines. To appreciate this turn of events, it will be helpful first to re-create the subsequent course of the Letter through the famous *experimentum crucis*, paragraphs five through nine.

After experimenting with the inverted parallel prisms, Newton decides to examine the effect of the slightly different angles of incidence of rays coming from the various parts of the sun. To this end he measures the distances and angles involved. The distance from the hole or prism to the wall is 22 feet; the spectrum is 13¼ inches long by 2⅝ inches wide; the diameter of the hole is ¼ inch. The angle through which the median ray in the beam of light is deviated from its original path is 44°56'; the refracting angle of the prism 63°12'; the angle of incidence of the median ray on the first face of the prism is 54°4', as is the angle of refraction at the second face (this means that the prism is at the position of minimum deviation). The sun's disk subtends an angle in the sky of 0°31', which turns out to correspond to the angle subtended by the breadth of the spectrum, whereas the angle subtended by its length is much greater, 2°49'. Using these numbers Newton calculates the sine proportion observed by the median ray and then, assuming that this single proportion holds for all the other rays, calculates further what a strict observance of this unique proportion by all the rays would entail – namely, that the length of the image should also subtend an angle of 0°31' and therefore the image should be circular. Because such a large discrepancy between the experimental phenomenon and the prediction according to the law of sines is so unexpected, Newton takes up the prism once more to investigate further by means of experiments. By rotating the prism to and fro about its axis, he is able to vary the angle of incidence on the first face by as much as four or five degrees without markedly shifting the colors from their place on the wall. If so large a difference in incidence produces so little change, a difference of 0°31' between the extreme rays coming from opposite parts of the sun will make even less of a difference.

Another suspicion then occurs to Newton: He wonders whether the rays might not move in a curved line after they are refracted, much as a tennis ball given spin by a racket will follow a curved path. This hypothesis is reminiscent of Descartes's rotating globules, though Newton mentions neither Descartes nor his hypothesis. This attempt to rescue the sine law in its original form is Newton's last; if this quasi-Cartesian hypothesis is correct, then the law of sines may still hold strictly at the moment of refraction, with the difference that the rays immediately begin to curve out of the rectilinear path. But he is unable to detect any curvature. Newton continues:

The gradual removal of these suspitions at length led me to the *Experimentum Crucis*, which was this: I took two boards, and placed one of them close behind the Prisme at the window, so that the light might pass through a small hole, made in it for that purpose, and fall on the other board, which I placed at about 12 foot distance, having first made a small hole in it also, for some of that Incident light to pass through. Then I placed another Prisme behind this second board, so that the light, trajected through both the boards, might pass through that also, and be again refracted before it arrived at the wall. This done, I took the first Prisme in my hand, and turned it to and fro slowly about its *Axis*, so much as to make the several parts of the Image, cast on the second board, successively pass through the hole in it, that I might observe to what places on the wall the second Prisme would refract them. And I saw by the variation of those places, that the light, tending to that end of the Image, towards which the refraction of the first Prisme was made, did in the second Prisme suffer a Refraction considerably greater then the light tending to the other end [Fig. 1.1]. And so the true cause of the length of that Image was detected to be no other, then that *Light* consists of *Rays differently refrangible*, which, without any respect to a difference in their incidence, were, according to their degrees of refrangibility, transmitted towards divers parts of the wall.

When I understood this, I left off my aforesaid Glass-works; for I saw, that the perfection of Telescopes was hitherto limited, not so much for want of glasses truly figured according to the prescriptions of Optick Authors, (which all men have hitherto imagined,) as because that Light it self is a *Heterogeneous mixture of differently refrangible Rays*. (*Corresp.*, 1: 94–95)

This ends the process of refutation and brings the ultimate confirmation: The *experimentum crucis* proves that light is a mixture of different kinds of rays. Even if what precedes is defective, it appears to demonstrate conclusively that light is differently refrangible, and without even mentioning color. The holes in the two boards select a ray of light out of the beam that is refracted by the first prism, and the fixed positions of the boards and of the second prism ensure that no matter what part of the spectrum falls on the hole in the second board, the incident angle of this ray on the second prism will be the same. Because the images

produced by these different rays are cast on different parts of the wall –
a criterion of geometry, not color – the rays must be differently refracted.

No one can wish to deny the phenomenon in question: It is one that
was performed not only to Newton's satisfaction, but to Hooke's, the
Royal Society's, and even Goethe's. Yet rather than rush to the conclusion
that Newton's presentation lets the phenomenon speak for itself, it would
be better to suspend final judgment until we have looked into the details
and the purport of the experiment and the experimental argument.

First, Newton's use of terms in paragraphs five through nine is rather
curious. Terms suddenly appear, then just as suddenly disappear without
compelling reason. "Color," which already has been variously used in
the Letter, does occur once, in the middle of the seventh paragraph, but
not at all in the course of the *experimentum crucis* and the statement of
differential refrangibility. Its general absence seems to support the contention that the doctrine of refrangibility is established independent of
color. But "ray," which occurs for the very first time in paragraph five
and then frequently in the three following paragraphs, also is not to be
found in the narration of the *experimentum crucis*; it appears again only
in the statement of the conclusion, that light consists of rays differently
refrangible. Instead of referring to the rays, Newton reverts to the kind
of phenomenal description characteristic of the first four paragraphs of
the Letter: For example, he mentions the "light," the "incident light,"
"the several parts of the image cast on the second board." Certainly no
one would want to argue that Newton thereby proved his doctrine irrespective of rays, because differential refrangibility is by definition the
differential refrangibility of *rays*.

"Refrangibility" itself is an interesting term. The word, according to
the *Oxford English Dictionary*, is probably Newton's coinage. The word
"refraction" is older by nearly a century; it describes first of all the
phenomenon of the apparent bending, deflection, or fracture of light out
of its original course when it passes from one transparent medium to
another and, derivatively, the action of the refracting media on the light.
Refraction thus refers to a visible event, a concrete and active process;
though some action of the medium on the light may be inferred, the term
is essentially descriptive. Refrangibility, on the other hand, is not truly
descriptive; it refers not so much to the visible phenomenon as to an
interpretation of it. Whereas refraction points to what happens when
light encounters different transparent media, and thus to a property of
both light and the media, refrangibility refers only to a characteristic of
the light, something that is intrinsic to light and that refraction serves to
reveal. Newton claimed to be the discoverer of this property of light, a
property revealed by the *experimentum crucis*. It is a property of rays of
light, and differential according to kind. Yet the experiment does not

really show us a ray of light in Newton's primary sense, but at best a bundle of rays. Moreover, what is visible is not a ray, but an image that is cast on the wall. What really makes Newton's investigations seem rigorous, however, is his apparent measurement of individual rays of light in the geometric sense. Clearly, the complicated interplay between the ray in Newton's sense, the beam of light, and the visible image is in need of explication.[12] In order to ascertain the real cogency of Newton's argument, we will have to pay close attention to the ray of light, particularly because of the major differences between Newton's and his predecessors' interpretations of what constituted it.

We have already pointed out that Newton avoids the term "ray" until the fifth paragraph of the Letter. Until then he uses unexceptionable, commonplace descriptions of the light and the visible image without implying that either is inherently divisible or compound. His depictions are phenomenalistic without being methodical or systematic. Once he begins to take measurements, however, he treats the light and the image as intrinsic and unproblematic aggregates – a bundle of rays conceived according to a geometrical model, a compact and continuous assemblage of points upon which these rays fall.

The geometry of light is as old as the origin of optics; for the period from Greek antiquity through the early seventeenth century, optics was synonymous with geometric optics. In the seventeenth century the emphasis began to shift from questions of geometry to speculations about the physical constitution of light and its mode of propagation through space, but not until Johannes Kepler had perfected geometric optics at the commencement of the century with his theory of the formation and location of images according to the concourse or focusing of geometric rays. Although his theory was introduced to account for the formation, location, and perception of sharp images, it gradually became objectified and divorced from the phenomenon of the visible image, so that the geometry of optics was taken more as a representation of real physical entities, of objectively existent rays.

Ever since then optics has been preoccupied with the physical interpretation of rays, the two main branches of which have conceived of light as an impulse (wave) or as a tiny body (corpuscle). Although we cannot follow the development of these ideas, it is important for our purposes to remark that, despite the exactitude that the physical interpretation of the ray helped bring about, it also tended to blur not only the distinction between the mathematical and the physical, so that a mathematical representation was implicitly identified with what occurs physically, but also the difference between the thing that is regarded as the physical cause or occasion of light and the experience of light or luminosity; the perception of luminosity was seemingly devalued to an imperfect indicator of objective light (see Ronchi 1970; cf. Guerlac 1986). Concomitantly, the chief goal of the physics of light became not the understanding of the phenomena seen but rather the understanding of the ray, in terms of which all the phenomena might be explained. The corresponding investigation and elucidation of the mathematicophysical reality underlying the appearances became a characteristic trend of modern science: To discover the mathematical principles underlying nature was to penetrate its innermost physical depths.

The shift from phenomenal descriptions in paragraphs one through four to the mathematicophysical depiction of what follows conforms to the changing temper of optical science in the seventeenth century. The visible image gives way to an image that is conceived as an epiphenomenon, the product of the really existent physical rays, which in turn have a mathematical interpretation. Newton's measurements, calculations, and discussion beginning in the fifth paragraph objectify the ray so that it is no longer subordinated to the visible phenomenon or merely coordinated with it but rather identified as the true essence of the event and the real cause of what is seen. What is visible is thereby reduced to the status of "mere" phenomenon, less worthy of scientific interest than the really existent rays because it involves a superabundance of subjectivity. What is seen is at best an indicator of what is there.[13]

In light of the historical development after Kepler, it is interesting to note that when Newton first brings up the ray he ostensibly defines it in relation to the image. "I then proceeded to examine more critically, what might be effected by the difference of the incidence of Rays coming from divers parts of the Sun; and to that end, measured the several lines and angles, belonging to the Image" (*Corresp.*, 1: 93). Up to this point, Newton's primary interest has been the shape and appearance of the image, but he effects a quick transition to a new level of discourse, to the infinity of rays flowing from the sun to the image. The several lines and angles belong to the image only in the sense that the different parts of the image, their positions, are used to quantify the passage of the rays. Furthermore, whereas traditional geometric optics employed rays to account for the focused image, so that the standard of judgment was the clear image that appeared in a particular place, refraction by a prism does not produce a focused image. With a lens there is said to be a unique place where *the* image of a given object is formed; at any other place the light that traverses the lens will produce a more or less hazy impression of luminosity, but not the sharp image we call the true or primary one. The spectrum is an image in a secondary sense: It is formed by rays that are diverging and thus do not meet in a focal point. It is of course quite natural and logical to want to use the ray to explain unfocused as well as focused images. But the relationship between the explanatory concept of the ray and the unfocused image is not identical to the relationship between the ray and the focused image. The sharp image, the primary image, warrants the validity of interpreting it as what is produced by focused rays issuing from a single point of the object and converging on a single point of the screen. The interpretation of a blurred, secondary image is derivative from this, and depends on the prior acceptance of the concept of the ray as legitimately applicable. Thus the sharp, primary image is prior both phenomenally and theoretically. (It is also prior practically: Lens makers concern themselves with producing lenses that are free of distortion, that make nearly perfect primary images.)

Although the geometric ray is a powerful theoretical and practical tool, a practical and perhaps even a theoretical optics is conceivable without it. Under normal circumstances, the best judge of a good image is not a theory of rays but the eye. When the ray becomes the primary object of investigation, however, we tend to lose sight of what constitutes the phenomenon and of the relationship between the theory and the phenomena. The ray, an explanatory device, albeit inferred from exacting descriptions of the phenomena, is increasingly used as a neutral descriptive term that becomes normative for both practice and theory. Newton fails to acknowledge a hierarchy of relationships between theory and phenomena, and that the former depends on the latter. It is possible to demonstrate that the light from the sun entering a dark room through a small hole produces a circular image that gets larger the further from the hole we move the screen and then to extrapolate therefrom the notion of the ray or beam as the thing enclosed by the geometrical boundaries that we can use to outline the places where images appear; it is even possible to talk about the parts of this phenomenally defined ray. It is misleading, however, to substitute geometry for the phenomena as though infinitesimal rays are unproblematically real.

From Newton's words and practice it is clear that the ray, abstractly and mathematically conceived and taken to be physically real as well, is the genuine subject of his inquiries, and that the phenomena serve to give evidence of the rays and their positions. Although he starts out measuring the distance of the image from the prism and its length and breadth, his way of conceiving the phenomenon soon changes radically. He measures "the angle, with the Rays, tending towards the middle of the image made with those lines, in which they would have proceeded without refraction"; he tells the reader that "the Rays fell perpendicularly upon those rays, which passed through the center of the said hole." In the next (sixth) paragraph he computes "the refractions of two rays flowing from opposite parts of the sun's discus." The reification is subtly but surely effected. The rays are not merely lines perceived by the mind's eye, they are present and active, they suffer refraction, they pass through apertures, they flow from the sun. When in the eighth paragraph of the Letter he asks "whether the rays, after their trajection through the prism, did not move in curved lines" (*Corresp.*, 1: 94), there can be no doubt about how thoroughgoing the reification has been. It is precisely at this point that Newton speculates about what might happen if light consisted of globules. Although he rejects the analogy of spinning balls because he cannot discover any curvity in the lines, the passage nevertheless reveals how far the geometrical model has led him. In the course of four paragraphs he has gone from the ray as a line to the ray as traveling corpuscles. The geometrical representation frees itself from subordination to the image and becomes the guide for all reasoning about light, and the image and even the colors become subordinate to the mathematical description. In the seventh paragraph, when Newton varies the incidence of the rays by turning the prism four or five degrees about its axis, he says that "the colors were not thereby sensibly translated from their place on the wall, and consequently by that variation of incidence, the quantity of refraction was not sensibly varied" (*Corresp.*, 1: 93–94). Here the colored spectrum is merely an indicator of what happens to the physical rays depicted mathematically.

This sentence contains the only occurrence of the word color in paragraphs five through nine. It would hardly have been possible for Newton to omit mentioning it here, because not merely the image and its shape are of consequence but even more the appearance, especially the order, of the colors. If color is disregarded, there is no criterion by which to determine that certain rays go to particular parts of the image. Only because there are regular color differences and because these different colors maintain the same order in the spectrum while the prism is rotated can Newton draw the conclusion that this degree of change in the angle of incidence has no material effect on the outcome. He presupposes that there are constant and identifiable entities that follow straight-line paths from prism to spectrum, and that what appears on the screen is wholly explicable in terms of these entities. As he rotates the prism, violet remains at one extreme, red at the other, and the rest of the colors retain their positions as well; consequently he can say, on the assumption that there are such constant entities as violet-producing rays, red-producing rays, and so forth, that there is no material effect because the colors were not sensibly translated. But if he did not take the colors as indexes of where these entities go, he would not be able to rule out the possibility that the overall appearance is unchanged although the behavior of the individual rays changes drastically (yet lawfully).

If, on the contrary, one rejects the color ray or maintains a certain skepticism about its reality, one could argue that the sidedness of the beam as a whole at least correlates with the order of the colors. One

might even decide to define the infinitesimal ray as the limit of an experimental phenomenon and then consider the visible beam's behavior
as the summation of the behaviors of innumerable infinitesimal beams –
of course, it would also be necessary to define what colors result from
mixing different kinds of color rays; however, by making this limiting
argument explicit, one would be quite aware that the ray is a fictive
approximation rather than a demonstrated fact.

Newton might object that phenomenal evidence for his ray theory can
be drawn from the second refutation in the Letter (in which he varied
the size of the aperture). As long as the prism is not excessively broad,
reducing or increasing the aperture does not much affect the size or colors
of the spectrum that appears on the wall 22 feet away. Reducing the
aperture in effect selects out of the larger beam a smaller one; increasing
it makes the original smaller beam a part of the new, larger one. Therefore, not only is the beam divisible, in that one can screen off parts of
it, but all these divisible parts are also independent of one another and
when refracted produce the same phenomenon according to the same
law. Thus the spectrum produced by a larger beam can be constructed
as the sum of spectra produced by the independent refraction of each of
its parts. But this amounts to the limiting argument mentioned in the
previous paragraph; it does not necessarily support the argument that
the spectrum is actually produced as the sum of many parts. The phenomenal evidence will not support Newton's desired conclusion without
the help of the geometric ray model, precisely what is in question. When
the aperture is reduced, the smaller beam is not really any longer a part
of the larger beam, but instead a new beam in its own right, defined like
the larger one by the boundaries of illuminated and unilluminated areas.
The smaller beam with its smaller image is as much a whole beam forming
whole images as is the larger beam. This thesis does not contradict the
fact that under the experimental conditions – with a refracting angle of
60 degrees, the screen at 22 feet, and so forth – a beam A admitted
through a hole half the diameter of another hole that admits beam B
does not produce a spectrum half the length of the one produced by B;
indeed, there is so little difference under the circumstances that one is
compelled to wonder about what happens at the limit of the practicable.
One might nevertheless still argue that the truly significant discovery is
that these various beams produce images that are basically circular and
mostly white with narrow fringes of color when a screen is placed near
the prism; multicolored and oblong in a changing proportion when the
screen is at intermediate distances; and tricolored and nearing a limiting
proportion of length to width at far distances. Although one might further
be willing to consider the possibility of analyzing the whole by dividing
it into parts in the manner of ray analysis, this analysis would merely be

a heuristic technique; the results would not be a demonstrated fact and would have to be tested critically in order to see whether they were sufficiently accurate and compatible with the totality of the prismatic phenomena, in particular with the rules of color mixing.

The presumption that the rays really exist and that they are what cause colors is in truth already implicit at the very opening of the Letter, when Newton says that he refracted a quantity of light to view the vivid and intense colors produced thereby; the colors are produced by the refracted quantity of light (i.e., the bundle of rays) and nothing else (cf. Goethe's comment at WA II, 4: 442). His words exclude the possibility, for instance, that color may be the result of an interaction of illuminated and unilluminated parts of a medium or of a mixture of light and darkness. External influences are discounted. The first refutations try to confirm this presumption by suppressing the idea that external factors like termination by an aperture, or darkness, or the matter of the prism itself is responsible for the phenomenon. The refutations not only bolster Newton's reputation as a Baconian, they also introduce certain hypotheses that might be suspect if they were made explicit. The measurements of paragraph five simply reify the unacknowledged implications of Newton's theoretical preferences. Thus, the success of the entire argument rests on a network of hypotheses that are hidden beneath the surface narrative.

The experimentum crucis: context and intent

The experiments that lead up to the *experimentum crucis* all deal in the same basic elements: the sun and its rays, the darkness of shadow and the camera obscura, a small aperture, at least one prism with a large refracting angle, the screen or wall, and the visible image. No special attention is given the sun as sun, because it is the constant source of light. The early refutations eliminate from further consideration the darkness of shadow and the room, the apertures or other boundings of the light, and the material of the prism. The position of the screen is a fixed constant, although Newton must have varied its distance from the prism to check for curvature in the paths of the lightrays when testing the quasi-Cartesian hypothesis of rotating globules, and the image, whether colored or colorless, elongated or circular, is taken as an index of what is happening (the same or similar results in the image suggest the same or a similar cause). By process of elimination there seems to be just one conclusion: The true and fundamental cause of the phenomenon – as things turn out, of both the color and the elongation – is the change in the direction of the rays of light brought out by the refractions at the faces of the prism, because the experiments appear to have conclusively demonstrated that (1) white light is divided into independent parts, into rays; (2) each and every one of the white-producing rays is spread out by refraction into an oblong, colored image; and (3) when multiple refractions return the beam to its original direction there is neither elongation nor color. What remains to be seen, then, is whether white light that has already been refracted once to produce an elongated spectrum is governed by the same law or laws as the light of the sun.

This question leads directly to the *experimentum crucis*, which shows that once the rays of white light have been spread out by a first refraction any subsequent refraction of some portion of the spread-out rays does not produce the same phenomenon as the original light. Any part of the white light of the sun is capable of producing a full spectrum, whereas different parts of a beam that has already been refracted once are refracted to different degrees by the second prism and produce truncated images. Moreover, the (violet-producing) light that is the most refracted in the first instance is also most refracted in the second: Its nearly circular or at least not very elongated image appears higher on the screen than light from any other part of the first spectrum. The (red-producing) light from the other end of the spectrum is least refracted in both instances; and the other kinds are refracted to an intermediate degree according to their positions in the first spectrum. Since the cause is to be sought only in the light itself (i.e., in the change of direction of its component rays), and since light is both experimentally and theoretically divisible into parts, the phenomenon must be due to differential refrangibility of light. This conclusion means that the apparently homogeneous light of the sun is really composite, consisting of different varieties of light that are distinguishable according to the extent to which they are refracted by a prism. Although in the Letter the statement of this "fact" is propositionally separate from the color theses in the second half of the Letter, the conclusion that each of these rays produces a different color follows inevitably from the premises of the mathematical model and from the presuppositions of the experiments. Those who wish to assert the simplicity of white light are refuted: It is impossible for a simple thing to have different effects, and because the only thing in these experiments that can have an effect is the light there must be multiple lights already present in the original light of the sun. The real "simple things" are the indefinitely many, differently refrangible (color-producing) ultimate parts of the white light; white light is intrinsically compound.

Newton's final coup is to announce that the sine law can be rescued after all in a modified form. Each of the different kinds of rays is refracted according to a constant sine proportion, but the proportion is different according to kind. Because there are indefinitely many proportions that correspond to the different points along the length of the spectrum, there must be indefinitely many kinds of light as well. Newton called this concept "the oddest if not the most considerable detection which had hitherto been made in the operations of nature." In his subsequent animadversions against Hooke, Newton argued that his theory explained the refractions according to a constant law without any irregularity (*Corresp.*, 1: 179). That is, each color ray always obeys one and only one sine proportion, whether it is intermixed with other kinds of rays or has been completely separated from them; it is not necessary to speculate about any irregularity supposed to be induced in an otherwise simple, colorless beam, because the beam is not simple but an aggregate. The effect of refraction is to order this aggregate quantitatively according to the property of the rays that Newton called refrangibility.

Now, although Newton erroneously portrayed all modificationist theories as necessarily implying that refraction was the result of accidental irregularities (i.e., governed by no law whatsoever), he was not wrong to claim that the law he had enunciated was constant, and that this distinguished his theory from those of the modificationists. By imagining the different kinds of rays as already present in the colorless beam he could say that they always followed the sine law proportion appropriate to their kind, regardless of what rays they were with at the moment. Modificationists, not accepting the notion that white light is originally composite, had to invent an explanation for why the second refraction in the *experimentum crucis* did not follow the same law as the first – that is, they had to appeal to a new or at least a modified law. Nevertheless, the experiments cited in the Letter and in the following controversy do not compel us to join Newton in his conclusion. The phenomenon of the *experimentum crucis* is important, but it does not necessarily support anything more than the assertion that light, once it is colored by refraction, no longer produces the same phenomenon as white light. If refraction changes white light in some significant way, a difference in subsequent refractions perhaps ought to be expected (see Sabra 1967, 249–50).

Newton's argument from the *experimentum crucis* seems to be purely geometrical; the rays that are refracted most the first time by the first prism – those that are most bent out of their original path and that appear at the top of the full spectrum when the refracting angle is turned downward – are also refracted most the second time by the second prism; and, mutatis mutandis, the same argument holds for all the other rays, all the way to the opposite end of the spectrum where the least refracted rays fall. But we have already seen that this interpretation depends on an unvoiced hypothesis that is instrumentalized in Newton's observations and experiments, and that most of the conclusions drawn on the way to the crucial experiment have at most a restricted validity if color is disregarded.[14] The conclusion of the *experimentum crucis* must be qualified similarly. The color of the part of the spectrum that falls on the hole in the second board (i.e., the color of the light that reaches the second prism) must be the same as the color of the partial spectrum formed after the second refraction. If a purportedly violet ray admitted through the hole produced a yellow image or even a violet image with markedly different fringes, Newton would have to explain how violet-producing rays could produce colors other than violet. That the color be essentially unchanged is a necessary condition for his conclusion that light is differently refrangible, for it is the chief criterion of ray identity.

Suppressing color in the *experimentum crucis* was an important tactic, however, precisely because it concealed such an experimental difficulty. More than a decade later the eminent French physicist Edmé Mariotte pointed out that in performing the *experimentum crucis* he had found that the images produced by the refraction of the second prism were decidely not circular, which they ought to be if that light is truly homogeneous, and that rather than being uniform in hue the images displayed several colors – that is, they had greater or lesser fringes of color different in hue from the presumed color of the light admitted through the hole in the second board, a fact that the Newton of the unpublished *Lectiones opticae* knew (*LO*, 164–65; Shap., 452–55). These fringes may be inconspicuous enough to be overlooked on a cursory glance; yet, although there are various methods for reducing them, it is not possible with the apparatus of the *experimentum crucis* to eliminate them completely. A Newtonian would dismiss these fringes by saying that the light had not been perfectly separated and might advise his opponent to learn better experimental technique. Yet this answer is scarcely satisfactory. Once again the experimental difficulties cannot prove Newton wrong; nevertheless, if a perfect demonstration of the theory is not possible, and if the geometricophysical interpretation can never be verified directly, how can anyone claim that the theory is proved directly from experiments as a fact beyond doubt? One must admit that the theory is indirectly inferred from the phenomena by speculating about what happens at the limit of the visible and with the assistance of various hypotheses and abstractions; it is not derivable from the phenomena alone, nor can the propositions about light and color be accepted as perfectly unproblematic.

In reflecting on Newton's controversies with his contemporaries and on Goethe's opposition to Newton and his epigones, we must keep in mind that Newton and his followers insisted that the theory of differential refrangibility was not hypothetical, that it was established beyond all doubt, and that one had only to examine the experiments to see the full evidence of its truth; however, the theory actually depends on a number of unstated premises and only partially explicit refutations that may be made plausible by experiments but are not self-evident. The only way to make them self-evident is to suppress inconvenient phenomena, use terms ambiguously, shift between different levels of description, and in general make a complicated and often convoluted argument seem to be the evidence of the senses.

The experimentum crucis as refutation

Newton seems to have borrowed the term *experimentum crucis* from Robert Hooke's *Micrographia*, a work that Newton read during his early studies of color and light. Hooke in turn apparently derived it from Francis Bacon by conflating (or perhaps confusing) the latter's *experimenta lucifera* and *instantiae crucis* (Lohne 1968, 179). By its nature an *experimentum crucis* is meant to perform two functions: It should place the experimenter at the intersection of two or more possible ways of accounting for phenomena, and it should exclude some of the possibilities from further consideration while perhaps also pointing to one or more alternatives as the most promising paths. An experiment that fulfills this office must be designed so that it yields unequivocal information. Even if it does not clearly identify a single path, it must at least point away from one or several alternatives. The nature of the *experimentum crucis*, then, is to refute even more than it is to confirm.

Seen in this light, the experiments in the Letter all have an element of cruciality, because they argue against certain hypotheses and provide information that ultimately leads to Newton's theory. Yet when Newton gave this name to the one experiment he considered definitive both pro and contra, he accomplished a significant transformation of the Baconian method and placed the new concept of the crucial experiment at the center of natural philosophy, at the center of science. The essential difference is that whereas Bacon advocated enumerating all relevant phenomena in tables and then determining the truth by a process of elimination, Newton merely alludes to alternative theories in the course of proving his own and virtually denies that any context is needed apart from the few experiments he describes. Newton's Letter, though quasi-Baconian in appearance, proceeds more positively than negatively in that it judges what is wrong from the perspective of what the theory requires; also, the phenomena are selected to test theories, rather than to provide a comprehensive array. The alternative theories, insofar as they are discussed at all, are not vigorous adversaries but pale shadows of their true selves and so hardly worth considering at all. Although the Letter seems to be a historical narrative that is a model of experimental caution and exactitude, it is really a tendentious reworking of events, theories, and phenomena for the sake of reaching a predestined conclusion.

In the *Lectiones opticae* Newton said that he could refute all other theories at length, if he wanted to, but would not, seeing that it would be tedious; and in any case their common error was to think that color was due to some modification of light rather than to an innate and original property of light (*LO*, 149; Shap., 436, 437). Newton rarely refuted theories exactly as others presented them, however, and from what we have seen so far it seems unlikely that even a tedious refutation would have been sufficient to do the job Newton thought could be done.

At the time Newton wrote the *Lectiones* and the Letter, the two premier theorists of light and color in England were Robert Hooke and Robert Boyle. Boyle, perhaps because he was more interested in outlining the various phenomena and theories of light and color, especially those germane to chemistry, than in establishing a particular theory of his own, did not take part in the controversy over Newton's theory. Hooke, of course, was the curator of experiments of the Royal Society; although hardly a dogmatist about the truth of his prolific ideas, he believed that the way to truth required the formation of mechanical hypotheses that save the phenomena. His interpretations of light and color are an example of the older type of theory that Newton's replaced, a modificationist theory. Anyone wishing to establish a new theory of light and color as true, particularly before the Royal Society of London, needed to explain its superiority to Hooke's theory. But although Newton considered Hooke wrong and thought it easy enough to refute his theory, none of the experiments in the Letter, not even the *experimentum crucis*, fulfills the task.

Hooke did not have a unified theory to account for all color in a single, constant way, so that perhaps one ought to talk of Hooke's theories of light and color; nevertheless, his theory of refraction was relatively well developed and can be treated on its own merits. It proposed that color is determined by a characteristic of the entire light beam or ray of light, the orientation of a so-called pulse front, rather than by different kinds of rays present in the original beam. Light is conceived as a pulse that is propagated through space; this pulse acts along a front that in white or colorless light is perpendicular to the direction of propagation – that is, the pulse front is like a moving cross-section of the beam. When the beam is refracted it undergoes not only a change in direction but also a change in the orientation of this front. The new direction of the beam as a whole is determined according to the familiar sine law; the new orientation of the front is then determined by the changed speed of light in the new medium. Hooke assumed that the ratio of the speed of light in the first medium to the speed of light in the second equaled the inverse

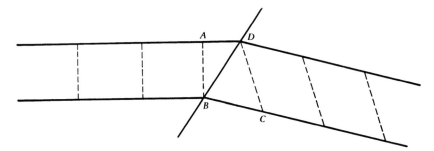

Figure 3.2   Refraction according to Hooke. Point B of the wave front (dashed line) enters the glass first. Assuming that the speed of light in the medium to the right is greater than in the medium to the left, the part of the front that enters the second medium first will travel faster than the opposite extreme of the front, which is still in the first medium. When point A of the front finally enters the second medium (at point D), the wave front will no longer be perpendicular to the direction of the ray's propagation, which direction changes according to the law of sines.

ratio of the respective indexes of refraction of the two media; thus, if the sine of incidence of a ray passing from air into glass stands to the sine of refraction in the proportion of, say 1.5:1, this same ratio would express the proportion of the speed of light in glass to the speed of light in air (sine of incidence from air divided by sine of refraction in glass equals speed in glass divided by speed in air). In the middle of the nineteenth century it was finally demonstrated experimentally that just the reverse is the case, that these two ratios are in direct rather than inverse proportion, and therefore, contrary to Hooke, light travels faster in rarer than denser media, fastest of all in a vacuum. But this defect in Hooke's theory was inherent as well in Newton's, so that it cannot be a criterion for deciding between them.

To picture Hooke's interpretation of what happens in refraction, imagine a beam of light in air that is approaching glass at an oblique angle (Fig. 3.2). The beam consists of unmodified white light, and so the pulse front is perpendicular to the beam's path. Because of the oblique incidence on the refracting surface, one side of the front will enter the glass and be refracted before the other side reaches the glass. Light, once it enters the glass, travels faster than in air; therefore, the part of the pulse front already in the glass will get ahead of the part still in the air, so that the wave front will no longer be perpendicular to the sides of the beam (or the direction of propagation).

By virtue of this induced obliquity of the pulse front, Hooke tried to account for both the color and the spreading or dilation of the beam.

Hooke first correlated colors with the relative strength and weakness of successive parts along the pulse front. He said "that Blue is an impression on the Retina of an oblique and confus'd pulse of light, whose weakest part precedes, and whose strongest follows. And, that Red is an impression on the Retina of an oblique and confus'd pulse of light, whose strongest part precedes, and whose weakest follows" (Hooke 1665, 64). The other colors produced by refraction result from the intensification, attenuation, and (in the case of green) mixture of these two basic colors. The "confusion" of the pulse begins at the two edges of the beam and spreads itself therefrom, but only when refraction has made the pulse front oblique to the direction of propagation rather than perpendicular. Thus, immediately beyond the surface of refraction only the *edges* of the beam are confused, weakened, or attenuated; the central portion remains unmodified and uncolored until the weakening effect spreads to it.

The color that one sees at any point along the oblique pulse front depends on the order in which the adjoining parts are stronger or weaker. Blue appears at the edge where the front is most advanced (the part of the pulse front that first comes into contact with the retina is relatively weak because it is nearer the attenuated edge of the beam). At the other edge it is the stronger part of the front that precedes the weaker, and so red appears. The center of the beam, as long as it remains unattenuated by the weakening effect spreading out from both edges, appears white because the adjoining parts of the pulse front still have equal strength. As for the diffusion of the beam, when the pulse front is oblique the beam communicates a weak impulse into the parts of the medium contiguous to the passing front; it therefore has a tendency to spread out or dilate.

Hooke's explanation is a rather complicated affair, full of ambiguities that he failed, for the most part, to clarify. The obliquity of the front, the dilation, and the appearance of color are all interrelated, but none is entirely reducible to one or both of the others. Refraction produces an obliquity in the pulse front, the obliquity leads to an attenuation and a spreading, and the attenuation to a differential strength of the pulse front that is able at the retina to make the impression of colors. On the other hand, despite its ambiguities and inexactness, it is not obviously self-contradictory, and it does fit a number of the phenomena of refraction with which we are acquainted.

Earlier we said that Newton used experiments involving two prisms to refute not only Hooke's theory but also all other theories that employ the concepts of modification and dilation. The inverted parallel prisms are intended to show that many refractions can result in no net effect, as though there had been no refraction whatsoever. The modern literature on Newton generally agrees that he was successful in demonstrating the

inability of dilation/modification theories to account for the effects of
the second prism (but see Sabra 1967 and Laymon 1978). It is true that
Hooke's and other contemporaneous diffusion theories are untenable by
today's standards, so that, for example, any attempt at justifying Hooke
cannot be taken as a rehabilitation. Our key consideration here, however,
is not whether a theory in all its details is adequate for the purposes of
twentieth-century science, but whether Newton's arguments refuted it.
The answer is no.

Newton's peculiar interpretation of the dilation theories is illuminated
by a two-prism experiment he introduced in the *Lectiones* and which he
cited in response to Hooke's criticism of the Letter.

Moreover to all these Objections is opposed the Experiment, where the latter
Prism is not placed parallel to the former, but perpendicularly transverse. For in
that Case, if the former Prism dilated the Image in Length from any other Cause
than the different Refrangibility of different Rays, then the latter Prism by a
transverse Refraction ought to dilate that oblong Image in Breadth, and so would
form a quadrilateral one. But upon trying the Experiment, the Thing came out
otherwise. (OL, 41–42; LO, 31–32; Shap., 306, 307)

Namely, the spectrum is still oblong, just as it is after a single refraction
– also more elongated, of course – but even more importantly it is oblique
with respect to the axes of both prisms; rather than being horizontally
or vertically elongated, the spectrum is diagonally elongated. The basic
argument is that because dilation elongates the image, and the two prisms
refract the image first vertically and then horizontally, according to dilation theories the final image ought to be elongated in both directions
and thus be more like a square than a narrow oblong. But this interpretation does not touch Hooke's theory. Even though Hooke himself seems
to have been surprised by the outcome of this experiment (*Corresp.*, 1:
195), his theory of dilation according to the obliquation of the pulse
front does not require that the twice-refracted image be nearly square.
The primary effect of refraction, apart from the change in direction of
the beam, is the induced obliquity of the front; dilation is a subsidiary
effect contingent on the obliquity. The beam of light and the quiescent
medium adjoining it interact with one another to produce a spreading
of the light impulse only when the pulse front is oblique, and the colors
that appear and the progress of the interaction of the beam and the
medium depend on the orientation of the front. What happens to this
orientation when the ray is refracted first by one prism and then by
another placed perpendicular to the first?

Diagrams used to represent the refraction according to Hooke's theory
can give only a two-dimensional representation of what happens in three
dimensions. Hooke's oblique pulse front is not the line it appears to be
in a drawing, but rather a circular or elliptical plane figure, a cross-

section of the cylinder or cone that represents the ray geometrically. Any single refraction that takes place on a plane refracting surface – all four refractions that take place with two prisms are of this kind – results in a rotation of this circular or elliptical front around an imaginary line formed by the intersection of the pulse front with the refracting plane at the moment when the geometrical center of the front enters this plane. No matter how many refractions of this kind take place, the net effect will be a sum of these rotations of the front as a solid unit, which is equivalent to a *single* rotation of this kind. Thus, after all the refractions are completed, the front will still be elliptical (or, in one case to be noted later, circular) and oriented as though it had undergone but a single refraction at an appropriately positioned refracting surface. Some point of this elliptical front will be furthest advanced with respect to the entire beam (the leading edge, as it were), its diametrical opposite will be hind-most, and the elongation of the image will take place, just as in every other case, parallel to this diameter. With two prisms placed perpendicular to one another, the resulting front will be an ellipse skewed with respect to the axes of both prisms; consequently the elongation will take place along a diagonal. Thus, Hooke's theory predicts what actually happens in the experiment.

Experiments with the parallel prisms are even easier to explain. When the prisms are arranged so that the second counteracts the effect of the first, the pulse front is returned to perpendicularity with respect to the beam's direction of travel, so that the pulse front is once again a circular section of the beam and the light is colorless once more. When the second prism intensifies the elongation by refracting the beam again in the same direction as the first, the obliquity of the front is increased further in the same direction; it would be quite natural to expect an additional elongation as the result.

Newton's argument assumes that the image is oblong as it leaves the first prism; but this assumption is contrary to the phenomenon, in which the image continues to appear as essentially circular and colorless in the immediate vicinity of the prism (cf. Goethe, *FL-P*, par. 88). Hooke's explanation, on the other hand, need not be construed as depicting the phenomenon in any way other than it appears.

Although Hooke did not explain in his theory whether colored portions of the beam should behave differently from uncolored portions, any color fringes that appear when the two prisms are placed close together should be no more disturbing to Hooke's theory than they were to Newton's. The demonstration that upon refraction colored light does not behave the same as white light does raise a problem for Hooke's theory, however, because it is not at all clear how this phenomenon could be incorporated into it without ad hoc assumptions. The premier accomplishment of the *experimentum crucis* was to call the attention of natural philosophers to the differentiation that takes place because of refraction and to the peculiar behavior of this differentiated light when it is refracted again. Yet surely Newton went too far in drawing the conclusion that this differentiation was in fact proof of the original and innate constitution of light and that theories like Hooke's were incapable of accounting for its implications. Hooke pointed out to Newton that the Letter contained no compelling proof that there were differentiated rays already present in the original light. (Even the recombination of rays to form white again might be explained in accordance with Hooke's notion of oblique pulse fronts.) If Newton could accuse Hooke of not having a constant law to govern repeated refractions once colored light was involved, Hooke could respond that introducing modified principles to explain the behavior of colored light is not worse than having to bring in an infinity of sine proportions – an infinite number of constant laws, one for each of the infinitely many kinds of ray. Newton had multiplied entities without necessity, claimed Hooke (*Corresp.*, 1: 113).

On epistemological and experimental grounds, then, and on the grounds of theoretical economy as well, Hooke could allow only that Newton's theory was an ingenious hypothesis: "I cannot yet see any undeniable argument to convince me of the certainty thereof" (*Corresp.*, 1: 110). He (and also Huygens) could not tolerate Newton's extreme claims to truth and factuality. He thought that Newton's hypothesis had many merits but believed as well that some of the relevant phenomena could be explained otherwise or were inadequately treated by the new hypothesis. Newton took his opponents' criticism and even their hesitancy as blindness to the truth and regarded all attempts to explain the phenomena by other means as inferior to his unhypothetical theory, and he suspected that their obstinacy was occasioned by partiality for their own hypotheses. He treated even his most eminent adversaries with barely concealed condescension and annoyance, which finally dissuaded Huygens from continuing correspondence about the matter; and the lesser participants had to endure pedantic lectures on the proper method of arguing and deciding the truth in natural philosophy. Newton was therefore never compelled to engage the profound issues that he himself had raised, the factuality, certainty, and exactness of his theory. Although, as we have seen, differential refrangibility depends on the sequential and often defective argument presented in the Letter, he tried to force his opponents to concentrate on the *experimentum crucis* alone, as though the experiment could make its argument out of context just as well as within it.

Newton's inability to understand what underlay his critics' observations and objections and his insistence that he had discovered an essential property of light and a mathematical doctrine of colors have aroused the curiosity of modern scholars to investigate the roots of this apparent dogmatism. The notebooks in which Newton recorded some early observations of light and color reveal that even before he had formulated his theory he was thinking of light as an aggregate of tiny bodies, and of color as a function of their properties of mass, speed, size, or shape (Hall 1948; cf. Shap., 5–17). The theory itself may well have dawned on him as he performed and pondered experiments of the kind presented in Goethe's *Beiträge*. Also to be considered is Newton's discovery that he could state his theory without committing himself to corpuscles or to pulses by resorting to the neutrality of geometry as a description of the phenomena. Although Newton never seriously entertained the notion that light was a pulse – chiefly because all known pulses and waves propagated themselves into the geometric shadow when encountering obstacles and so did not appear suited to account for the well-defined shadows cast by light (*Opticks*, 362) – this generalized version of the theory seemed to justify the claim that it was free of hypothesis.

Yet although his theory was not hypothetical in the same way as Hooke's theory (which constantly resorted to ad hoc principles, like pulse front obliquity, not observable in the phenomena but at best only inferable), it was only less obviously hypothetical. Hooke realized that what he had to advance were hypotheses without any indubitable certainty, but that did not deter him, for he believed that hypotheses would contribute to the eventual progress of science (Sabra 1967, 187). Newton, however, was avid for truth in the present. As he wrote to Pardies, if he had thought that his theory of light and color were only a hypothesis he would have rejected it as vain and empty.

Maurizio Mamiani (1976) has argued persuasively that Newton's optical works are the key to his philosophy of scientific method and thus to his natural philosophy as a whole. According to Mamiani, it must have become clear to Newton early in his color studies that this science might be raised to the mathematical status of optics and the other mixed sciences handed down from antiquity, and that his approach would unify in a single mathematicophysical science the hitherto separate sciences of optics and color. His method of experimental demonstration would transform the purely mathematical hypothesis of geometrical optics (that all line rays are refracted according to a single sine relationship) by making clear that light was physically composite and that the ray paths reveal characteristics of the rays themselves. That would turn a mathematical hypothesis into a mathematicophysical certainty; and at the same time it would replace the purely speculative study of color with a rigorous, experimentally manifested theory. The theory of colors would thus become mathematical – or apparently so, for although Newton struggled for nearly thirty years to prove his fundamental tenet, that the disposition to diverse refrangibility and different colors was intrinsic to the rays even before refraction, he did not achieve that goal. In the words of one of the most eminent contemporary historians of optics, commenting on Newton's work on the *Opticks* in the 1690s:

The youthful confidence of the newly appointed Lucasian Professor that he would found a new mathematical science, a science of color, had been frustrated. As brilliant as we may judge Newton's optical work to be, by his own standards he had not fully succeeded, and the *Opticks* remained a patchwork of mostly thirty-year-old writings with internal contradictions and no underlying mathematical structure. . . . In part, Newton's youthful hope to found a new mathematical science of color was just misdirected; he did indeed found such a new science, but it was mechanics. The success of the recently completed *Principia,* I believe, gave him the confidence – even arrogance – to return to his earlier optical work and attempt to give to it a veneer of certainty which was simply not there. (Shapiro 1979, 127–28)

Despite the brilliance of Newton's optics, then, despite the apparently immediate self-evidence of his experimental theory, one might reasonably wonder whether it would not have been better had he, like Goethe, come to realize and admit the problematic nature of experimental proof rather than conceal and ossify it ever more completely with masses of experiments, improperly qualified claims, and a veneer of mathematics. For in Newton's case we are talking about a scientific success that decisively influenced the natural sciences for generations. Insofar as these shortcomings and this dogmatism went unnoticed and uncriticized, we have to deal with a significant failure of early modern science itself.

Goethe's critique of the experimental argument

The entire mistake [of Newton] rests on the fact that a complicated phenomenon was to be made the foundation and the simpler to be explained by means of the composite. (*HA,* 14: 263)

In the historical part of *Zur Farbenlehre* (*HA,* 14: 145–53) and in the 1793 essay on diverse refrangibility (*LA* I, 3: 152–64), Goethe focused on the inadequacy of Newton's attempted refutations of theoretical alternatives. These critiques were for the most part logicoexperimental, in that Goethe evaluated the character and cogency of the argument and the ability of the experiments to support the generalizations based on them. In the "History" he went through the series of refutations up to (but not including) the *experimentum crucis* and adjudged, one by one, whether Newton had really settled all questions. Is the different thickness of the prism decisive for the phenomenon? Newton quite rightly answered no, says Goethe, although if one considers the refractive and especially the dispersive power of different media, then thickness is not insignificant (*HA*, 14: 147). Is the size of the windowshut opening important? Though Newton denies it, this factor is crucial: The larger the opening, the longer the center of the image will remain uncolored as the screen is moved farther away from the prism (ibid.). Do irregularities in the glass bring about the appearance of color? Against the seventeenth-century opticians who thought that the colors were accidental and ungoverned by law, Newton quite rightly argued for its lawfulness and excluded accident as the cause; nevertheless, he failed to acknowledge "the real foundation of this lawfulness" (*HA*, 14: 149–50). Was it the different incidence of the rays on the prism, or the quasi-Cartesian deviation of rays from a straight-line path that produced the dispersion of colors? In both cases Newton was quite right, and in the former he properly applied mathematics to make his case (*HA*, 14: 150).

On the question of the importance of the contrast between light and dark, however, Goethe took vehement exception to Newton's procedure. In his didactic *Farbenlehre* (and already in the *Beiträge*), he had shown that without a boundary (a contrast between brighter and darker or between different hues) no colors appear. That is, the boundary condition is fundamental; if one prescinds from it, one fails to obtain any spectrum (or edge spectrum) whatsoever. "There arises no prismatic color phenomenon unless an image is displaced, and there can be no image without a boundary.... The kind of investigation through which Newton convinced himself that no influence on the appearance of color is to be attributed to the boundary must move anyone who is not depraved to astonishment, indeed to horror" (*HA*, 14: 148). He briefly describes the experiments in which Newton obtained the same effect (a colored spectrum) first by passing light through an aperture before refracting it, then by reversing the sequence. Goethe comments:

From this he concludes that the aperture has no influence on the coloring of this [spectrum].

We summon all our present and future opponents to this spot. From now on it is here that the battle over the tenability or untenability of the Newtonian system will be fought, here, right at the entrance to the labyrinth and not within, inside the confused maze, here, where Newton himself has preserved for us the way in which he arrived at his conviction.

We therefore repeat what has already been frequently emphasized by us didactically and polemically: Refracted light shows no color unless it has been bounded; light shows a color upon refraction not as light but insofar as it appears as an image, and it is indifferent whether an image appears first that is subsequently refracted, or whether a refraction occurs, within which an image is bounded. (*HA*, 14: 148–49)

A few pages later Goethe sums up:

Now we have seen that his chief error consisted in too quickly and hastily setting aside and denying those questions that chiefly relate to whether external conditions [*Bedingungen*] cooperate in the appearance of color, without looking more exactly into the proximate circumstances. Consequently on some points we had, and were able, to contradict him completely, on others in part, on yet others not at all; and we have tried to make clear which points are tenable or not and how far they are such. (*HA*, 14: 152)

Apart from his aversion to the astonishment and horror of the undepraved observer, Goethe's tone here is measured, fair, objective. He selectively brings to bear the immense historical and experimental knowledge he had acquired in the course of almost two decades to show that Newton's argument is defective because the evidence does not bear out the full scope of Newton's assertions, and therefore the argument must fail because not all the premises are true. In particular it does not succeed in completely excluding the possibility that a factor external to the light (i.e., something other than intrinsic refrangibility of the rays, for instance some chemical or physical property of the refractive medium) affects the outcome in an essential way. The argument is not only not self-evident, it is not cogent or correct, and it ignores crucial circumstances of the phenomena. Logically one is not entitled to affirm the theory's truth, much less its factuality; nor is one able to rule out all the conceptions, hypotheses, and *Vorstellungsarten* that Newton thought he had devastated.

From what we have already seen of Goethe's project for color science, however, we can be sure that this basically logical conclusion was not enough to satisfy him. Although he would already have considered it a major step forward for natural philosophers to claim less than certainty or factuality for differential refrangibility according to color, it would still have been easy for them to counter that it was the best theory of refraction and color available and so accurate that there was no need to be overconcerned about flaws in the logic. Goethe of course believed he had identified fundamental shortcomings in the theory that made it unsuitable as a basis for color science in general. He therefore needed to examine the theory closely to show how theoretical convictions had worked themselves into Newton's presentation (thus Newton's work represented not the naked truth but rather one *Vorstellungsart* among others), how the theoretical convictions produced distortions in seeing and description (therefore one had to break free of the Newtonian conceptions even to see things adequately), and how the selectivity of Newton's experimental demonstration concealed his failure to explain the relevant phenomena in their entirety (and so the method of crucial or decisive experiments did not deserve its paradigmatic status and needed to be reconsidered in light of a more adequate method of advancing and supporting assertions in experimental science).

One way to achieve this was by a combined logical, phenomenal, methodological, epistemological, historical, and rhetorical explication of Newton's writings. In a sense this type of approach falls under the general rubric laid down in the epigraph of this section: Newton's work seems simple and straightforward, but a careful investigation shows it is complex. Thus it needs to be carefully articulated into its divisions and episodes, checked against the experiments Newton performed and certain significant variants, viewed against the appropriate historical and conceptual background, and read not only as an exercise in deductive or inductive reasoning but as a text employing various strategies of persuasion.

The examination to which we subjected the Letter above is precisely such an analysis, the model for which was Goethe's (unfinished) critique of the Letter prepared in the last phase of the composition of *Zur Farbenlehre* (*WA* II, 4: 441–65). In it Goethe showed in detail the failure of Newton's refutations, both logically and phenomenologically; he analyzed the tendentious and arbitrary way in which Newton had narrated experiments, taken measurements, and described phenomena; he discussed the theoretical viewpoint implicit in Newton's approach and vocabulary; he offered alternative experiments to correct misleading impressions that Newton's work had produced. All this was to be seen, of course, against the dual background of the experimental history of the phenomena (the didactic part) and the temporal history of chromatic experience and science (the historical part).

In our analysis of the Letter we recognized that the issues of the geometry of the spectrum and its coloration were not kept distinct by Newton because they could not be. The doctrine of refrangibility lays the basis for the ray analysis of color, but color in turn provides an ineludible perceptual criterion, without which one cannot be sure of the consistent identity of rays. Goethe never took seriously the claim that refrangibility and color had been treated separately. Indeed, he thought that Newton's real interest was the ray of light; that is, all his descriptions were adapted to the exigencies of proving the ray theory, and therefore Newton neglected as much as possible whatever might have created difficulties for it. Even the way in which Newton used the word color and the various color names led Goethe to conclude that the rays were his chief concern: More often than not they refer not so much to the visible hues as to the inferred rays that produce them. His usage was guided more by the momentary demands of the demonstration than by descriptive need or accuracy. Newton's optics was a science of rays, not of color. He had hoped to establish a perfect correlation between the mathematical criteria of refrangibility and the perceptual qualities of chromaticity; wherever the correlation failed, he tried to conceal the failure by measurements, by punctilious but irrelevant detail, by equivocation and other stratagems.

According to Goethe, it was not color that was mathematical but the theoretical schema that had been superimposed on it and by means of which the phenomena were seen theoretically. The mathematics can be applied to the phenomena only by constantly hedging and equivocating (in Goethe's terms, only by mixing incompatible *Vorstellungsarten*; see, e.g., *FL-P*, par. 457). Newton's usual preference was a mechanical way of conceiving things; he sometimes seems to imagine that rays are like grains of powder or sand that when combined are still actually present in the mixture. Yet the perceived result of color mixing is more like a chemical combination in which the constituents lose their separate identities and qualities than like a mechanical mixture; to conceive this appropriately requires a more dynamic way of understanding the phenomena (see *WA* II, 4: 463). Goethe thus argued that Newton had tried to establish an isomorphism between incommensurables, between the undifferentiated continuum of degrees of refrangibility and the visibly articulated and changeable colors of the spectrum. This attempt at an isomorphic function between the two endowed the spectral or homogeneal colors – incidentally, as it were – with ontological priority: They were the real colors, in terms of which all other colors needed to be explained. Bodies, as a corollary, did not have colors per se, only a tendency to reflect or absorb certain kinds of rays.

Goethe had become suspicious of the ray concept at an early stage of his investigations. He had used the term on occasion in his own work, usually when he was dealing with the objective (observed on a screen) rather than the subjective prismatic phenomena; he preferred in general, however, the term "image" *(Bild),* and even where he had used "ray" he clearly meant to indicate the entire beam of light rather than infinitesimal rays (e.g., *LA* I, 3: 118–24, 164–89). By 1794 he had begun to insist that the light ray be treated as a convenient fiction derived from the evidence of visible images (*LA* I, 3: 210; cf. 222). He had also started consistently to call his work chromatics, color research, color doctrine, or color science, terms that at the earliest stages of his work he had tended to use almost interchangeably with optics – a further sign that he was working out the implications of his historical studies and their bearing (see *LA* II, 3: 161 and *LA* I, 3: 135).

Around 1800, as he became more deeply absorbed in the history of the science of color, Goethe wrote of the subtle but pervasive theoretical bias the very notion of the ray had introduced into optics and color theory.

Light rays, ray bundles are hypothetical entities, of which one ought not to speak in experience.

When we demonstrate a phenomenon, others doubtless see what we do. When we articulate, describe, discuss a phenomenon, we are already translating it into our human language. The kinds of difficulties already present here, the inadequacies threatening us, are obvious.

An initial terminology suits a restricted, isolated phenomenon; is also applied to yet others. Ultimately something no longer at all suitable still continues in use. (*LA* I, 3: 300–301)

Although a concept like the ray had its usefulness – for instance, in geometrical optics – it could be misleading if it became detached from the phenomena that had given it birth or if it were used as an unproblematic term at the basic levels describing phenomena (cf. Klein 1940 on "sedimentation"). The first duty of the experimentalist, we recall, was to try to describe as thoroughly, accurately, and unhypothetically as possible the visible phenomenon and the circumstances under which it comes to appear. Accordingly, rather than excluding the use of concepts like the ray, one had to try to draw distinctions between the phenomena that occur, the attempts to describe them, and the introduction of ever more comprehensive and generalized notions and hypotheses – distinctions that in practice are by no means simple. Goethe's primary objection to the ray was essentially an extension of his concerns about the confusion between theory and phenomenon that he had expressed already in "Der Versuch als Vermittler von Objekt und Subjekt," and this objection was the basis of many of his specific criticisms of Newton.

In his close reading of the Letter, in truth in all his critiques of Newton's theory, Goethe constantly called attention to Newton's use of the term ray and how it revealed theoretical proclivities and produced tendentious descriptions. He even balked at harmless-sounding statements such as Newton's reporting that he had let in a "convenient quantity of the Sun's light" at the beginning of the Letter, because this way of speaking cultivates the impression that light consists of small, quantifiable parts that can be taken in greater or lesser amounts ad libitum; thus, even Newton's locution promoted the ray concept. Goethe contended that it is not a quantity of rays but an image in its whole integrity, in this case an image of the sun, that is admitted through the hole (*WA* II, 4: 442). From this visible image Newton silently inferred the objective existence of light conceived as a bundle of rays and thereby discounted whatever cannot be embraced in such terms. Darkness, for instance, must be conceived as not-light, not-rays – an empty negation, nothing at all – and then of course it seems inconceivable that darkness can in any way influence the phenomenon.

By ignoring the bounding of light (i.e., the production of an image),

Newton overlooked the fundamental condition for the appearance or visibility of light – the formation of an image or, at the very least, the encounter of light with matter. The undifferentiated white light that falls upon objects in our field of vision is delimited, determined, bounded by them; if there is nothing to form an image or otherwise affect the light, then we see not the light but empty space (recall that the space between ourselves and any object we perceive we understand to be suffused with light radiation that for the most part we are unaware of, and that the light that enters our pupils usually appears under the aspect of localized colored images, not as pure brightness). Although we easily talk of beams and rays of light, we tend to forget that they are postulated from experiences such as successively viewing the circular image produced by a projector on a screen at a range of distances or filling a camera obscura with dust or powder and noting the image(s) formed simultaneously therein. The ray concept is a way to unify these experiences; but it is also possible to conceive that one is dealing primarily with a (changing) image that is bounded on all sides, and that the effect of refraction on such an image is to be correlated with the boundary's different characteristics (e.g., the orientation with respect to the axis of the prism) in its various parts.

Let us recall the subjective prism experiments that Goethe described in part 1 of the *Beiträge* that placed white rectangles on black grounds: At one edge the white side of the boundary is above the black side – one could describe this more generally by saying that the white side is the leading edge of the prismatic displacement of this boundary of the image (and at this edge red and yellow appear); at the other edge the black side is above the white, the black is the leading edge (here violet and blue appear). If one uses a circular image instead, there is a continuous variation of the boundary's orientation with respect to the refracting angle of the prism, but the same basic principle of the above and below, or the leading edge and the trailing edge, still holds. The apparently simple refraction of a ray of light is in Goethe's view complex because there are two kinds of boundary rather than one, two types of boundary condition to take into account. If one proceeds to add more apertures, prisms, lenses, and other variables, one is adding to the complexity. The basic Newtonian spectrum, then, is in Goethe's view the sum of two edge spectra; from this point of view, the fundamental Newtonian phenomenon, Newton's Urphenomenon, erroneously puts something artificial and complex in place of the naturally simple.

Put this way, Goethe's objections take on a more problematic cast than does his purely logical and phenomenological analysis of Newton's arguments. It is not so much that Goethe is wrong as that his theoretical preference, his *Vorstellungsart*, becomes an essential part of the case. It is one thing to say that the ray is a fiction – today most physicists might well agree – but quite another to claim that it is the image of the sun rather than a ray or beam that enters the room and is refracted. Perhaps we are simply too accustomed to thinking and seeing with Newton; but it seems the part of common sense, the *gesunder Menschenverstand* that Goethe so highly esteemed, to say that it is the ray, not the image, that is refracted. Rays produce images, even if they are at the same time inferred from the images.

The *Bild*, or image, which was not at all a crucial term for Goethe in the period of the *Beiträge*, gradually became one of the key unifying concepts in the Farbenlehre. By joining this concept with the dual Urphenomenon of *Zur Farbenlehre*, he hoped to take a significant stride toward explaining the physical and even the chemical colors.

The Urphenomenon was introduced under that name in the didactic part of *Zur Farbenlehre*, although as early as 1793 Goethe seems to have appreciated its importance (*LA* I, 3: 140–41). When a light shines through a medium that is not perfectly transparent – what Goethe calls *ein trübes Mittel*, a turbid medium – it appears yellow; as the medium's turbidity increases, the color tends toward orange or even orange-red. An example would be the sun shining through the atmosphere. When the air is relatively dust free, the sun is yellowish; as the air becomes dust laden or as the amount of atmosphere through which the light must travel increases (as when the sun is on the horizon), it appears orange or even red. When darkness is seen behind an illuminated medium, on the other hand, one sees a shade of blue, from pale bluish white to indigo. The sky in the course of the day, from noon to late evening, gives an example. In the one case the warm colors appear; in the other, the cool colors (*FLD*, par. 145–77).

On the basis of these phenomena of turbid media, Goethe thought he could account for all the physical and chemical colors, including the colors of the prism. By analogy to other cases in which a double image is formed by light, Goethe postulated that a peripheral or secondary image (*Nebenbild*) was created in the body of the prism; that this secondary image was itself semitransparent or turbid; and thus, with the primary image considered as the source of light, that the dual Urphenomenon could be cited to account for the appearance of the spectrum, with warm colors at one end and cool at the other (see Appendix for a fuller explanation). This explanation was not well received by critics, because, as they pointed out, there is no evidence of such a secondary image; and Goethe himself later granted that it was hardly convincing (*WA* IV, 42: 167). What is immediately relevant to our purposes, however, is that once again Goethe endows the image with material and efficient powers that the Newtonian theory reserves for the ray. Goethe now interpreted the sequence of experiments from the two installments of the *Beiträge zur Optik* – which was incorporated, for the most part with relatively minor changes,[15] into the didactic part of *Zur Farbenlehre* – as Urphenomenal. When an image is displaced by the action of a prism, the warm colors are formed at one type of boundary, the cool colors at the other, all by virtue of the way in which the primary and peripheral images interact within the body of the prism. This process holds even for colored images and colored light, which, however, produce in addition effects of canceling or enhancement depending on whether the edge colors are in harmony or in contrast with the color of the image or light. Thus a red image will be truncated on the side where the cool colors are formed; a violet image will be truncated on the opposite side, where the warm colors tend to form. According to Goethe, this process, and not differential refrangibility of infinitesimal rays already present in the light before refraction, is responsible for the outcome of Newton's crucial experiment.

Goethe became so wedded to this conception of prismatic colors that he refused to believe conflicting evidence. In the historical part, Goethe quoted at length an article by Robert Blair on the unequal refrangibility of light that had appeared in the *Transactions of the Royal Society of Edinburgh* in 1794. In it Blair reported that by combining prismatic media with different dispersive powers in the manner of Dollond he was able to produce compound prisms and lenses that refracted homogeneal green light more than any other. Although Goethe perhaps rightly complained that from Blair's descriptions it was difficult to know the precise circumstances of the experiments (in particular, whether in any single case Blair was using a prism or a lens), he simply tried to explain away what Blair had reported, because according to his explanation by way of the Urphenomenon and the images interacting within the prism green could be produced only where the blue of one kind of edge mixed with the yellow of the other: Therefore, it can never appear at the extreme edge of an image when white light is refracted (*LA* I, 6: 399–412; cf. *HA*, 14: 248–51).

It is also noteworthy that Goethe was never able to explain the appearance of the rainbow. It could not be assimilated to his explanatory schema precisely because it seemed to present a case in which the entire Newtonian spectrum appeared at a single edge; moreover, the warm colors appear at what seems to be the wrong side, the side adjoining the relatively darker part of the sky outside the primary bow.[16]

Goethe's attempt to achieve explanations by means of the image and Urphenomenon was ambitious, especially insofar as the underlying cause of what appears was analogous to the appearance itself (the hidden realm was to duplicate the phenomenological structure of the visible realm), but most of the explanations he gives are lame. The *Beiträge*, we recall, did not venture causal explanations, but remained content with an account of correlations; in *Zur Farbenlehre*, by contrast, Goethe tried to found phenomenological principles of causality. Although one might argue that this approach was not inconsistent with his *Vorstellungsart*, the *Beiträge* show that a causal theory was not a necessary prerequisite for producing a useful, potentially instructive natural and experimental history of the phenomena; moreover, Goethe was well aware from his historical studies of the dangers of premature investigations into causes. Goethe's failed attempts at causal explanations are doubtless responsible for the widespread assumption that his work had the sole aim of replacing Newton's theory of refrangibility with his own theory of turbidity, and they exposed his entire project for chromatics to unnecessary misunderstandings and to derision.

Contrasting the polemical part of *Zur Farbenlehre* with the earlier polemical writings and even with the historical part, we see that Goethe lost perspective on his undertaking. His ridicule of the *Physiker*, the physicists, inalterably alienated those who needed to be recruited for his project. Not surprisingly, many of them responded in kind and seized upon the occasional errors, exaggerations, obfuscations, and inaccurate translations in *Zur Farbenlehre*.[17]

Once one understands the aims and methods of Goethe's argument against the *Opticks*, the "Polemic" begins to appear far less vitriolic than it does on first reading (although the invective stands out all the more when it is the only thing one really understands). Nevertheless, one cannot exculpate Goethe for initiating the insult and scorn that poisoned the reception of the Farbenlehre for over a century. In an important sense, by not restraining his quite humanly understandable impulses Goethe encouraged in his followers a type of positivism that was at odds with his purpose and that tended to undermine the advancement of his science.

Not least problematic was his concentrating the attack on Newton's ray. Insofar as the ray theory and the color theory are indissolubly linked it made sense, yet Goethe did not really establish his right to banish the ray from discussions of color. For, properly speaking, all one could do was to show that the ray is a limiting concept and thus fictive; that there is not such an exact correlation between Newton's rays and colors as he claimed; that it was not established that the rays exist already in the unrefracted white light; that even if the rays exist, features such as their nature, divisibility, and sidedness are not finally determined; and that it is not just the ray but also the material with which it comes into contact and other related circumstances that need to be studied.[18] Goethe shows that the premature introduction of the ray — for example, into the basic descriptions of phenomena — leads to tendentiousness and distortions, but there can be no proof that it is completely useless as an auxiliary, or even as a central, concept. Today, of course, spectral analysis is a sine qua non of the physical study of color, and even in the studies of physiology and perception it is crucial as a control on light.

What Goethe did not recognize, or at least did not emphasize (perhaps because of his *Vorstellungsart*, perhaps because of the blindness that anger had induced), was that his own method of investigation is ideally designed to keep the ray concept under control. First, by means of the method of progressive variation, he could have shown that the ray is derivative from a certain class of refractive phenomena and other phenomena of light and shadow that suggest an extrapolation to the hypothetical line ray and its possible nature and behavior. In this way the ray is conceived in the image of certain classes of phenomena, rather than vice versa. Second, he could have applied his method to investigate what happens when one varies the experiments of the *Beiträge* by substituting different pigments and materials for those originally used in the display cards; the edge colors that arise with the new displays then could have been compared with the edge colors in previous experiments. The results of such comparisons would have enforced a qualification on Goethe's phenomenological theory of the edge colors of images, for one would find, for example, that pigments that look the same to the naked eye are different when observed through a prism. Third (and this would have pushed Goethe closer to Fraunhofer), he could have examined the different sources of light. Although in Goethe's day there were not many sources from which to choose, it still should have been possible to take steps in this direction. In the long run, at any rate, the practitioner of the Goethean method would not have been able to take light for granted as Goethe did in the general foreword to *Zur Farbenlehre* (HA, 13: 315). Although there was a certain logic to Goethe's decision not to investigate or discuss light per se in *Zur Farbenlehre*,[19] it would have needed examination in the next phase of the Farbenlehre, as is underscored by the frequent references to light in the fourth section of the didactic part, which was both a summary and an outline of a program for future research.

Goethe's fundamental error may thus have been in a certain sense the complement of Newton's. If Newton reduced the study of color to a study of rays of light, Goethe tried to hold the study of light at arm's length from the study of color. Color science is in need of both, however. A comprehensive chromatics is impossible without a detailed examination of light that considers its propagation, effects, and other features – an examination that will often find the ray an extremely useful notion; however, color cannot be comprehensively understood by reducing it to rays and color-mixing functions. Goethe was perfectly aware of the latter point. If he had reminded himself of the breadth of his projects for other sciences, for instance of the programmatic importance he had assigned to chemistry in studying living things as a science that investigates what is for the most part hidden from sense (*HA*, 13: 122–23), he might have somewhat abated his passion for executing an autonomous science of color along almost exclusively phenomenological lines.

It would be misleading, however, to imply that Goethe's attempt at a positive doctrine is nothing but a tissue of errors and problematic assertions, and that the phenomenal method is good only for launching a critique of established theories, or just for establishing the foundations of psychological and physiological approaches without having anything substantive to offer to physical or psychophysical approaches. Consider, for example, Goethe's stubborn resistance to the idea that when all the kinds of rays are recombined in prism experiments the result is white. Noting that all chromatic hues are lighter than black and darker than white, he often referred to colored light as half-light, light that has been darkened by coming into contact with matter. When one mixes all the differently colored half-lights, one does not thereby eliminate the previous darkening; although the colors may cancel one another, the result is not white but gray. In saying this, Goethe of course had pigment mixing in mind, which since Helmholtz we know to be subtractive color mixing as opposed to the additive mixing of combining lights.

However, this Goethean conception of color as *skieron*, as a kind of shadow, should not be dismissed as a personal idiosyncrasy. It fits into a long tradition of thinking of color as some kind of mixture, blend, or other interaction of light and darkness, a tradition that goes back to Aristotle and frequently influenced modificationist theories of light and color. There are also important phenomenal considerations. First, the brightest, most energetic light appears white (*FL-D*, par. 150); dimmer lights, like that of candles and stars, most often appear tinted with a chromatic hue (*FL-D*, par. 81–88). Second, under the same illumination, whether colored or white, white surfaces appear brighter than surfaces of any other color (see esp. *LA* I, 3: 194, 199; cf. *BzO*, par. 102); put another way, colored surfaces in some as yet unspecified way obscure the light that shines upon them, whereas white does not. Third, uncolored light tends to take on color when it traverses a semitransparent or turbid medium (the Urphenomenon); color involves, then, an attenuation, a shadowing of light. Fourth, even the Newtonian in a sense grants that we can see the darkness in colors. Very few natural colors exhibit the pure luminosity of spectral lights (this feature is a matter of relative saturation and brightness of the colors). Some objects illuminated in, say, spectral red appear bright red, others dusky red or even black; and a surface that reflects all rays equally but in reduced quantity appears not white, which the Newtonian spectral analysis predicts, but gray.

One of the reasons Goethe rejected Newton's claim of having recombined all the rays into white light is that he did not trust Newton's color names. Any gray he is willing to call white, and in the *Opticks* he justifies this practice by experiments showing that grays can be made to appear white by being brightly illuminated and true whites made to appear gray by putting them in shadow. For example, Newton recounts how he put a white sheet of paper in the shadows of a room and gray powder in the direct light of the sun, then asked a friend to look in at the window and judge which was the better white; the friend said that both were equally good (*Opticks*, 152–53). Goethe does not dispute the experiment, just the conclusion and the criteria of judgment by which it was reached: The proper way to determine the color of bodies is to compare them in the same light (see *FL-P*, par. 563–91; cf. *LA* I, 3: 202–206). With regard to the recombining of the rays, then, the question for Goethe is whether the final image is as bright as the original light, for in camera obscura any colorless light appears white. Because Newton's color-mixing circle did not take into account differences in brightness and darkness, his standard is insufficient to distinguish what for Goethe is a crucial dimension in the appearance of color. Newton's spectral standard informs us we are seeing white when we actually see gray. Insofar as the color-mixing function cannot distinguish between dusky and intense colors of the same hue, the science of color is not yet complete; it is in need of additional fundamental principles (see *FL-P*, par. 556).

Another question Goethe asked is whether the experiments in which Newton reconstituted white light were not really defective in design. Both the Letter and the first book of the *Opticks* conclude with such an experiment (more complicated in the latter). In the Letter white light is refracted by a prism, then intercepted by a lens, which focuses the rays to a bright, colorless image. The experiment is certainly striking, but perhaps not compelling. If, after the initial refraction, the colored light is intercepted by the lens before it has become completely colored (i.e., if the light at the center still produces white – and this will be the case unless the lens is large enough to be placed far from the prism so that a full spectrum may appear at the lens), then the proof is rather less than perfect.

Moreover, whether the recombined light is as bright as the original light – that is, whether it is gray (shadowed) or white – turns out to be not the question of a controversialist trying desperately to confute the theories of his opponent but a query that touches on an important and surprising result of modern color research. Traditional color theory, based on the notion of summing up the effects of each component of compound light in order to determine the result in the manner of the ray theory, assumes that brightness is additive: Two differently colored but equally bright lights will yield a light that is twice as bright as either taken alone. However, Wasserman (1978) reports an "absolutely relia-ble" experiment with both naive and trained observers that demonstrates the failure of additivity.

Using an instrument called an anomaloscope in the experiment, the subjects are presented with patches of color that are yellowish green, yellowish red, and pure yellow, where "pure" indicates psychological purity (the yellow appears to be neither greenish nor reddish) and there-fore "impure" indicates that the color tends toward either one neigh-boring hue or the other. First the subjects combine the yellowish green and yellowish red in varying proportions until they match the pure yellow in hue. Let YG represent the quantity of yellowish green in this matching mixture, and YR the quantity of yellowish red. Then the subjects continue by making *brightness* matches: How much pure yellow ($Y1$) is needed to match the brightness of the yellowish green in the mixture (thus $Y1 = YG$ with respect to brightness), how much pure yellow ($Y2$) is needed to match the brightness of the yellowish red in the mixture ($Y2 = YR$), and finally how much pure yellow ($Y3$) is needed to match the brightness of the mixture itself (i.e., $Y3 = YG + YR$)? According to the laws of additivity, you expect that if you add $Y1$ (which is as bright as YG) to $Y2$ (which is as bright as YR) the result will be as bright as $Y3$ (i.e., $Y1 + Y2 = Y3$); but in fact $Y1 + Y2 = Y4$, which turns out to be considerably brighter than $Y3$. Thus the experimental outcome is that the mixture of the two impure colored lights YG and YR looks consid-erably darker than the mixture ($Y1 + Y2$) of pure colors that are in-dividually only as bright as the individual impure colors (Wasserman 1978, 141). Wasserman gives a table with the results for ten different observers. Not only is the impure mixture less bright than expected in every case, but in seven out of the ten it is darker than either component alone (where the two components are of equal brightness). The brightness of the impure mixture varies from 18.7 to 58.9 percent of the brightness predicted by additivity, with a mean of 31 percent (Wasserman 1978, 143; if the mixture were as bright as just one of the components, the value would have been 50 percent).

This result cannot be explained on the Newtonian principle of addi-tivity (which is canonized in the so-called component theories of color vision), but seems to support opponent theories and zone theories (Goethe's work is considered to be a forerunner of the former; the latter attempt to reconcile the virtues of the different *Vorstellungsarten* implicit in component and opponent theories).[20] "A new interpretation of New-ton's classic experiment is implicit in opponent theories. Newton said that white light is *produced* by mixing all the colors. The opponent interpretation is that every wavelength evokes some white and some color.

Mixing spectral lights causes the color responses to cancel, *revealing* the white which has been there all along" (Wasserman 1978, 93). Thus one might possibly obtain a white by combining lights of many different colors, but less bright than one expects according to additivity; in comparison with the brightness of originally unrefracted light, the resulting white would be gray, and there would then seem to be some reason to assert that there has been a darkening that is not eliminated when the lights are recombined. To understand these phenomena, it is necessary, as Goethe insisted, to understand not only the physics of color but also the physiological functioning of the eye; at the very least they reveal that the psychophysics of color is not a simple function of the physics of radiation.

These of course are matters to be decided by empirical research and are adduced here as points of reference rather than as proof. The same applies to work like Land's, which emphasizes that studying small patches of color in camera obscura is not always relevant to understanding color in natural surroundings (where the complex workings of the eye, the effect of the total field of color, and the relation of the field to its parts are important, and where the exact spectral composition of the light is subordinate to the overall polar relationship between longer waves and shorter waves). Yet it is not insignificant that Land, like Goethe, uses colored and black-and-white displays that abstract from the natural setting such essential features as boundaries and geometrical forms; that he has identified new conditions that contribute to understanding the genesis and appearance of color; that his retinex theory highlights certain polarities and the relative darkness and lightness of colors in comparison to one another; that he correlates the polarity of long and short waves with the psychological polarity of warm and cool colors; and that he argues against the casual belief that bodies cannot truly be said to have natural colors by adducing the essential constancy of body colors under an enormous range of variation in the spectral composition of light (see, e.g., Land 1978, and Land and McCann 1971).

These parallels to Goethe, however near or distant, suggest that even if the Farbenlehre is seriously flawed in parts, and even if his critique of Newton is one-sided and sometimes unfair, his project for a new science of color included much that was sound and much that was pregnant; thus it might have led to interesting and significant results if it had been pursued in the spirit of many-sidedness that Goethe advocated, at least in principle. As profound and influential as Newton's optical work has been, it is perhaps unfortunate that it was for so long considered to be the centerpiece of color science. For Newton's real interest was the ray, but he ended up coopting the science of color in the form of a mathematical theory because he needed those colors as indicators of the kinds of refrangible rays that were present in the light. It was fateful for Newton, Goethe, and the science of color, then, that the "Analogy 'twixt colours, and refrangibility" was nowhere near as "precise and strict" as Newton had claimed (*Corresp.* 1: 97–98).

4

Factuality, certainty, and the organization of science

> The highest thing would be: to grasp that everything factual is already theory. The blue of the sky reveals to us the fundamental law of chromatics. Do not search for anything behind the phenomena: They themselves are the teaching.
>
> — Goethe (*MR*, no. 575)

The shifting focus of the debate about color

By making the science of colors mathematical, Newton made it possible to dispense with most of the phenomena. A theory needs the evidence of only a few experiments, the rest amounts to working out the mathematical theorems. The chief evidentiary instrument is the crucial experiment, which does not leave room for doubt about which explanations are true and which are not. Beyond the crucial experiment one may certainly go, but anything more will be illustration of the now-established theory rather than proof. Furthermore, proving the theory wrong by offering new experimental evidence is virtually impossible. Experimenters make mistakes, but mathematics does not. Thus, natural philosophy no longer concerns itself first and foremost with nature but instead with the mathematical abstractions of theory. Theory takes full possession of the phenomena and gives them weight and consistency; the theory turns isolated events and facts into evidence, or at least consequences, of the theory. Under this dispensation phenomena are turned into mere phenomena, and descriptive science becomes little more than the prelude to genuine science.

Newton was not a little astonished and perplexed by the opposition his theory aroused among supposedly perspicacious natural philosophers like Hooke and Huygens, not so much because he did not anticipate opposition as because he thought he had met their objections in advance. Time and time again he referred to his original letter or buttressed what was there with additional evidence bearing the same tenor. His opinion of them must have fallen, because, like nonmathematicians, they required superfluous proofs. He insisted that they show him exactly what was wrong with his experiments or adduce experiments of their own that would directly contradict his theory. On occasion he restated his theory for their benefit, so that they might see as he did; when they failed to assent, he ascribed their refusal to partiality for hypotheses, love for disputation, or incompetence. What he himself failed to recognize was that his theory was founded on a sequence of arguments from the phenomena, and that despite his intentions he had let hypothetical elements that were not beyond suspicion of doubt enter into his discourse. He did not grasp the methodological and epistemological issues raised – though not always clearly – by his opponents, and insofar as they questioned his experimental accuracy or offered alternative explanations he considered them in the wrong. Unfortunately for the course of the debates, the only consistently tenacious disputant was Newton; not before Anthony Lucas began questioning Newton's method and claims to certainty in 1676 did anyone undertake a sustained and well-planned critique. But Lucas was saddled with the burden of being the successor to two less competent disputants of the English College in Liège, and by this time Newton had reached the limit of his patience with a controversy that had dragged on for over four years and with what he took to be aspersions on his scientific integrity from the Liègeois Jesuits.

Lucas was the first to recognize explicitly what he called the "neat Sett of very ingenious and naturall inferences" (*Corresp.*, 2: 9) of Newton's theory, the chain of argument, which, if he could break it at any point, would fall apart; and he tried to adhere to Newton's prescription that his opponents tell him what was wrong with the experiments or offer others that contradict them. In his first letter Lucas reported a number of "experimentall exceptions" that seemed to contradict the theory. For instance, he placed many differently colored rulers side by side at the bottom of a basin of water, then peered over the basin's edge to see which color appeared first; all appeared simultaneously, said Lucas. Newton's response disappointed him, for Newton devoted most of his letter to the question of the proportions of the refracted image, which had been a major point of contention since the first Liègeois Jesuit, Francis Hall (also known as Linus or Line) had affirmed that the length of the spectrum was due to the reflection of light from clouds. Lucas conceded that Hall had mistaken Newton's meaning, but he went on to report that in his own experiments with the prism he had not been able to confirm Newton's proportions of 5:1; the closest he had been able to come was a length 3.5 times the breadth. (Lucas was the first of the Liègeois to specify the size of the refracting angle, in this case 60 degrees, the diameter of the aperture, the distance of the prism from the aperture and from the screen, and the computed refractive index of the prism.) Newton was

exasperated by the repeated failure of the Jesuits to confirm his results
and even, in the case of Hall and, after Hall's death, his first successor,
John Gascoines, to perform the experiments according to prescription.
He must have felt that his reputation was in the hands of semicompetent
bunglers who could not follow his instructions or measure correctly. But
the disparity may have been due to differences in the color dispersion of
the prisms used; if this possibility had been explored, Newton very likely
could have discovered a way to perfect the refracting telescope that remained unknown until the middle of the eighteenth century, the search
for which was discouraged by Newton's affirmations in the *Opticks* that
the improvement of refracting telescopes was "desperate" (*Opticks*, 102).

As for Lucas's new experiments, Newton shifted his ground.

It will conduce to his more speedy & full satisfaction if he a little change ye
method wch he has propounded, & instead of a multitude of things try only the
Experimentum Crucis. For it is not number of Expts, but weight to be regarded;
& where one will do, what need of many?

The main thing he goes about to examin is ye *different refrangibility* of light.
And this I demonstrated by ye *Experimentum Crucis*. Now if this demonstration
be good, there needs no further examination of ye thing; if not good ye fault of
it is to be shewn, for ye only way to examin a demonstrated proposition is to
examin ye demonstration. (*Corresp.*, 2: 79–80)

Thus criticism of all but the *experimentum crucis* was ruled impermis-
sible. After more than four years of debate Newton was still willing to
place the entire burden of proof (he refers to the "demonstration," a
word that in the seventeenth century was the equivalent of "mathematical
proof") on this single experiment.

Because only Lucas's first letter and Newton's response to it were
published, the public (and Goethe) never saw Lucas's second letter, in
which he argued that Newton had failed to establish one of his premises,
and that therefore the *experimentum crucis* could not be esteemed "a
demonstrative proof of this new Theory without the assistance of further
experiments" (*Corresp.*, 2: 104). Lucas thereupon presented several other
experimental tests designed to ascertain whether the *experimentum crucis*
definitively showed that unequal refraction necessarily implies an unequal
refrangibility in rays differently colored (e.g., with the apparatus of the
crucial experiment, he found that the most refracted light contained not
just violet-producing rays but also red light, which is supposed to be least
refrangible) and concluded that his experiments "jointly defeate[ed] the
pretended difference of refrangibility in rays differently coloured" (ibid.,
105). In case Newton thought these experiments were of less weight than
the crucial experiment against which they were directed, Lucas turned
the tables on him: "I shall also be of his opinion when he hath showed
the defect of mine.... Till then his distinction between *number* & *weight*

of experiments may possibly appeare to some more subtill than weighty" (ibid., 107); and as for measurements of spectra, Lucas remarked that he "h[e]ld it improper, not to say preposterous, to spend time on the precise length of the spectrum by severall prismes, before the fundamental point be agreed on, namely the different refrangibility of rayes differently coloured" (ibid., 108).

Newton in his likewise unpublished response demanded that the issue of the spectral proportions be settled once and for all and charged that "the examining my Theory is but a new attempted digression" (*Corresp.*, 2: 183–84). He further declined to answer any of Lucas's experimental ˙objections until the Jesuit should have told him "which of his experiments he would have me begin with" (ibid., 184). Precisely who was attempting digressions here is certainly arguable; after all, even while remarking their absurdity, Lucas had been earnestly trying to meet Newton's terms for debate. Another letter from Lucas finally prompted Newton to reply to the experiments; but besides being hastily conceived and ill tempered, Newton's answers, in focusing on how the phenomena were to be interpreted in accordance with the principle of differential refrangibility, tacitly assumed that the theory had already been proved, exactly the point at issue (*Corresp.*, 2: 254–60).

Newton's behavior in this episode could seem duplicitous, but it is just as likely that he truly believed there was no room for debate.[1] He had at one time described the propositions that the sun's light consists of rays differing by indefinite degrees of refrangibility, and that rays different in refrangibility also differ proportionally in the colors they produce, as matters of fact (*Corresp.*, 1: 293). Then how could anyone dispute them? They were established by the mediation of experiments concluding directly without any suspicion of doubt. But what does it mean to evince something by a mediation concluding directly? The statement is somewhat oxymoronic. Far from being a semantic quibble, this question locates the crux of the debate – or rather the lack of debate – about Newton's theory, for natural philosophers soon lost sight of the difficult and subtle problems involved in the relationships between the experiments and the propositions, between the phenomena and the theory, between the fact and the interpretation. Whereas Hooke, Huygens, and Lucas recognized the extravagance of Newton's claims, the generations that followed simply accepted them.

Newton's experiments "demonstrated" differential refrangibility according to color, about which fact there could be no dispute, although the precise nature of these rays was still an open topic. The supporters did not always use terms in a way that would have pleased Newton – it would have infuriated him to hear Joseph Priestley call it a hypothesis, even when Priestley went on to call the hypothesis true and evident from decisive experiments (Priestley 1772, 250) – but, whatever the words, they did not think it any less certain than Newton did. As far as they were concerned, the relationship between the experiments and the theory was unproblematic. As Gehler noted, "these propositions about colors ...rest not on any hypothesis about their nature but directly on the experiments themselves" (Gehler 1787–96, 2: 137). The revised second edition of Gehler was even bolder in its claim: For the most part Newton's optical writings contain "nothing other than pure expressions of experience" (Gehler 1825–45, vol. 4, pt. 1: 43). No one with any sense would presume to controvert Newton's theory because any other way of conceiving the phenomena was false.

What for our purposes is the most interesting thing about the earliest controversies is that they settled very little. Although Henry Oldenburg told Newton that the Royal Society was pleased with the new theory, those best able to judge remained unconvinced. Above all it was the vehemence and certitude with which Newton pressed his claims that induced them to withdraw before the major issues could be settled. Thirty years later the *Opticks* appeared, but by then Newton was the president of the Royal Society and the undisputed master of British if not European science. There was no longer anyone foolhardy enough to resist, if someone had been so inclined (Hooke, by the way, had died in 1703).

In France, however, the *Opticks* was not an immediate success, largely, it seems, because of Edmé Mariotte's experiments with refraction, first published in 1681. Mariotte, as the leading French experimentalist of the seventeenth century and a theorist of note as well, had impeccable credentials as a natural philosopher. In trying the *experimentum crucis* after Newton's fashion, he failed to confirm Newton's conclusion, much as Lucas had a few years before. When he passed just the violet rays of a once-refracted spectrum through a second slit and refracted the light again, he found that the resulting violet image was tinged with red and yellow, and so decided that the coloration was due to a modification of light, not to an original and connate property of rays. As Guerlac (1981) has argued, Mariotte's results impeded the entry of Newton's theory into French science, and it was not until after the appearance of the Latin translation of the *Opticks* in 1706 that differential refrangibility according to color became topical. One of the first to adopt Newton's color theory (and adapt it to his own theory of light as the vibrations of a subtle matter) was Malebranche, but he probably "simply took Newton's account at face value" (Guerlac 1981, 111). Around this time de la Hire, a mathematician and a friend of Mariotte's, tried to verify Newton's experiments without success. His failure provoked the interest of Leibniz, who urged that some able person be charged with the task of verification; for, he wrote, "since M. Newton has worked at them for so many years, and since one cannot doubt his ability, it is not credible that he has recounted imaginary experiments." In 1713 the *Acta eruditorum* expressed the hope that someone would test Mariotte's results again: "To us, Mariotte's experiments will only appear decisive if indeed pure blue [*sic*] light changed into something else" (Guerlac 1981, 117). It seems that Newton took this as a challenge and requested that the young experimentalist Jean Théophile Desaguliers, the successor to Francis Hauksbee as the Royal Society's curator of experiments, begin verifying the separation from one another of the heterogeneous rays of compound light by means of an improved version of the *experimentum crucis*.

A shift had taken place in the controversies even during Newton's lifetime. The focus of the earliest debate was the degree of certainty of the theory and of its inference from the phenomena, whose depiction by Newton was generally accepted by critics as fact; that is, Newton's argumentation was the issue. But the present debate took for granted that if Mariotte was shown to be wrong and Newton right about a single phenomenon, then the theory was to be considered proved. The truth or falsity depended on the results of a single, crucial experiment. Apparently, the objections raised by Newton's early opponents had simply been forgotten, not answered; the methodology of the crucial experiment had been accepted as binding and authoritative.

Goethe in particular wondered whether Desagulier's counter-demonstration ought to have been as decisive as it was taken to be. For one thing, it showed the reasonableness of the objections raised by Lucas and Mariotte on experimental grounds; Desaguliers confirmed their results, given the experimental setup of the *experimentum crucis* described in the Letter, which until the publication of the *Opticks* was the authoritative document in the public domain. Even more significant is the process Desaguliers used to verify Newton's experiments. He did not merely produce a refined version of the crucial experiment; rather he performed nine experiments in all. Only the last few directly tested and improved the crucial experiment; the first several were various experiments from the *Opticks* (beginning with the first, the differential displacement of colored rectangles) designed to provide an ocular demonstration of the principles of differential refrangibility. That is, Desaguliers presented the witnesses with didactic instruction in the theory rather than just a test of a refined crucial experiment. Goethe expressed his consternation at this coaching of witnesses.

What Desaguliers did is thus divided into two parts: The first seven experiments are to prove diverse refrangibility and fix it in the minds of the observers; in the eighth and ninth, on the other hand, which are the first to be directed against Mariotte, what was proposed is thought to be really achieved.

... Experiments, however, on the one hand so important, on the other so easily and conveniently repeated, are now to be declared once and for all settled, completed, dispensed with, and repetition of them decried as unnecessary, absurd, indeed presumptuous, just because they were performed a hundred years ago in England by a society that was eminent, to be sure, but not fully reliable either in theorizing or in experimenting. Is there the least sense here of what experimental science is, on what it rests, how it can and must grow, how it gradually discards all by itself what is false in it, how the old discoveries are supplemented by the new, and how through this [process of] completion the older *Vorstellungsarten*, even without polemic, fall into ruin? (*HA*, 14: 165–66)

Goethe is not inveighing against the improvements in experimental technique that Desaguliers introduced. At issue is whether the experiment was accurately described and the spectral phenomenon truly portrayed, whether the experiment has meaning apart from the series of experiments in which it appears, and whether the entire theory can be proved on the basis of a single experiment, or even nine.

Another point to be made is that Desaguliers reported some imperfections in his results; he went on to prescribe precautions that are necessary to get really homogeneous light, and then assured his readers that a few days after performing the experiments recounted in his memoir he made the same "Experiments over again before several Members of the *Royal Society* with better Success" (Desaguliers 1717, 447). This "better success" may well make one wonder whether the perfectly homogeneal light was perhaps just adequately homogeneal, whether all the colors gave the same good results, and whether membership in the Royal Society was sufficient warrant against seeing with preconceptions. Lastly, one may also ask whether the experimental setup, with no less than three apertures, two prisms, a plane mirror, and a collimating lens, is not itself an instrumentalization of the theory that prejudices the judgment in its favor.

Certainty in science

The concept of the crucial experiment transformed science and the role of phenomena. When Hooke invented the term it was used to describe an experiment that disproved a hypothesis of Descartes; in Newton its confirmatory value was emphasized instead. A single phenomenon became the foundation of the theory and the threshold to the truth about light and colors.

The context of a crucial experiment is problematic, of course. Insofar as a putatively crucial experiment disconfirms a given proposition, the necessary context would appear to be minimal (i.e., whatever is necessary to understand the sense of the proposition and what counts as disconfirmation). Insofar as it is designed to give positive information, however, we already need a substantial network of theory and phenomena that make the proposition in question not merely plausible but probable as well, because an isolated instance has little confirmatory value. For Newton the context was provided by the implicit and explicit refutation of a series of competing theories and their consequences. In the Letter, the *experimentum crucis* gives a result that apparently disconfirms one of two remaining possibilities, an interior modification of light (the second refraction does not modify the color or further disperse the light), and confirms the other, the innate differential refrangibility of light. Or, rather, a hypothetical consequence of the modificationist theory as interpreted by Newton conflicts with the evidence, whereas the evidence not only agrees with the prediction of his ray theory but gives ocular proof of the existence of the various kinds of ray. But now we have moved to a different sense of cruciality: The experiment reveals, immediately and without suspicion of doubt, the essence of the theory – that is precisely what makes it a theory rather than a hypothesis. Thus the crucial experiment seems no longer in need of a context other than itself. The theory becomes a matter of fact, because it is the direct expression of an experiment.

A little-studied indicator of the development of this "certaintism" in science is the change in usage of the word "fact" in the eighteenth century. The original sense of the word (in Latin and the Romance languages as well as in English) was something done, a deed, and, derivatively, anything that has occurred. In the primary sense there was always a doer of the deed. The fact was thus definite in that it had a doer, a time, and a place; in the extended sense, it had at least a time and a place. In either case the actor or the event was visible, in evidence. The more modern acceptation is further derivative, with an added, subjective component: something known by actual observation or authentic testimony (and thus opposed to mere inference) – a datum of experience. This shift in meaning seems to have taken place in the eighteenth century, at least in English.[2] French *fait*, although capable of the new construal, to this day retains a strong verbal aspect that assimilates it to the older usage, perhaps because it is the past participle of *faire*. German *Tatsache* (or *Thatsache*) is an especially interesting case, because its introduction into the language can be exactly dated, 1756 (see Grimm and Grimm 1854–1919, vol. 11, div. 1, pt. 1: 322); within a quarter century the German writer Gotthold Ephraim Lessing noted with bemusement how meteoric had been the rise of the term, so that everywhere one looked one came upon facts (ibid.)[3]

The dogma of facts was also an essential prerequisite for the rise of positivism. Comte's explanation of the meaning of "positive" in "positive philosophy" reveals its utter dependence on facts: "In adding the word 'positive' I announce that I am considering that special manner of philosophizing that consists in envisaging theories, in whatever order of ideas it may be, as having for their object the coordination of observed facts" (Comte [1830] 1968, xiv). One might add to these historical reflections the centrality of fact in the epistemology and ontology of twentieth-century philosophy, although there is considerable disagreement about whether facts are things of the world or things of language (see Nelson 1967 and Londey 1969).[4] The foundation for such thoroughgoing disagreement about the nature of facts was already laid by Newton, however, in the conflation of the fact as thing, act, or event with the fact as proposition, so that the proposition was reified as something simply given.

Approximately during the period of Goethe's most intensive work on color, German scientists acquired a passion for the facts. Comparing general scientific texts from as late as the 1790s with works from the 1820s, one finds that *Faktum* and *Tatsache* rarely occur in the former. Instead there are references to objects (*Gegenstände*), things (*Sachen, Dinge*), experiments (*Versuche*), and phenomena (*Phänomene, Erscheinungen*); these in turn are distinguished from propositions (*Sätze*), conclusions (*Schlüsse, Folgerungen*), and explanations (*Erklärungen*) that express or describe things. In Gren's *Grundriss der Naturlehre*, for example, *Thatsache* occurs infrequently, with no particular programmatic significance attached to it. Works from a quarter century later show a marked contrast. For instance, in the second edition of Fischer's *Lehrbuch der mechanischen Naturlehre* (1819), the fact has become the foundation of science. Fischer emphasizes that a sharp boundary must be drawn conceptually between facts on the one hand and hypotheses and *Vorstellungsarten* on the other: "A well-ordered doctrinal edifice of an empirical science should be nothing other than a careful, systematic compilation of *facts*. Such a building stands eternally firm in its essential parts, and new discoveries can of course serve to add on to it and to better fit out the interior, but never to destroy it and tear it down" (Fischer 1819, 1: xi).

A fact is thus an indestructible building block in an edifice proof against all disturbances. In striving for the utmost conceptual clarity in his account of the foundations of science, Fischer endowed the facts and their interconnections with an eternal and unshakable certainty. Gren, in principle at least, had acknowledged that there was a limit to the certainty of empirical science when he said that Newton had endowed his "immortal theory with the degree of evidence that can be reached with objects of experience" (Gren 1793, par. 586); Fischer took this utmost degree of evidence as a matter of course. The more that one conceives theory as the construction of an impregnable fortress out of absolutely indestructible elements, however, the less room there is for any methodical distinction between propositions and what they give an accounting of. The demand for conceptual clarity in science, the radical distinction between hypotheses and facts, led instead to the confusion of proposition, experience, and reality in the omnibus term "fact." A similar transformation is visible in the quotations from the two editions of Gehler cited in the previous section: The earlier one discriminates between the propositions and what they rest on (experiments), whereas the later one calls Newton's words the pure expression of experience. As the sense of the distinction between proposition and experience was lost, so was the awareness that describing phenomena is a problematic task.

At the very moment when Goethe was discovering the complex interrelationships of *Vorstellungsart* and fact – and Goethe typically used the word fact to signify experiments and phenomenal events rather than propositions about them (see, e.g., *LA I*, 3: 306) – the scientific and philosophical world was placing its trust in objective certainty and factual truth. The physicists of 1810 must have picked up *Zur Farbenlehre* in hope of finding mathematical theory, new facts, and crucial experiments; what they discovered instead seemed to be a mere rehearsal of facts already well known and perfectly well explained by the Newtonian theory. They are unlikely to have been looking for a new scientific method that paid careful attention to the complex relationship between what happens in the experiment and the way in which the event is described. Goethe and the physicists were headed in opposite directions: Whereas they sought to construct theoretical edifices out of isolated facts, he was learning that the attempt of the *Beiträge* to draw sharp boundaries between descriptions and hypotheses was untenable, because theorizing is inherent in all intelligent seeing. This implied that facts are not isolated and single experiments not crucial, for both depend on the context in which they are understood and viewed; from the perspective of another *Vorstellungsart* they might have a different significance, and so the facts need to be frequently recalled and reexamined, not forgotten just because someone somewhere once "ascertained" them.

The *Beiträge* tried to be comprehensive in arraying experimental certainty next to experimental certainty, each analyzed according to the conditions that conduced to the appearance of a phenomenon; the point was to make this array as natural as possible. *Zur Farbenlehre* retained the method of the earlier works but then complicated it by taking cognizance of the inescapable partiality in ways of conceiving things; thus, the certainties that Goethe could offer on the printed page were no more than provisional and would have to establish their worth when they were applied to actual phenomena. Every use of the theory is consequently also a test. According to Goethe, not *Zur Farbenlehre* alone but every theoretical text had, as it were, to be held in one hand while the other was busy with experiments, and while the eye and the mind's eye were comparing and criticizing. Unlike the method of Newtonian theory, which regarded experimentation as problematic only insofar as the experimenter was careless or inaccurate and which focused its attention on the inferred entities supposed to underlie the phenomena, Goethe paid close attention to the phenomena, the experimental process, and the contribution of the experimenter. Far from being subjectivist or metaphysical, Goethe's science attempted to keep in view both the knower and the known. In comparison, the so-called objective sciences of his day had a naive conception of the relationship between subject and object. They distinguished between what was proved and what was not, but failed to make a consistent discrimination between phenomena, descriptions, hypotheses, and theories, and so were incapable of giving a reasoned account of themselves. As the mathematization of the most scientific of the natural sciences, physics, went on apace, the reduction of the phenomena to mathematical data drove the problems of phenomenality and language ever further from view.

Goethe's great misfortune was to fall out with a well-developed theory of long standing precisely at a time when optics and the physical sciences in general were undergoing transformations that moved them further away from any common ground with him. In the first decade of the nineteenth century, optics received new life from investigations into the phenomena of interference and polarity, which in the next decade led to the enunciation of a wave theory in the form that ultimately supplanted Newtonian corpuscularism. Compared with this transformation, Goethe's concerns seemed peripheral if not atavistic, and the struggle of the wave theorists against corpuscularists was carried out on a different battlefield (the wave theorists saw no reason to dispute the basic Newtonian theory of differential color refrangibility). Goethe nevertheless applauded this attempt to replace the complicated ad hoc hypotheses invented to save Newtonian corpuscularism with a simpler and more economical theoretical schema based on a renewed and exacting investigation of the phenomena, and he further thought that the wave theory had the additional advantage of being a more dynamic way of conceiving the phenomena (*LA* I, 8: 276, and *LA* I, 11: 289–94).[5] Still, Goethe's primary interest was the science of color rather than the science of light, and he regarded the battle over the nature of light as quite another question. His goal was to establish the science of color in its own right.

But science was changing along rather different lines. European science was already undergoing a process of professionalization and redefinition toward the end of the eighteenth century (see Heilbron 1979, 12–19). The French revolutionary occupation of territories across the Rhine appears to have contributed to this process in Germany. Even if it was only at first in principle, the ethos of French physics brought with it the imperative of specialized research, standardized methods, quantitative rigor, and a new division of the scientific disciplines. *Naturlehre* was giving way before *Physik* in the modern sense. Moreover, German physicists wanted to distance themselves from the Romantic philosophy of nature that was emerging under the influence of Schelling, a philosophy that, despite its being rooted in the sciences of the day, exceeded the bounds of the empirical. As it won adherents among scientists as well as nonscientists, many in the German physics community began to regard it as a threat. Consequently, anything that smacked of speculation became an anathema, the highest virtue became the sober enunciation of facts, and the ultimate goal became a theory that could explain the empirical data. Clearly, the mathematizers would be at odds with Goethe about the foundations of natural science, but neither were the empirical fact gatherers his allies. Although many physicists recognized that Goethe's penchant for the concrete distinguished him from most of the *Naturphilosophen*, he was nevertheless counted as a fellow traveler. Goethe did indeed have close personal and scientific ties with Schelling and some of his adherents, but he must not be casually assumed to have been one of them. He was in fact rather cool to their speculative excesses and transcendentalizing and liked to think of himself as intermediate between fact gatherer and speculator (*LA* I, 3: 305, 324, 326–27; see also Jungnickel and McCormmach 1986, 27).

But even those who could appreciate Goethe's dedication to empirical work did not understand the polemical and historical parts of his magnum opus. Perhaps it was inevitable that proponents of factual science would have difficulty conceiving of the historicity of science, except in an accidental sense. Enlightenment historiography tended to see the rise of science as the gradual overcoming of obscurantism, superstitions, and vague ideas (von Engelhardt 1979, 39–44). The past is thus by and large a weedlot of error that is redeemed by flowerings of clear thought and scientific genius, and in the course of centuries the facts and theories that are no longer useful are discarded (Shklar 1981, 652–53). It is no accident that scientific texts of the late eighteenth and early nineteenth century devoted progressively less space to the history of their subjects, for factual truth is present truth and displaces what is past. What Goethe attempted to show in the historical part of *Zur Farbenlehre* (that the triumph of Newtonian theory owed much of its success to Newton's wearing down his opponents, to the antiphilosophical temper of the Royal Society, to the authority of the elder Newton, and to other similar factors, and that science is inevitably subject to influences other than the object of investigation because of the nature and necessity of *Vorstellungsarten*) was contrary to the physicists' understanding of science; or perhaps one ought to say that, given this understanding, Goethe's conception of science was completely unintelligible. After all, facts are facts, no matter when or by whom discovered, and insofar as there is a history of science it is a narration of discoveries and the removal of obstacles to discovery. Goethe's insight that "a history of the sciences, insofar as these have been treated by men, exhibits a completely different and most highly instructive face than when discoveries and opinions are merely arranged one next to another" (HA, 14: 10), that the history of the sciences is a series of events in the realm of spirit (LA I, 3: 314), was simply the wrong way of conceiving things. Science was the end product, not the process; it was purified of any alloy with personality, particularity, and speculative thought.

Goethe remained true to his insight into the Vorstellungsarten till the end of his life. Many of his later essays on scientific topics deal with the historical appearance and disappearance of Vorstellungsarten, with their pervasiveness and their modes of influence (for instance, in one essay he considered the recurrent tendency of successful sciences to dominate the imagination of an age and set the standard for all other sciences; see LA I, 11: 273–83). He analyzed contemporary and past controversies in their light; sometimes he suggested ways in which disputed questions might be better approached with the help of a new way of conceiving things that tried to reconcile the strengths of different Vorstellungsarten (see D. Kuhn 1967). He recognized controversy as an intrinsic part of science that leaves its imprint on the "end product," and asserted that in a deep sense the history of a science is the science itself (HA, 13: 319).

The organization of science

It is doubtful that even under the best of circumstances Goethe could have succeeded in stimulating a renewed investigation of problems of color along the lines he intended. Goethe's Farbenlehre was a science in search of an audience that never developed and perhaps never could develop. It aimed at stirring interest not only among professionals but among the general public as well, and he was firmly committed to the notion that intelligent amateurs can make small but important contributions to observational sciences, both because they might notice things that escape the attention of experts and because, not having been indoctrinated into the ways of the discipline, they might interject into the sciences new ways of conceiving things (we might compare the importance of younger investigators in bringing about scientific revolutions).

We have already mentioned many reasons for the failure of Zur Farbenlehre: Goethe's own errors and missteps and his decision to polemicize; the prevailing dogma of factuality; the lessening of historical consciousness among natural philosophers; the fear of speculation among the anti-*Naturphilosophen*; the rise of the wave theory of light; and the professionalization of science. This last point needs further elaboration. Scholars in recent years have made great strides in correcting the erroneous but once prevalent notion that German science at the beginning of the nineteenth century was dominated by *Naturphilosophie*. Kenneth Caneva has argued that *Naturphilosophie* and "romantic science" are often catchall terms for a complex constellation of movements and currents in German science of the period. In his studies of the science of electromagnetism, he discovered an influential school of antispeculative science, which he calls concretizing science. Concretizing science was based on *Anschauung*, qualitative (rather than quantitative) experiments, inductivism, and the rejection of hypotheses, and it sought explanations of particular phenomena in terms of their association with other known phenomena (Caneva 1975, 23–28). It therefore displays certain marked affinities with Goethe's methodology at the time of the *Beiträge*; it is not impossible that Goethe had some influence on this school.[6] In its epistemological standards, however, concretizing science was at odds with both Goethe's early and his later method, in that it cultivated the crucial experiment as its chief methodological tool and aimed at proving its theories beyond the shadow of doubt. Goethe's scientific writings in contrast were always marked by a rejection of the crucial experiment and by an epistemological modesty that was not characteristic of the concretizing scientists, who accordingly did not recognize any special value in plural approaches.

However, although German science in general was more resistant to the theoretical and hypotheticodeductive method than French and English science, there was a commitment in principle to the importance of mathematics and to the ultimate goal of achieving quantitative accuracy. It is not always so much what has been accomplished that governs science as the promise of what might be achieved. Indeed, the ideal can be all the stronger when it has not been put to the test. German scientists did not always practice the mathematical ideal when they preached it; and insofar as they were not organized to practice an ideal, Goethe's theory of color was doomed. Goethe's science could thrive only where color was an object of intensive research, where theories could easily and routinely be checked against phenomena. But the chromatics that existed was conducted occasionally rather than systematically (see Burwick 1986, esp. ch. 1). Moreover, the university tradition of transmitting established knowledge rather than producing new research discouraged the cultivation of any genuinely pathbreaking sciences (see Turner 1974). In addition, the most scientifically progressive of eighteenth- and early nineteenth-century German universities, Göttingen, had decidedly Newtonian views on color; both Erxleben and Lichtenberg were professors there (see *HA*, 14: 214). Nor did the relative isolation of German scientists help Goethe cultivate scientific interest in color. Germany had no center similar to Paris or London, and its political fragmentation prevented the concentration of scientific forces until later in the century. As government minister Goethe himself had tried to build the University of Jena into a center of intellectual and natural scientific activity, but in the wake of the Napoleonic wars its gains were rapidly lost; on the other hand, Berlin did not become the intellectual capital of Germany until after the restoration of 1815. Science thrives best where it is concentrated, and the simplest way to concentrate science is to bring scientists together. Where this does not or cannot happen, scientists are more likely to become purveyors and preservers of the work of others. The dispersion of scientific forces tends to produce a kind of scientific scholasticism, which in turn reinforces the influence of figures of authority. What Goethe wanted and needed above all, however, was a science that actively both preserved and innovated.

The historical part of *Zur Farbenlehre* documents a late eighteenth-century interest in color and nonstandard, even anti-Newtonian approaches (see esp. *HA*, 14: 215–51; cf. *LA* I, 6: 353–412). The colors Goethe called physiological had already drawn the attention of Scherffer in 1765 and, twenty years later, of R. W. Darwin; the anonymous H. F. T. (probably Jean Henri Hassenfratz; see *HA*, 14: 324, editor's note) collected observations on colored shadows in the 1780s, as did the Portuguese Diego de Carvalho e Sampayo. Guyot, Mauclerc, Gülich, Delaval, and others took an interest in color printing techniques, the properties and uses of dyes, and other technical matters, while both natural philosophers and artists (e.g., Philipp Otto Runge) tried to single out the primary colors and to place them with all their mixtures and nuances into two- and three-dimensional color space. Westfeld tried to explain the workings of the retina in color perception, while artists and theorists like Mengs and Hoffmann philosophized about the principles of color harmony. There were scores of people besides who had at least noted particular color phenomena as worthy of attention, among whom were scientific eminences like Franklin and Count Rumford.[7]

Although there was no lack of interest, there was also no organization of the researchers and their work, no theoretical schema with any authority other than the Newtonian one, no project to unify the manifold scientific labor that needed to be pursued. The Farbenlehre was intended to provide the core for such a project. But in a sense Goethe had outstripped most of the potential collaborators with his first-hand knowledge of the full range of phenomena and experiments, his scholarly command of the history of the subject, and his sophisticated philosophy of science; he could only be a leader and director by 1810, no longer just another worker in the field of chromatics. Yet he had alienated those who were essential to his project by polemicizing against Newton. No matter how just it may have been in principle, the critique of Newton made Goethe an outsider, in the eyes of both the remaining heirs of eighteenth-century experimental science and the proponents of mathematized physics, because both groups recognized in Newton a key symbol of their heritage and their identity. Goethe therefore had no natural audience for his case, except the general public – and they of course were largely inclined to leave the matter to the experts, to the natural philosophers, to the physicists.

5

Goethe and the ethos of science

If ultimately I rest content with the Urphenomenon, it is, after all, but a kind of resignation; yet it makes a great difference whether I resign myself at the boundaries of humanity, or within a hypothetical narrowness of my small-minded individuality.

– Goethe (*MR*, no. 577)

Urphenomenality and the basis of science

The *Opticks* spurred the growth of eighteenth-century experimental science by teaching investigators to see theoretically, mathematicophysically. Both the *Opticks* and the *Principia* provided decisive paradigms for exploring in detail the substructures of everyday appearances. The *Opticks* in particular showed how from within the bewildering, apparently arbitrary domain of colors one could gain virtually self-evident mathematicophysical knowledge about the nature of light and colors by fusing the way of experiment with mathematical demonstration. Thenceforth, wherever the physicist saw light, he also saw geometrically conceived color rays. The eye became little more than a passive detector, even an undependable one, for it could be deceived when it was fatigued or when the rays were mixed with one another.

Almost every early nineteenth-century critic of Goethe's *Zur Farbenlehre* had been initiated into this kind of seeing and took for granted the factuality of Newton's interpretation (indeed, Goethe complained that not just physicists but also almost every intelligent layman had been indoctrinated as well; see *LA* I, 3: 116). By and large the critiques were conducted at the level of abstracted theory, with only occasional glances at experimental phenomena – usually cited according to Newton's descriptions – a cruel irony for Goethe, whose first hope was to induce physicists to reexamine the experiments and phenomena of color in a more or less comprehensive way independent of the standard theory. Not a few of the earliest reviewers hit upon the approach that Helmholtz would canonize in 1853 – to argue that the poetic nature disables one from genuinely comprehending the power of mathematical abstraction and the rigorous methods of physical science.

Goethe cannot be held blameless of the misunderstandings of his critics, however. Reading the foreword to *Zur Farbenlehre* and the introduction to the didactic part one can easily miss the concern for comprehensiveness and even Goethe's disavowal of intending merely to put a hypothesis of his own in place of Newton's (*HA*, 13: 319); and by stating in the foreword that the "capital intention" *(Hauptabsicht)* of the work was to apply "the language of nature" (*HA*, 13: 316), a language of polarities, to color, he gave the impression that *Zur Farbenlehre* was chiefly devoted to drawing the study of color into the ambit of speculative *Naturphilosophie*. What some were quick to interpret as a confession of allegiance was more an acknowledgment of affinity, however. Well before Goethe invited Schelling to take up a professorship at the University of Jena (1798), Goethe had become convinced that polarities in the phenomena of color (such as those made apparent by the *Beiträge zur Optik*) demanded a vocabulary of polarities.

Goethe was perhaps too subtle for his own good and overrated the ability of his readers to penetrate the complexities of the phenomena and the rich density of his prose. A more explicit statement of his method and purpose at the outset might have more effectively forestalled misunderstandings than the occasional pithy remarks in the body of the work. Certainly his labeling the phenomena of turbid media Urphenomenal, then trying to extend this Urphenomenon as the principle of explanation for refractive colors, convinced many that this was the sum and substance of his theory, perfectly analogous to Newton's principle of diverse refrangibility. Of course, the Urphenomenon is not so much a single, objectified phenomenon, conceived at a high level of abstraction, as it is a rubric for a determinate and naturally unified sequence of experiments and phenomena. The Urphenomenon was intended to unify the phenomena of color. Yet the very multiplicity of the phenomena presented in the didactic part defeated Goethe's synthetic powers, despite his having devoted the better part of two decades to the project. It is hardly surprising that those for whom theoretical seeing in the manner of Newton had become second nature found themselves wondering what all the phenomena in *Zur Farbenlehre* were meant to prove. At least the ray concept gave the investigator something definite and inalterable to look for in any event of color, no matter what one did to the light; in contrast, the Urphenomenon, as the phenomenal first principle of color, is for the most part not immediately isolable in new classes of color phenomena. The encounter of light with a turbid medium is supposed to occur in all the physical and chemical color phenomena, but its particular manifestations depend on the specific circumstances of the event/

experiment, and so one cannot presume that the addition of further circumstances, such as the interposition of a lens, will not introduce something unanticipated. There is therefore no inalterable entity to quantify; instead, there are appearances to be compared with one another and (experimental) conditions to be classified.

Goethe of course argued that Urphenomenality was not incompatible with mathematics; for example, Galileo's kinetic law of freely falling bodies was based on an Urphenomenal unification of manifold individual instances (see Chapter 2, note 19). Yet we might still like to distinguish between a quantitatively formulated Urphenomenon like Galileo's and a qualitative one like Goethe's; furthermore, we might decide that any quantitatively formulated theory ought to be favored over any non-quantitative one (and perhaps that a more fully quantified one should be favored over any that is less quantified). We might argue that Goethe, despite his attempts to forestall the empirical aimlessness of Baconian method and his awareness of how difficult it is to survey an entire science, succumbed to the sheer impossibility of grasping the whole, that like any Baconian he was ultimately overcome by the profusion of nature.

Mathematical theories, accordingly, are not simply aids to science but of its essence. They abstract from nature's profusion, and that is precisely their strength. They help pick out one by one the various strands and elements that nature comprises and that otherwise are likely to stay hidden. The precision and economy of mathematics encourage the rapid progress of science better than any Goethean community of researchers with various *Vorstellungsarten* could, for mathematized theories can be applied and tested more swiftly and certainly than what is not quantified or otherwise exactly specified. This possibility of application and test concentrates and directs the efforts of scientists to seek ever greater exactness. Against the profusion of nature we must pit the ability of the scientific imagination to seize the main chance with determinate and bold hypotheses, not just with modest generalizations. More than any other single factor, the well-defined (and thus preeminently mathematical) hypothesis creates the discipline and rigor of science. If restricting the application of hypotheses or postponing their introduction until after a phenomenal base is laid ends up dispersing the energy of researchers and retards scientific advancement, might we not reasonably decide that the price for a Goethean science is too high?

The legitimacy of this question is reinforced when one considers Goethe's ever more frequent acknowledgment of a conceptual aspect to the Urphenomenon and the inevitable gap between idea and experience. In the essay "Bedenken und Ergebung," written ca. 1818, Goethe asserted the existence of an essentially unresolvable tension between theory and phenomenon (*HA*, 13: 31). This gap was already apparent to him no later than 1798, when in the posthumously published "Erfahrung und Wissenschaft" he wrote:

Since the observer never sees the pure phenomenon [*das reine Phänomen*; presumably this can be identified with the later *Urphänomen*] with his eyes, but rather a great deal depends on his mood, on the momentary state of the organ, on light, air, climate, bodies, [method of] treatment and a thousand other circumstances: One has to drink up a sea if one wants to hold on to the individuality of the phenomenon and to observe, measure, weigh, and describe that individuality. (*HA*, 13: 24)

In practice this means, as he remarked two paragraphs before, that "there are, as I am often able to note particularly in the subject that I am working on [color theory], many empirical gaps one must dispose of to obtain a pure, constant phenomenon; but as soon as I let myself do this, I am setting up a kind of ideal" (ibid.).

If Goethean method at best provides us with an ideal, not with an inductive truth or proven fact, we might again wonder whether ultimately it is not more efficient and more productive to cultivate hypotheses at the very beginning of a science. Rather than keep the imagination in check, as the Goethe of both the *Beiträge* and *Zur Farbenlehre* had done, it would be better to give it free rein. Strict empiricism, whether or not it posits certainty as its object, rarely produces great science; at best it can lead up to it. The cautious method and discipline on which this kind of empiricism is founded may be laudable, but there is a rigor of another kind involved in taking a hypothesis and putting it to work. One might agree with Goethe's assertion[1] that "there is nevertheless a great difference, whether one, like the theorists, casts whole numbers into the breaches on behalf of a hypothesis, or whether one offers up an empirical breach to the idea of the pure phenomenon" (*HA*, 13: 24), but come to the opposite conclusion: that in the sciences we must choose the way of number, more generally the way of mathematics, as quickly as is practicable.

This kind of argument against Goethe and in favor of abstract hypothesis is not simply answerable. One question that would first have to be posed would be about the goal science is pursuing, and another would ask about the horizon within which we gauge scientific progress. These would take us too far afield at present, although they are questions that are implicitly and sometimes explicitly posed by Goethe, especially in the great literary works of his maturity (e.g., *Elective Affinities*, *Wilhelm Meisters Wanderjahre*, and *Faust* II). It is more pertinent to restate a basic Goethean contention: That to be genuinely scientific, a science and its practitioners must develop a coherent understanding and a clear conception of what part of nature they are attempting to investigate and how they ought to go about it. This procedure is in fact part of the science

itself, not pre-science; it is a necessary preliminary to, and constant concomitant of, all hypothetical science. Furthermore, no matter how powerful theories, hypotheses, and mathematics may prove, scientific
understanding is not simply reducible to them. One cannot properly
understand scientific theories unless one comprehends their role in seeing
and knowing. Goethe would insist that science cannot avoid beginning
with and returning to a relatively concrete sense of how the field in
question is articulated and how it is related to other fields. Although this
articulation will almost surely be modified in light of one's results, it is
the concrete field that makes sense of the results; and, as Goethe once
remarked, the human spirit possesses and must reassert "its old right of
putting itself directly in touch with nature," a right that he believed
nineteenth-century science was neglecting but that had to be exercised if
science was to be fully scientific (HA, 13: 50).

The truth embodied in this old right is often overlooked because of
enthusiasm for new hypotheses and the apparent regularity with which
scientific results can claim to overthrow naive intuitions, but it is conceded, tacitly or expressly, in virtually every scientific work. The Opticks,
for instance, is divided not according to properties of the ray but according to the different classes of phenomena (reflective and refractive,
those of thin films, those of diffraction). Where he can, Newton tries to
assimilate them to a single property, but where he cannot he is willing
to introduce new properties (e.g., repulsive forces) to account for a class
that refuses assimilation. That is, the articulation of the class is prior;
the explanation (property) follows the lead of the preliminary and largely
"intuitive" classification. What Goethe's Urphenomenon does is to elaborate and articulate the principle of unity of these classes: It draws out
what is common to all the events of a given type, or rather it is an explicit
constitution of the type, not as a single, isolated phenomenon nor as
matter for theoretical proof, nor as a highly abstract concept, but in the
form of a phenomenal abstraction made as concrete, as full of content
as possible. In pursuing the Urphenomenon one is trying to give scientific
articulation and expression to what would otherwise be an unexamined,
and in that sense prescientific, understanding of the field under
investigation.

This approach does not abolish hypothetical or abstract science, but
rather provides a method of binding hypotheses and abstractions concretely to the entire field. Goethe would argue that every science is constructed on, in fact begins in, such a field. It is characteristic of scientific
discipline not to abandon an investigation the moment a new hypothesis
comes into view but rather to go about things methodically and with due
care. A surveyor would not rush off to the other end of the field just
because he saw something interesting there; nor will he let himself be

absorbed by every blade of grass. What he does in the first place is orient himself to the natural landmarks of the field and note their relationship to the surrounding countryside. The initial survey then provides a map by which others can in future find their bearings. It can be changed in light of future developments and projects. Someday, perhaps, there may even come a botanist who will extend the work closer to those very blades of grass, or a cosmologist who will place the field in relationship with the universe.

A summary catalog of Goethean criteria for science might, then, read as follows. Any theory that is unbound by the necessary qualifications, conditions, and restrictions that enable it to be used as a genuine instrument of knowing is inferior to a theory that acknowledges bounds. Any theory that uses mathematics to appear more exacting than it really is – a phenomenon not unknown in the history of the modern sciences (see, for instance, Westfall 1972 on Newton's fudge factor) – is inferior to a theory that obligates itself to follow with care the manifold courses of nature's evidence. The best way to foster scientific knowledge is to ensure that one is completely familiar with the phenomena before going behind or beneath them in search of causes – that is, one first ought to grasp and conceive the Urphenomena. Nothing in principle prevents the subsequent or concomitant mathematization of Urphenomena (Goethe's understanding of Galileo's law of falling bodies underscores this) as long as the mathematical theory is presented with the requisite caveats about complicating circumstances, acknowledges the inevitable margins of error, and disavows trying to supplant the phenomena themselves.

The manifold project of Zur Farbenlehre

Zur Farbenlehre, as a natural and experimental history, as a way of approaching and seeing color (i.e., as theory), was a new beginning for color science, not an end, a project rather than dogmatics. Its project for a science of color may be conceived as fourfold. First, the *Farbenlehre* aimed at reforming experimental natural science by introducing a program of ongoing pluralistic research based on natural and experimental histories. On this level Goethe was addressing major issues in natural science itself – for example, the proper relationship between theory and phenomenon, the tendency of hypotheses to sclerose into exclusive schools and dogmas, the general inclinations of human beings to apotheosize propositions as the single truth of things. Second, the *Farbenlehre* attempted to constitute a science specifically about color, chromatics, so that the subject would no longer be studied merely as an appendage of other sciences. Third, it tried to develop a particular *Vorstellungsart* within the larger program of pluralistic research, what Goethe called the genetic and dynamic *Vorstellungsart*. Fourth, it provided a comprehensive articulation of the phenomena of color that, despite its orientation toward the genetic/dynamic *Vorstellungsart*, was to be of use to all researchers in chromatics.

These four aspects of the project are not logically, materially, or temporally independent of one another. Goethe understood his articulation of the phenomena in the didactic part of *Zur Farbenlehre* (fourth aspect) as an example of reformed natural science (first aspect) that would serve as a foundation of chromatics (second aspect) while simultaneously representing a provisional attempt to elaborate the Goethean *Vorstellungsart* (third aspect).

Even if we prescind from questions of historical influence, we can recognize that Goethe did not succeed equally in each of these aspects. If he managed to lay the foundation for a science specifically about color, he did not demonstrate the consistency and power of the genetic *Vorstellungsart* in a convincing way (even if we exempt him from the requirement of providing a theory of the same type as the ray theory), nor did he sufficiently emphasize his major intentions of reforming method and encouraging pluralist science. If we consider further how perplexing, even bewildering, the sudden appearance of *Zur Farbenlehre* must have been, a massive work seeming to come, as far as the general public and even most of the physics community was concerned, out of nowhere, nearly twenty years after the last *Beiträge*, and the imprudent vehemence of the polemic against Newton and the Newtonians, we realize how difficult it would have been for anyone unfamiliar with the history we have traced to begin to appreciate this work.

Going about things as he did, Goethe seems to have forfeited his chance to persuade the scientific community, which, despite Goethe's hope to reach the nonexpert, was more important to win over than the general public. Yet, as especially Chapter 4 has made clear, it is not at all certain that Goethe could have accomplished the reorientation of chromatics, not to mention of the general method and the historical conception of natural science, even if he had avoided all errors of execution and tactical and strategic judgment. It would not have helped, for example, simply to publish a series of researches like the *Beiträge*, because the proper understanding of the parts relied on a significant apprehension and demonstration of the whole. Sporadic oral and written communications with physicists at Jena and Göttingen did not suffice to win support or clarify the purpose of his project, and he could not very well force them into his camera obscura for reeducation (see, e.g., *LA* I, 3: 474). *Zur Farbenlehre*, ambitious and far reaching enough for a diverse research team, was too enormous a work for a single scientist and his small circle of occasional helpers, no matter what their native endowment.

As has already been mentioned, the German physics community around the start of the nineteenth century had come to profess more intensely the physicist's reliance on mathematics, had weakened the sense of difference between event and account in its understanding of factuality, and had affirmed rather than abandoned proofs of truth as the major goal of science. From Goethe's perspective, of course, these were all changes for the worse. Yet it cannot be said that Goethe himself only changed for the better, and it was not only Newton and his followers who sometimes failed to abide by professed principles. Goethe's scathing dismissal of the experiments with colored shadows performed by his secretary Eckermann, which tended to show that these colors are in some cases attributable to the hue of the illuminant rather than to the eye's propensity to perceive complementary colors (Eck., 19 February 1829), recalls the treatment he had suffered almost four decades earlier. Eckermann recorded for us what Goethe had to say in justification of his irate reaction.

Things have gone with my *Farbenlehre* just as with the Christian religion. For a while you think you have true pupils, and before you know it they deviate and form a sect. You are a heretic just like the others, for you are not the first to deviate from me. I have quarreled with the most excellent men on account of disputed points in the *Farbenlehre*. (Eck., 19 February 1829)

Goethe had criticized the sectarian spirit of the Newtonians and decried their dogmatism. Is, then, Goethe's treatment of Eckermann, Schopenhauer, and other "heretics" admissible? Certainly we can criticize the manner of Goethe's reaction, and on Goethean grounds. A science founded in a pluralistic spirit requires two virtues above all, patience and irony: With irony, one may not be overwedded to the supposed perfection of the truths one holds; with patience, one may not rashly reject as impossible alternatives one violently disagrees with. One must be as reticent in uttering a definitive no as one is in giving a final yes. In particular, one must be as cautious about refutations as about proofs, and there is perhaps even an obligation not to let a failed *Vorstellungsart* disappear completely even when one was an opponent of it. Yet we must also recognize as legitimate the tendency of trustees of a *Vorstellungsart* (or, alternatively, the proponents of a theory) to be protective of it. This protectiveness is necessary, for without it no one would ever develop a scientific idea beyond its first glimmerings. Goethe, as an embattled proponent of the genetic/dynamic *Vorstellungsart*, was bound to resist efforts to undermine (especially from within) what was not merely his approach but also a long-standing tradition, though contemporarily out of favor, in the history of chromatics (*das alte Wahre*, the old truth, as Goethe sometimes called it). Even if Goethe in some significant way was wrong about colored shadows, he could not permit Eckermann, who was still very much a beginner in the study of color, to pronounce judgment on the *Farbenlehre*.

From his historical studies Goethe realized that to be an isolated figure in the history of a science was to be essentially without influence. He needed a school, he needed a group of followers who would carry out the project of *Zur Farbenlehre*. As he said in the "Konfession des Verfassers," from the very outset he had hoped to rouse in another the same aperçu that he had observed so that he might share his burden (*HA*, 14: 264; cf. 262). Newton, especially after becoming president of the Royal Society, had little trouble in winning adherents; Goethe, on the contrary, had difficulty in finding and keeping any. The most faithful was probably Leopold von Henning, a follower of Hegel at the University of Berlin, who offered lectures on the *Farbenlehre* every summer semester from 1822 to 1835; but I am aware of no one who took up Goethe's cause as a direct result of them. The subsequently eminent physiologists Johannes Müller and Jan Purkinje acknowledged the influence of Goethe's method in their early works concerning vision; but their interest focused solely on the physiological section of the didactic part of *Zur Farbenlehre*, and later in their careers they fell silent about (or even criticized) the *Farbenlehre*. A very few mathematicians and physicists made efforts to carry on the work Goethe had begun. For instance, J. Friedrich Christian Werneburg, a mathematician residing in Weimar, tried to show ways in which the prismatic phenomena according to the *Farbenlehre* could be quantified. Thomas Seebeck, a physicist who had collaborated with Goethe as the latter was concluding *Zur Farbenlehre*, actually published some of his own research on photochemical reactions and the colors of polarized light in the supplementary part of *Zur Farbenlehre*; but upon moving from Jena shortly thereafter he gradually let his connections with Goethe's project lapse.[2] In the 1820s a few young physicists argued that the *Farbenlehre* had anticipated the principle of interference of the new wave theory of light, in that it attributed the colors that appear at the boundaries of colored images to an enhancing and canceling effect; and both during and after Goethe's lifetime a handful of physicians, attracted first by the physiological part, became proponents of the entire work.[3]

But most of Goethe's defenders were readers of science rather than practitioners; they were chiefly artists, literati, and philosophers, many of whom were more attracted by the beauty and ambition of *Zur Farbenlehre* than by its science, or by the spectacle of Goethe and the Newtonians trading insults (it was perhaps amusing to contemplate the foolishness of the scientists who, it seemed, had been hoodwinked for more than a century). It could not have been part of Goethe's project to further the split between amateurs and professionals that ultimately led to the dichotomy of the humanities and the sciences; but too many of his followers helped drive the two cultures further apart by polemicizing against natural science without understanding its practice.

It is easy to begin polemics; it is much harder to stop them, to decide that enough is enough. Goethe essentially refrained from polemicizing after 1810. He even told Eckermann that, if for reasons of space it was necessary to eliminate something, the polemical part of *Zur Farbenlehre* could be dropped – not because it had been wrong or unnecessary, but because it had served its historical purpose of loosening the stranglehold of the Newtonian theory of colors. The historical part on its own contained sufficient polemical material, and the real key to *Zur Farbenlehre* was in any case the didactic part. Moreover, said Goethe, "at bottom all polemical action is against my proper nature, and I take little pleasure in it" (Eck., 15 May 1831). Although it is hard to believe that Goethe did not at all enjoy being on the attack after twenty years of ridicule and neglect from the "guild of physicists," we probably do not need to question the basic sincerity of this disclaimer. Yet when we observe how the polemical part has ever since encouraged warfare between proponents and opponents, when we see how many of Goethe's votaries have shown more ability in lashing out at Newton than in doing service to knowledge, when we realize how much the polemicizing has obscured the central purposes of *Zur Farbenlehre*, we may doubt Goethe's wisdom not so much in writing a critique of Newton's *Opticks* – polemic in the high sense – as in giving reign to the passions and resentments that had festered in his spirit for two decades – polemic in the baser but unfortunately more common sense.

No matter how justified or true, polemics appeal to our lower natures and induce us to act against our better judgment. Like all warfare, polemics tend to be demoralizing, in that they lead us to act like our enemies. Perhaps Goethe's willingness to omit the polemical part from a reissued *Zur Farbenlehre* was tacit admission that there is something wrong with the polemical attitude when it gets out of hand – and there is little that gets out of hand so quickly. The polemical mode itself works against Goethe's fundamental insights into the character and history of the natural sciences and their proper methods. It encouraged in principle and, despite Goethe's caveats about experimental proof to the contrary, encouraged in fact the notion that Goethe expects us to adjudge a serious and sustained approach to the science of color (i.e., Newton's) as simply right or wrong, that the reader is faced with an exclusive alternative of two sets of propositions that claim to represent the truth. The problem is that Goethe had long since come to realize that truth resides less in propositions than in experience, less in statements about nature than in the adequacy of one's approach to it. The truth of science is to be judged fundamentally not by checking a single experiment, nor by measurements and margins of error – these are derivative – but by adherence to a way (method) that corresponds to and amplifies the encounter of human beings with nature.

Aperçus, language, and the problematics of truth

The color science of *Zur Farbenlehre* was far more complicated than anything Goethe had envisioned in 1790. The problem of science, as posed by the essay "Der Versuch als Vermittler," was to restrain the exuberant impulses of the imagination long enough to secure the phenomenal and experimental basis of science. As with all naive inductivism, there was a belief in the possibility of uncorrupted perception and of the accurate translation of this perception into propositions (although even at this early stage Goethe had doubts about the ease of this translation). In contrast to naive inductivism, however, Goethe never thought that discovery was simply a matter of painstaking induction from the particulars, and he always approached science from the perspective of the whole of nature.

The aperçu enabled Goethe to evade the quandaries of strict induction and to make the claim of being directed toward phenomenal wholes and ultimately the whole of nature. Scientific work proceeds from an interest focused by these aperçus, provisional glimpses of comprehensive truths – for example, Goethe's aperçu that a boundary is a necessary condition for the appearance of colors in cases of refraction. Yet it may be misleading to assert that interest precedes aperçus, for interest itself is the product of an aperçu that engages the human being in pursuit of the whole that an aperçu has manifested. If we look back at the introductory paragraphs of the *Beiträge zur Optik*, we see that Goethe's progression from the whole of phenomenal nature, to its aspect of color, to specific questions about the science of refractive colors is really a succession of aperçus – some more comprehensive, some more particularized; some no more than mentioned, others carefully examined.

The aperçu in itself is speculative and in need of development and confirmation. It anticipates the results of scientific labor, but is no shortcut, for it must be justified and deepened (i.e., concretized, analyzed, deconstructed, and reconstructed) by the effortful method of identifying and varying the conditions needed to bring about the phenomena to which the aperçu pertains. In this sense, the aperçu is the first phase of "the experience of a higher kind" (*HA*, 13: 18), which was the goal of the method of the *Beiträge*. In the course of this labor, which progressively arrays the phenomena into natural groupings, new aperçus arise. In general the aperçus will be formulated as hypotheses, but it is important to recognize that they are not in themselves the same thing as hypotheses. A hypothesis is a proposition; it can be formulated or conceived in a more or less mechanical way, quite apart from any experience, and can be adopted (or tested) by anyone who exhibits an operational understanding of the terms of the proposition. The aperçu, on the other hand, is an anticipatory experience. It is a seeing through a set of given phenomena to a higher or more elemental level of (putative) truth; it is therefore intrinsically transcendental – that is, a going beyond the previously given. Once this going-beyond has been effected, it is possible, indeed necessary, to concretize the experience in a formula. The method of the *Beiträge* was precisely to bring exactness and comprehensiveness to this task of expressing the results of scientific experience and going beyond its immediately given content.

In the period of the *Beiträge*, the aperçu was still relatively unproblematic. It was a more or less passive registration of the true state of affairs; there was a relatively sharp distinction between theory and phenomena, and a single, unambiguous truth was to be pursued through cooperative work that would systematically unfold the content of the aperçu. But insofar as the aperçu implied the activity of a consciousness particularized thus and so, it pointed ahead to the more sophisticated scientific pluralism based on *Vorstellungsarten*, a pluralism that did not deny the essential unity of science but did acknowledge that unity and the corresponding consensus among scientists as problematic. In this later understanding, each aperçu represents not only a synthesis of, or at least within, the phenomenal field but also an individualization of the standpoint from which the field is viewed. The standpoint is implicit in every apprehension and conception of the subject and is reflected in how we separate and collect the different experiments and phenomena into significant groupings. One therefore cannot presume any longer that two researchers will place the same emphasis on a given experiment or phenomenon, or that they will relate it in the first instance to the same things. The mechanist sees reflection and perhaps attributes it to the rebounding of perfectly elastic particles; the Goethean dynamist sees the same event and thinks that some yet-to-be-explained power must reside in the surface of bodies to affect the light with color. The question is no longer, as in the *Beiträge*, whether two individuals can agree on a short, concise sentence describing the phenomenon, but in what ways one can still legitimately claim to be able to talk about a single science.

Even within one *Vorstellungsart*, however, there is probably an inescapable multiplicity of ways of experiencing and expressing aperçus,
which would lead to an important consequence: Even if one infirms by
experience a particular formulation (or hypothesis), the infirming experience does not necessarily extend back to the initial aperçu that gave
rise to the formulation (e.g., the refutation of one geometrical hypothesis
about refraction does nothing to infirm geometrical hypotheses themselves). Some aperçus are foundational for a *Vorstellungsart*; they are
not so much sources of hypotheses as the cornerstone of a program of
investigation. This kind of aperçu is tantamount to the founding act of
a *Vorstellungsart* in a given science or even the emergence of a new
science itself (Goethe's basic aperçu in its intention of creating a science
of color that was not merely the outgrowth of another science is of this
latter type). The science-founding aperçu singles out and unifies a part
of nature as the first synthesis of the subject matter into a coherent
scientific object with an appropriate method of investigation. One may
even say that it is only with the occurrence of such a fundamental aperçu
that what can be called a phenomenon is fully constituted. Beforehand
one has more or less isolated appearances, scattered instances, relatively
incoherent data. Only the aperçu can effect the required preliminary
unification and, as it were, redaction from the whole of nature into a
phenomenon.

Here it is possible to see Goethe as a precursor, ca. 1800, of twentieth-
century developments in the philosophy of science. In his studies of the
perception of color and the history of color science, Goethe was con-
fronted with the question of the principles that unify the sciences and
their changes, much as studies on the multivalence of perception and the
lack of strict progressivity in the history of science led philosophers like
Hanson and Kuhn to ask about the commensurability of theories and
the rationality of scientific change. But a perfect analogy is forestalled
by Goethe's claim to have appeal to a basic instance that by and large
is not accessible to twentieth-century philosophers chiefly concerned with
sciences that have as their objects entities remote from direct experience.
Anyone who does not suffer from total color blindness is able to perceive
chromatic hues, and among those with normal vision there is, despite
individual variations, a remarkable similarity of color experience from
person to person. The sine qua non of color science is color, and although
chromatic science utilizes mathematical theories and complex instru-
mentation to articulate and analyze the appearances of color, it cannot
displace the appearances without becoming something other than chromatics (by replacing colors with degrees of refrangibility, for instance,
one turns chromatics into a branch of geometric optics). The common
experience of color and the basic aperçus shared by those with normal
vision provide the foundation and the fundamental articulation of the

science of color. The subsequent results and aperçus of scientifically disciplined experience may significantly modify and amplify the common experience, they may even force a rearticulation and reconception of the foundations, but they cannot abolish those foundations or simply prescind from the common experience.

The common experience of color does not imply identical experience – there can be sameness without strict equality in all respects. Scarlet and carmine are the same without being identical: We call both red, a convention more dependent on common physiology and psychology than on language. What makes the common experience scientifically exploitable is that researchers can set up experiments to imitate it and can thus analyze and control the circumstances and explore correlations. The more broadly they conceive the subject the more complex this task becomes, and even simple experiments can lead to differences in result and analysis. As long as the aim of research is to comprehend a significant natural object òr a set of natural phenomena, however, the long-range goal is to make one's analysis parallel, as far and as comprehensively as possible, to the course of nature. Researchers may well have (at least temporarily) greater success and sureness in treating one aspect of the subject than another, but the science as a science of nature cannot be judged merely by its most successful part, or by its most backward; it must be judged by its faithfulness to the totality of the relevant phenomena.

In this world of Goethean science, the chief criterion of truth is comprehensiveness, and the chief locus of truth is the conformity of scientific discourse and practice to the experience, both scientific and everyday, of nature. But neither this comprehensiveness nor this conformity is at all a straightforward matter for Goethe (unless we are talking about the period of the *Beiträge zur Optik*): Comprehensiveness must include not only the object in its manifold relationships but also the variety of human subjectivity, the many ways of experiencing the object; and the conformity is not, indeed cannot be, a mere one-to-one correspondence of statements and facts.

Goethe certainly does not aim at a science that is merely a deductive system. A deductive formulation, for one thing, turns the science in the direction of being treated as an essentially linguistic and logical formulation. For another, a deductive system bears a certain implicit reductionism, in that the truth of the conclusion is reducible to the truth of the premises, whereas Goethe's science is antireductionist. To be sure, Goethe believes that when nature acts, it acts in accordance with basic laws and elemental principles, but what happens is not a mere consequence of elements and laws. Elemental events and appearances in their lawfulness lay the groundwork for more complex phenomena; these in turn are the basis for the even more complex, but this progression is not necessarily an automatism. Goethe's disinclination to resort to the category of causation is thus not due to obscurantism but to a conviction that nature is essentially creative, that the event that arises from a given set of conditions, the phenomenon, is not simply the sum of its parts or the mere result of the operation of fixed and unchanging laws; a phenomenon is a novel entity, or rather a novel unity in the sense that it is not entirely precedented in what has come before it and what has gone into it. The urge to single-mindedly axiomatize and "causalize" events is tacitly to deny that the phenomenon itself is a genuine reality and that the unprecedented can occur. Moreover, the quest for causes, insofar as it suppresses the reality of the appearances for the sake of the reality of causes, starts science down a slippery slope along which reality can slide ever further away, from appearance to substructure to sub-substructure; and yet the fundamental reality always has to be justified by appealing to the appearances. Goethe would argue that the appearances are inalienably real, and that to deny this point is to foster hopeless confusion about reality. Indeed, if there is a most fundamental reality of all, it is phenomenality – that is, the appearing (being) of one thing to (for) another.

For Goethe the core of a science is its subject matter, comprehensively worked out from everyday experience and amplified by technical praxis. If scientists do not have a clear understanding of this core, then they really do not know what their science is about. Although science does not stop at this core, it begins there and also eventually returns. Even about this core there can and will be disagreement, in some sciences probably more than others (in particular those that have a narrow basis in direct experience). Yet it is still imperative that scientists cooperate at this basic level, which means that they need to work together, share conceptions and results, offer comment and criticism, and discuss fundamental issues and advance bold hypotheses. Not only will they learn from one another, but they will also find it easier to agree on what questions are foundational, what issues need explanation, and what kinds of explanations are acceptable. In so doing they will fulfill one of Goethe's chief hopes, that scientists will devote careful attention to the groundwork and purview of their science as a basis for more highly speculative work. If these conditions are met, the science can be understood as single and continuous, despite changes over time, because the constant reference to phenomenal foundations, even in cases of amendment, returns the science to its point of origin.

Although in certain areas more rapid theoretical and technical advances may be made by concentrating forces on a narrower set of questions and by allowing hypotheses to define the phenomena rather than conforming to them, the science thereby risks losing touch with its foundation. The more autonomous the science and its hypotheses become, the more ten-

uous are the relationships to the whole called nature and the less justification there is for calling the science natural, an understanding of nature.
As the science becomes one-sided, it becomes less true to the whole, less
true to nature. Goethe's science certainly does not scorn technical and
theoretical advances (indeed, one of his major criticisms of Newton's
theory was that it had brought virtually no technical innovations during
the entire eighteenth century, and in his own Farbenlehre he drew on
and tried to systematize the experience with color of the technical arts
and crafts in hopes of enriching both theory and practice), but it aims
at an equable progression of the whole. Science demands specialization,
but the specialists need to act responsibly and responsively toward the
core that holds the specialties together and makes ultimate sense of them.

By cooperating, human beings focus their attention on a common
object and learn from one another. This point is obvious, but it is easy
to underestimate the importance of the obvious and to think that it reveals
its full meaning to a momentary glance. One of humanity's most characteristic potentialities is learning, a potentiality on which all labor and
progress in the sciences is built. Each human being has the capacity to
incorporate information and thoughts that are not properly his own.
Although each person's way of thinking and understanding bears an
irreducibly individual aspect, each also possesses the capability of understanding not just one but many ideas, not just one but many *Vorstellungsarten*, not least because the *Vorstellungsart* of any individual is
conglomerate (there are no pure mechanists, atomists, dynamists), and
because one can conceive what one does not believe. The human being
is, potentially and actually, many-sided. In this many-sidedness, directed
toward a common object, in the breadth of the interests and the depth
of the formation of human beings, lies the counterweight to the centrif-
ugal effect of the *Vorstellungsarten*.

According to Goethe,[4] the history of science – but not only of science
– shows a a tendency toward the predominance of individual theories
and ideas. Because few human beings are sufficiently independent to resist
the pressures of the many, and because the ideas that have the broadest
appeal are usually the ones that are most readily conceivable (i.e., familiar
and accessible to an average understanding, although the average may
be higher or lower, depending on the character of the group), this historical tendency is perhaps unavoidable. But Goethe nevertheless contrasts with it an ideal ethics of science. This ethics recognizes that even
though our speaking, thinking, experiencing, and acting are diverse and
sometimes incommensurable with one another, we all live within the
truth as the basic fabric of our lives, and even if our ways in this truth
are sometimes errant we must realize that this very errancy reveals something, that along each path truth appears, though often under different

aspects. Experience, as the cumulative apperception of the world and ourselves, is the locus of truth. Because it is guided by aperçus, experience and its truth have an inevitably transcendental character; because they are lived, they are subject to the test of further experience. Moreover, experience is affected by what we hear from others and what we experience with them. Our experience is by its nature both private and public. It reflects ourselves, our neighbors, our world. Every expression of this complex of experience, however, is problematic; the expression is not identical to our own experience, it does not conform exactly to the experience of others, and it also unavoidably diverges from the object it aims to comprehend. This constellation of experience and expression is the ethos of science, and as ethos, it is the proper place for science's ethics.

The very problematic of the ethos of science gives rise to a politics for science that establishes the community where science is cultivated and preserved. This politics is tolerant but not feckless; it requires a vigorous, even exhausting confrontation of the variety of experience and expression. The object of this politics, however, is neither simply to cultivate the maximum of variety nor simply to assume that there exists a single expression of the truth, but rather to raise the science to a new and higher level (*Steigerung*), to enhance the depth and breadth of human experience, and not least to put us in surer touch with what we know by recalling us to the foundations of our science. Ultimately the chief criterion of the success or failure of this politics is the sense of wholeness and completeness that arises in the practitioners of science. That is, the political recurs to the ethical, and the ethical leads again to the political; in the way of the classical understanding of politics, the community cultivates virtue in its members (e.g., tolerance, a critical spirit, irony, many-sidedness) and is in turn made stronger by their virtue. In the classical polis, not just a single kind of activity was needed to sustain the life of the city; so too in the community of science, the life of science depends on many different kinds of people and activity. To prosper it needs the help of all who are interested in the way things are, and it must be constituted so that the intelligent, well-situated nonspecialist – perhaps even a layperson – may contribute observations, aperçus, and inventions. It is therefore important that the sciences not be so overprofessionalized that laypersons can only be passive recipients of popularized (not to say vulgarized) results, and crucial that the profession not be de facto identified by adherence to a particular hypothesis.

Every philosophy of science, at least implicitly, holds to some belief about science's place in human existence, and most see the proper pursuit of science as contributing to a higher, more mature, more desirable kind of existence. Science is thus considered as a vehicle of what in German is called *Bildung*, the formation of human beings in the fullest sense. It was no less Goethe's conviction that science is necessary for the perfection of *Bildung*, because the inner being is tested and formed by facing and accommodating the public world and the world of nature. Science cultivates human beings. It is, as it were, a metaphor for the achievement of a human and humane balance of powers accompanied by the recognition that not every particularity of the individual can or ought to be preserved, but that it is of the nature of the human being to be various within limits, and of the essence of nature to bring forth the unexpected against the background of the familiar. Insofar as Goethe was at odds with modern natural science ca. 1800, it was because it tended toward an imbalance of the mathematical over the physical/natural, of the complex over the simple, of the abstract over the practical and phenomenal, of the abstruse over the familiar, of the partial over the total.

One might add – of the present and future over the past. Science is not unique in often leaving behind past accomplishments as outdated and thus risklessly forgettable; but in the project of knowledge, forgetting is a risky and irrational business, and there are very few accomplishments, no matter how feeble from a modern perspective, that turn out to be completely false and useless. This important lesson Goethe himself learned from his attempt to overthrow Newton's theory. The passion for refutation not only aims at discarding something that may later be useful to science – modern histories of the sciences abound in cases where there is a strange, often partial, yet almost always unexpected return of the past – but it also cultivates a not always justified belief in the superiority of present over past and implicitly reaffirms the notion that science is based on proof, even if only in the mode of reductio ad absurdum.

The past is fecund with possibilities that have already, if but partially, been realized. The major problem involved in the strategy of just waiting for a brilliant new scientific solution to emerge is that one must rely almost totally on accident – that it occur to the right person, at the right time, in the right place (viz., among the right people). Of course, trying to provide research funds for every interesting nonstandard notion would be absurd. There is, however, an alternative to investing in the future, and that is investing in the past. The history of science and, more broadly, the history of interest in the subject matter of a science, is the archives of science, a trove of already-discovered approaches that at one time had something to be said in their favor and that might well reveal important present and future pathways. Indeed, even without considering these archives, the sciences are resonant with history. Goethe's analysis of Newton's theory showed how certain traditions and decisions, not all taken with full consciousness, had become embodied in the theory, woven into its fabric (e.g., the fusion of mathematical and physical conceptions of light and color, the identification of color with the ray, the abandonment of the notion of a primary image and the corollary reduction of the image in general to a ray indicator). In our own day we need only recall how the seemingly innocuous term "monochromatic light" (light of a single wavelength or frequency) is laden with the Newtonian way of conceiving color. Without a genuine understanding of the history of the science, not the least part of which is a careful rereading of the key documents and a reconstruction of how people obtained their evidence and what it looked like, we do not realize in what diverse ways we are bound to the past.

Of course, it is impossible for each individual to execute the whole of a science, and we should not be deluded by Goethe's almost single-handed composition of *Zur Farbenlehre* into thinking he wants us to follow this example. His solitary approach was motivated by frustration and resignation, and often enough in the various parts of the work we find Goethe's confessions of his personal inadequacy (see esp. the fifth section, "Nachbarliche Verhältnisse," *HA*, 13: 482–93). This predicament is why the community of scientific workers became so important a concept for Goethe, why despite the idiosyncrasy of *Zur Farbenlehre* the essence of his science is comprehensive cooperation, amplification (*Vermannigfaltigung*), and mutual enrichment. The historian of color science, the physiologist, the chemist, and the physicist should not arbitrarily encroach on one another's work; but by talking with one another, by informing one another of what they have found, suspected, and hoped, they can often assist one another better than if all worked in a single specialty, and can learn how to profit from one another's ways of conceiving things.

Goethe realized (see esp. *FL-D*, par. 751–57) that the question of *Vorstellungsarten*, the ways of conceiving and representing things, was intimately bound to the question of *Darstellung* (presentation); the question of presentation, in its turn, is a question of language and rhetoric. By now we have seen that rejecting Goethe's science as the imaginings of a poet is false; perhaps it is not fanciful to suggest that as poet Goethe recognized with unmatched clarity the role of language in science, its symbolic and inalienably metaphorical character. At the end of the section "Nachbarliche Verhältnisse" in the didactic part, Goethe said:

People never consider sufficiently that a language is really just symbolic, just figurative [*bildlich*], and that it never expresses objects immediately but only in reflection. This is especially the case when it is a question of things [*Wesen*] that only approach being [directly] experienceable and that can be called activities more than objects, things that in the realm of natural philosophy are constantly in motion. They do not let themselves be held fast, yet one must speak of them; thus one looks for all kinds of formulas in order at least to come at them by way of simile. (*FL-D*, par. 751)

It is not just between different individuals, then, but already within the consciousness of the single individual that the different ways of expressing what is and what is experienced become manifest. The individual who is alive to what he experiences becomes aware of a certain discrepancy, a certain incommensurability, between what he thinks and what is; the more alive this sense is, the more keenly present to him this central problem of science is.

We should remember, in reading these words and those that are about to follow, that they are written by a man whose poetic work is widely regarded as among the greatest achievements in any language, a man who could write within almost any genre and form with mastery, and who, especially in his late work, could seemingly change style at will. When such a sovereign of language gives witness to a fundamental incapacity of language, we should pay close attention. Language, he seems to say, cannot encompass the truth, except by indirection, "in reflection." It would be a corollary, then, that scientific truth cannot be intrinsically propositional or a simple correspondence between sentences and facts. Indeed, a sentence is not merely a sentence, it is an expression of a way of seeing things and a style of thinking, as well as the expression of a particular seeing.

Immediately following the paragraph just quoted Goethe goes on to consider, in passing, the advantages and disadvantages of several of these styles, in particular of metaphysical, mathematical, mechanical, corpuscular, and moral formulations, and concludes that

if we could nevertheless make conscious use of all these kinds of conception and expression [*der Vorstellung and des Ausdrucks*] and deliver our observations about natural phenomena in a manifold language, if we would keep ourselves free of one-sidedness and comprehend a living sense in a living expression, we would be able to communicate many refreshingly welcome things [*manches Erfreuliche*]. (FL-D, par. 753)

Two dangers we face, he reminds us, are putting symbols in place of things and applying alien terminologies to express our views of simple or elemental nature. The latter is to some degree unavoidable, he says, yet it risks covering up the elemental with the complex, of obscuring the universal with the particular. "Most desirable of all, however, would be to take the language through which one wants to denominate the particulars of a certain sphere from that sphere itself, to treat the simplest appearances as a basic formula and to derive and develop the more manifold ones from it" (FL-D, par. 755).

This simplest appearance treated as a basic formula is another name for the Urphenomenon, which is at once the transcendental unity of phenomenal experience, the center of gravity of the science, and the origin of the words and symbols that most naturally – though not necessarily perfectly – express and perhaps explain the appearances. Even though "through words we fully express neither the objects nor ourselves" (*LA* I, 3: 417), the attempt to grasp and express the Urphenomenon comes as close to bringing together experience, word, and object as is humanly and linguistically possible. The real core of science, therefore, cannot be method or language, not even mathematical language – of which Goethe wrote that its symbols have the potential to "become in the highest sense identical with appearances because onlookings [*Anschauungen*] likewise lie at their basis" (*LA* I, 3: 418) – but rather the experience and activity of the human being, or, to use a more Goethean expression, human spirit.

Not language in and for itself is right, fit, graceful, but rather the spirit that embodies itself in it; and thus it is not a question of whether a person wants to endow his calculation, speeches, or poems with the most desirable qualities; the question is whether nature has endowed him with the appropriate spiritual and moral qualities: the spiritual – the capacity for onlooking and penetrating vision [*An- und Durchschauung*]; the moral – that he be able to renounce the evil demons that might hinder him from giving the true its proper honor. (Goethe 1982, 313)

All these things seem to imply that science is an endless task, because of the nature of language, because of the variety of experience, because of the characters of individual human beings, because each new generation must be initiated anew into old experience while they discover truth for themselves. But despite its endlessness, science always aims at unity, and in some sense we must approach it as though it were completable. In a sense, it is; for although we can never finish the work of science, by holding fast to the ideal of comprehensiveness and striving to realize it we are already anticipating the presence of that ultimate goal and keeping faith with the human and scientific conviction that nature and the universe constitute an intelligible whole. This anticipation (aperçu) of the whole as we labor to understand the particulars is the beginning of science and, insofar as we cannot possess the whole except in anticipation, its end as well. In this way science resembles art, which aims at producing not parts but wholes that point toward ever more comprehensive wholes. It is appropriate in a manifold sense, then, to conclude with these words of the Goethe who was, among his many sides, simultaneously scientist and poet.

Just as art always presents itself as complete in every single artwork, so should science always show itself whole in every single thing it treats.

But to come close to meeting such a demand we must not exclude any of the human powers from scientific activity. The abysses of intuition [*Ahndung*], a sure view [*Anschauen*] of the present, mathematical depth, physical precision, sublimity of reason [*Vernunft*], sharpness of intellect [*Verstand*], agile, yearning fantasy, loving joy in the sensuous: Nothing can be foregone if there is to be a lively, fruitful seizing of the moment, through which alone a work of art, whatever its content may be, can arise.

Even if these required elements may seem to be, where not contradictory, yet nonetheless opposed to one another in such a way that even the most excellent spirits could not hope to unite them: They nevertheless still reside manifestly in the whole of humanity and can emerge at any moment, as long as they are not (through prejudices, through the wilfulness of the individuals who possess them, or through any of the other mistaking, terrifying, and exterminating negativities there may be) suppressed in the very moment when alone they can be effective, and the phenomenon [*Erscheinung*] annihilated in genesis. (*HA*, 14: 41–42)

Appendix

Two aspects of Goethe's Farbenlehre have historically produced great confusion – his contention that white light, pure and simple in itself, must be darkened if it is to produce colors; and his attempt to elucidate the phenomena of refractive colors (*FL-D*, par. 218–42) on the basis of his doctrine of the *trübes Mittel* (*FL-D*, par. 145–77). Goethe's teaching about white light is treated briefly at the end of Chapter 3; the present appendix is concerned chiefly with the doctrine of refractive colors.

What is a *trübes Mittel*? If we translate by cognates we would say "turbid medium." The problem with this, however, is that turbid has stronger connotations of dark and muddy than does *trüb,* which is rather more akin to cloudy or milky, perhaps even semitranslucent. A *trübes Mittel* is, in the first instance, a semitranslucent medium. Goethe introduces the term to describe the beginning of opacity in an otherwise transparent medium. We can imagine empty space without matter; this space would be perfectly transparent. As soon as we introduce matter, however – for example, by releasing into the space a small amount of colorless gas – we encounter the first degree of nontransparency; ever greater amounts of the gas would begin to produce a noticeable dimming of a light shining through it. Light that passes through transparent matter is, to a very slight degree, obstructed or obscured. It is in light's being obscured by its encounter with matter that the light becomes visible and displays color. Color thus can be described as an interaction of light and darkness (though not a mixture, for a mixture of light and darkness yields the achromatic grays), in that matter has a dimming, darkening effect on light. Progressive increases in the turbidity of the medium would not turn the medium dark, but white, because "perfect turbidity is whiteness" (*FL-D*, par. 147); the darkening is of the light that traverses the medium.

When colorless light is observed through a turbid medium, it appears slightly yellowish; the more turbid the medium is, the more the color tends toward yellowish red. On the other hand, if one looks through a turbid medium into a dark background while the medium is suffused with light, one sees blue. When the medium is dense and the suffuse light bright, the blue is relatively light or less saturated (i.e., whiter); when the medium is rare and the light dim, the blues are darker, tending toward indigo, perhaps even toward violet. (This last assertion, however, is not really well substantiated; for example, one does not see the sky as violet before sunrise, after sunset, or from mountaintops.) Some instances of these phenomena are colors in illuminated milkglass and the changing hues of sun and sky through the day. (The atmosphere is the turbid medium: The light of the sun, as it approaches the horizon, must pass through more of the atmosphere and so changes from yellow to orange and finally to orange-red; the darkness of space is perceived as bright blue when the sun is high in the sky and bright, darker blue as the light dims. Ernst von Brücke [1852], although he considered the Farbenlehre a "web of deception," was spurred by Goethe's emphasis on this phenomenon to give the first mathematically sophisticated account of it in terms of wave theory.)

At the conclusion of his discussion of the phenomena of turbidity, Goethe first mentions the concept of the Urphenomenon.

What we have just presented is such an Urphenomenon. We see on the one side light [*das Licht*], the bright [*das Helle*], on the other darkness [*die Finsternis*], the dark [*das Dunkle*]; we bring what is turbid between the two, and out of these opposites, with the help of this mediation, there develop, likewise in an opposition, colors, which, however, immediately point back again, through a reciprocal relation, to something in common. (*FL-D*, par. 175)

It was Goethe's hope that this Urphenomenon would be the unifying principle for all phenomena of color.

Goethe immediately tries to adapt this theory of turbidity to the colors of refraction. He emphasizes that the experiments with refraction deal primarily in images, not rays, and points out a number of phenomena in which double images appear (e.g., in reflections from glass and in the refraction of light by Iceland crystal, a polarizing substance) and argues by analogy that in ordinary cases of refraction a secondary or peripheral image (*Nebenbild*) is produced next to the principal image. He then explains that the peripheral image itself acts as a turbid medium. "Where the advancing border of the turbid peripheral image stretches itself over the light from out of the dark, there appears yellow; contrariwise, where the bright boundary goes out over the dark surrounding area, there appears blue" (*FL-D*, par. 239).

Even in full context this explanation is tentative and not perfectly clear. Years later Goethe admitted that it was not very good, especially in the case of objective experiments (when the refracted light is cast on a wall or other screen rather than received directly into the eye) (see the letter of 3 May 1827 to Chr. D. V. Buttel, *WA* IV, 42: 167). But although it is confusing, it is not prima facie absurd or self-contradictory, as some have claimed. For example, Wells (1968, 111–13) argues that the pe-

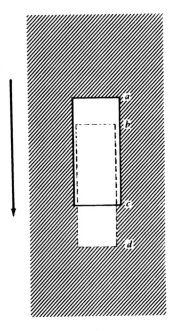

Figure A.1   A diagram depicting the emergence of the Nebenbild,
or peripheral image, in the course of refraction.

ripheral image (which he calls the accessory image) would act as a turbid
medium at only one edge of the spectrum. In Figure A.1 let the solid-
line rectangle represent the primary (white) image and the dotted-line
rectangle the peripheral image; the arrow shows the direction in which
the image is displaced by refraction. According to Wells, who follows
Schopenhauer on this point, the peripheral image slides over and ahead
of the primary image; thus between *c* and *d* one will get blues (the
darkness of the surroundings appears through a turbid peripheral image,
which is illuminated by suffuse light), between *c* and *b* red and yellow
(the white primary image shines through the turbid medium), and between *b* and *a* white (because there is no turbid medium intervening
between the white light and the eye). But white should be at the center,
so that the doctrine is self-refuting.

I believe, however, that Goethe conceived of it somewhat differently.
He emphasizes that he is not talking about a second image detached from
the first image (*FL-D*, par. 226, 230); we must think rather of an image
that is not genuinely separated from the first image, but rather a kind of
stretching out or extension. Moreover, we recall from the *Beiträge* that
the emergence of the full spectrum is a phenomenon that evolves from
two boundaries (discussed in Chapter 2 in the section on the experiments).

There are, as it were, two peripheral images, or perhaps we should say peripheral boundary images, or just blurred boundaries. The blurring is very turbid close to the primary image at *a*, so that the light shining through is reddened; toward *b* it is less turbid, so one sees yellow; between *b* and *c* there is white (the turbidity does not yet extend this far) until, in the evolving phenomenon (as one moves further away from the white rectangle that one is viewing through the prism in the subjective case or as one moves the screen further from the prism held next to the windowshut aperture in the objective case), the turbidity spreads all the way to *c*; at the opposite boundary, by *c*, the blurring is once again very turbid and very much suffused with light, so that it appears blue; toward *d* the turbidity decreases, as does also the suffuse illumination, so that violet appears. This explanation is more or less in accord with what appears in fact. One might note certain formal similarities between this explanation and Robert Hooke's account of the spread of a disturbance toward the center of the beam of light and outward into the darkness (see the discussion in Chapter 3 in the section on the *experimentum crucis* as a refutation).

Goethe thought his explanation was more satisfying in the case of subjective experiments, probably for two reasons. First, when one holds the prism with the refracting edge downward, the image appears displaced not only downward but also toward the observer; that is, objects near the bottom of the field of vision seem to move closer to the observer than those near the top. This finding seems to have suggested to Goethe that at the upper boundary the darkness is so to speak drawn over the original image, and at the other the light is drawn over the darkness. Second, it is fairly clear what "looking through" the turbid medium into darkness beyond means if one is looking through the prism, but in the objective case we are obviously in need of some projection of illumination onto the screen so that we may see blue and violet there. Is there also some accompanying projection of the darkness, which in the subjective case is seen through the turbidity? How can suffuse light be projected toward the screen? It is precisely in cases like this, requiring some understanding of the transmission of light, that Goethe's explanations are weakest.

In paragraph 173 of the didactic part, Goethe expressed the hope that future researchers would ultimately be able to extend the Urphenomenon of turbidity to all other phenomena, but the hope was stillborn. There is perhaps some similarity to Newton's failed hope that all the phenomena of reflection, refraction, diffraction, and so forth could be explained by a single theory made in analogy to other fairly well-understood phenomena like the behavior of light-corpuscle masses in force fields or in an aetherial medium that exhibits variations of density at optical interfaces (see Bechler 1973). This failure to provide an explicit unifying principle does not vitiate the more basic undertaking of the *Farbenlehre*, however; the need for a systematic and comprehensive presentation of the phenomena of color remains intact. Although Goethe's explanation is far from adequate, subsequent developments in the wave theory of light showed that there is an intimate connection between the colors produced in a turbid medium by scattering and the colors produced by refraction. Consider the following statements from a work that has long been a standard university textbook on optics.

The fact that the velocity of light in matter differs from that in vacuum is a consequence of scattering. The individual molecules scatter a certain part of the light falling on them, and the resulting scattered waves *interfere* with the primary wave, bringing about a change of phase which is equivalent to an alteration of the wave velocity. (Jenkins and White 1976, 471)

The scattering from liquids and solids [as opposed to gases, like the atmosphere] in directions other than forward is very weak indeed. The forward-scattered waves are strong and play an essential part in determining the velocity of light in the medium. (Ibid., 469)

The clue to the explanation of [refractive] dispersion lies in the secondary waves which are generated by the induced oscillations of the bound charges [of molecules]. These secondary waves are identical with those which give rise to molecular scattering, as in the explanation of the blue color of the sky. (Ibid., 492)

Goethe cannot take credit for this kind of discovery; it cannot be said that it was spurred by the *Farbenlehre*, and there can be no more than very limited merit in his vaguely anticipating a later unification of apparently disparate classes of phenomena. Yet given Goethe's efforts to understand refractive colors as due to a disturbance set up in the refractive medium; given his attempt to describe the fringes produced by an originally colored image as the result of an enhancement and interference; given his general approval of the wave-theoretical approach and some of his followers' claims (in the 1820s) that the new optics was confirming Goethe's insights (see Bratranek 1874, 110; Schmid 1940, 333–34, 339); and given, finally, the possibility in wave optics, as demonstrated by Gouy, of conceiving the original white light as an undifferentiated pulse out of which the various wavelengths are subsequently produced by the pulse's encounter with matter (in the form of diffraction gratings, thin films, prisms, etc.), we must grant at the very least that what we understand as the theoretical progress of optics and physical science is compatible with Goethe's project for chromatics, the physical (i.e., natural) science of color.

Notes

1 The most common English rendering of this word is "theory of color(s)," which I find problematic because it tends to obscure by parallelism the differences between Goethe and Newton on the nature of theory. Some alternatives are "science of color," "teaching about color," and "doctrine of color," all of which I sometimes use for the term Far-benlehre. The first choice is probably the best when the full scope of the Farbenlehre is considered, whereas the latter two would seem to refer more narrowly to what Goethe called the didactic part of *Zur Farbenlehre*. Given these problems and implications, for the most part I shall leave the term untranslated. Moreover, I shall use the unitalicized Farbenlehre to denote Goethe's science of color in general; *Farbenlehre*, on the other hand, will denote more specifically the multivolume work *Zur Farbenlehre* or, by extension, the specific project for a color science contained in that work.

CHAPTER I
Defining the questions of the Farbenlehre

1 Thomas Young described *Zur Farbenlehre* as "a striking example of the perversion of the human faculties" (Young 1814, 427). Few scientists, and virtually no physicists, have defended the overall scientific merits and character of the Farbenlehre (Jaki 1969 finds it astonishing that the physicists have conceded as much as they do). Goethe's chief supporters have been philosophers, artists, and physicians; in the scientific community there has been occasional support from researchers studying the physiology and psychology of color perception, especially since the later nineteenth century. The reader interested in surveying the abundant literature for and against Goethe should consult Braun 1883–85, vol. 3; Sepper 1981, pt. 1; Burwick 1986, 31–36. Bibliographies include Richter 1938 (annotated); Schmid 1940, 326–88; Pyritz 1965, 485–528; and the annual bibliographies of the *Goethe-Jahrbuch* since 1952.
2 I am referring to the appearance of a complete spectrum and, indirectly, to the relatively small number of hues that can be discriminated if narrow bands are separated from the rest of the spectrum. In both cases the number of colors is much smaller than most people would guess; in the latter, Raman gives empirical data and theoretical reasons for placing the number between 50 and 200 distinct hues under the very best circumstances (Raman 1968, ch. 8). The number of color metamers producible by isolating and then mixing any number of segments of the spectrum is not at issue here.
3 In the view of most recent philosophers of science, the "facts" cannot be established independently of theories: They are theory laden. Therefore it is not clear that there can be such a thing as a crucial experiment, a single experiment that forces one to accept or reject a theory. See Hanson 1958, Kuhn 1970, Feyerabend 1975, and Lakatos 1978. Goethe, as we shall see, had reached this conclusion by the late 1790s.

CHAPTER 2
The Farbenlehre in its origin

1 The epigrams were published in Friedrich Schiller's *Musenalmanach* for 1797. Goethe probably did not decide to discontinue the *Beiträge* before late 1793 at the earliest. The years 1794 through 1797 were transitional; then by late 1797 the project of *Zur Farbenlehre* began to take shape in correspondence with Schiller. The didactic part of *Zur Farbenlehre* was finished in 1805–1806; the following four years saw the composition of the polemical and the historical parts.

2 The writings mentioned here may be found in *LA* I, 8 and 11. In addition, notes and manuscripts on color not published in Goethe's lifetime are available in *LA* I, 3; II, 3; II, 4; and II, 6; and in the second division (scientific writings) of the Weimarer-Ausgabe (also called the Sophien-Ausgabe), in particular *WA* II, 4, and II, 5, pts. 1 and 2.

3 Although this term is not standard, I use it as a reminder of the intimate connection between *kind of ray* and *color* in Newton's theory, which is still an integral part of our thinking about color. It is not meant in any way to imply that the rays themselves are colored, a notion that Newton forestalled in the section of the *Opticks* titled "Definition" (*Opticks*, 124–25).

4 There were six editions of Erxleben's compendium from 1772 to 1794 and at least one edition thereafter. From the third edition on the work was edited by Georg Christoph Lichtenberg, who made additions and then, beginning with the fifth edition (1791), minor revisions. All editions through the sixth retain the same paragraphing, though not pagination. I cite by paragraph number according to the fourth edition (1787).

5 For example, the compendia of Gabler (published in 1778), Kratzenstein (1782), Titius (1782), Hobert (1789), and Bruchausen (1790); see *HA*, 14: 212–13, for a discussion. Goethe mentions Karsten (1781) and Klügel's German translation with commentary of Priestley (1776) as rare examples of caution *(HA,* 14: 212–213, 227). I highlight Gren 1788 and 1793 and Gehler 1787–96 in subsequent remarks both because of their relative eminence (Gren was editor of the *Journal der Physik,* and Gehler's dictionary was the most thorough German compendium in its day) and because they give greater detail and therefore can be held to higher standards of accuracy.

6 Gehler asserts that the "experiments prove without contradiction" Newton's theory of the diverse refrangibility of white light and the strict correspondence between refrangibility and color; he asserts that the propositions "rest not on any hypothesis about the nature of colors but directly on the experiments themselves," and that in these "propositions is nothing at all hypothetical, nothing which experience did not confirm" (Gehler 1787–96, 2: 136–37, 139–40). Gren (1793) calls Newton "the immortal inventor" (par. 574) and affirms in par. 586 that by means of experiments Newton "provided his immortal theory with that degree of evidence that is possible to achieve with objects of experience."

7 This use of "subjective" and "objective" is Goethe's, and appeared already in the *Beiträge*.

8 On Goethe's career as scientist, one of the best sources of information is D. Kuhn 1967, 16–63.

9 Boyle 1664 is an experimental history that attempted to give an overview of the phenomena of color; see *HA*, 13: 323, and 14: 122–23. The other forerunner Goethe acknowledged was Aristotle's successor as head of the Lyceum, Theophrastus; see *LA* I, 6: 16–35.

10 Of course Descartes and Galileo had enjoined a mathematical approach to experiments half a century earlier, but Descartes held no brief for induction and Galileo's method often involved a kind of explicitly analogical reasoning that is foreign to Newton's approach. The key difference is that Newton believed that experiments could be arranged so that the mathematical theory would, as it were, reveal itself. By joining mathematics to induction in this way, he superseded the skeptical fallibilism that had arisen from Baconianism and that set the tone for British science in the mid-seventeenth century: One might speculate tentatively, in full consciousness that the powers of the

human mind were too weak and uncertain to guarantee the truth of any of its beliefs and that a single future disconfirming instance would undermine any hypothesis (on the tradition of fallibilism, see especially Bechler 1974, Lakatos 1978, and Popkin 1979). Baconian fallibilism would be aided, of course, if there were some way to sketch out the full range of possible hypotheses without waiting for the completion of the natural and experimental history. Goethe's conception of *Vorstellungsarten*, introduced in the last section of Chapter 2, is a step in this direction.

11 The *os intermaxillare*, known in English as the intermaxillary or premaxillary, holds the upper incisors and is usually present in mammals even when the incisors are not. It characteristically has three sutures, one of which is never seen in human skulls. Goethe's "discovery" is problematic because, first of all, much of the evidence that Goethe advanced had already been noted by others (and another researcher, Vicq d'Azyr, has a claim to priority); also because the bone itself does not appear in most human beings (it is fused with neighboring bones). To dispute Goethe's title to discovery, however, is something of a red herring, for what mattered most of all to him was not that the thesis was original – aware as he was of the general state of research, though not of Vicq d'Azyr's work, he knew it was not – but that he could demonstrate the bone's presence by means of a new method, a way of seeing things genetically, of recognizing form in the process of mammalian development. For an account of Goethe's work on this subject, see Bräuning-Oktavio 1956.

12 The account given here will be interpretive as well as expository, and draws on both published installments of the *Beiträge*, part 1 (1791) and part 2 (1792); they can be found in *LA* I, 3: 6–53. The two *Beiträge* are numbered consecutively; part 1 contains paragraphs 1–88, part 2 paragraphs 89–122. The same class of phenomena is treated in the didactic part of *Zur Farbenlehre*, par. 195–302, much of which was simply taken over from the *Beiträge* with slight modification. I shall occasionally give at the end of a paragraph of my text an indication of the paragraphs of the *Beiträge* that I have been narrating, and shall use notes to point out major divergences between Goethe's account and my own.

13 This motivating paragraph is based on themes of paragraphs 14, 15, and 18 of the *Beiträge*.

14 It should go without saying that the reader ought to obtain a prism and perform these simple experiments. Only then will he or she be able to judge the truth of expressions like "essentially a single hue" or "for the most part quite distinct" and experience the difficulty of describing spectra. A few points here may be helpful as a guide, chiefly with respect to the solar spectrum. First of all, there is the problem of determining how to produce a "standard" spectrum: One needs to specify the kind and intensity of the light source, the size and shape of the aperture, the manner of viewing (through a spectroscope, cast upon the wall, etc.), the distance of the prism from the screen, and so forth. Then there is the problem that, especially with quite brilliant solar spectra, the colors and their boundaries are not absolutely fixable. Seen as a whole from some distance, the solar spectrum appears with fairly distinctly bounded areas of constant hue; closer up, if one gazes intently at some small part of it, there can appear a finer but elusive gradation of color that may vanish with a blink. Given the traditional representation of the spectrum as a continuum containing all possible hues from violet to red, however, it is astonishing how few can be seen in fact. This conventionalized spectrum is an idealization at best, at worst a falsification. Goethe's spectra and edge spectra, produced by viewing his black-and-white displays, are more determinate and less evanescent and thus simpler to describe than the solar spectra. One of the few researchers to describe these variations in the appearance of the spectrum depending on the conditions of illumination is the Nobel-prize-winning physicist Sir C. V. Raman (see Raman 1968, esp. 22–28). See also note 2 of Chapter 1.

15 Goethe in the *Beiträge* does not mention this orange. It is most evident at very bright levels of illumination, though even then it is elusive. However, Goethe classifies both orange and spectral red (which is an orangish rather than a pure red) as varieties of yellowish red. On the problems of naming and numbering colors, see Goethe's reflections at *LA* I, 3: 437–39.

16 Obviously there are some obscurities in the account of what happens with colored rectangles; not all of them are due to the compression of my account, in the last two paragraphs, of part 2 of the *Beiträge*. Some of these Goethe attempted to resolve with his color circle, first evidence of which dates from 1792 or 1793. The circle (Fig. 1.2b) is divided into six equal sections, with magenta (Goethe's name for this color varied over the years, from peach to purple and finally to red) at the top, then (moving clockwise) violet, blue, green (at the bottom), yellow, and yellowish or spectral red. One may get some idea of how Goethe systematically employed the circle from the fourth and sixth sections of the didactic part of *Zur Farbenlehre* and from Matthaei 1941, 175–200. The circle does begin to define more precisely what colors are opposites of one another, but still leaves many questions unanswered.

17 A brief introduction to the chemical revolution can be found in most histories of modern science; more detail and documents are available in Conant 1964. Gren's revision and extension of the phlogistic system can be found in Gren 1793. On Goethe's lifelong interest in chemistry, including his relationship with Göttling, see D. Kuhn 1972. I have not been able to ascertain whether Goethe had actually read Lavoisier's *Traité élémentaire de chimie* (1789) before writing part 1 of the *Beiträge*, but there are unmistakable affinities between Lavoisier's conception of the proper way of presenting a science and Goethe's; see Lavoisier 1952, 1–2.

18 We shall not discuss "the more general things" about color presented in par. 22–32: light and darkness (and their interaction); the difference between chromatic hues and black, white, and grays; the relationship between the "absolute colors" of the spectrum and the colors of bodies and pigments; and the two colors that appear purest, *yellow* and *blue*, their mixture, *green*, and the color that is never completely pure because it inclines now more to yellow, now more to blue, *red*. At least some of these begin to verge on the problematic, especially his assertions about yellow, blue, and red; and they suggest that one cannot begin genuinely without presuppositions. In his advertisement of the *Beiträge* Goethe said that to a certain extent he would have to unite the experiments through theory and hypothesis (*LA* I, 3: 4); perhaps these paragraphs yield to this necessity. But he also asserted that if he were writing just for experts he would not have to introduce theories and hypotheses of any kind. As his understanding of scientific method deepened, however, this concession to necessity would turn out to be unavoidable even for the expert audience. "Das Allgemeinere" may thus be seen as the kernel of a *Vorstellungsart*.

19 Thus the Urphenomenon is phenomenal, but not a phenomenon in isolation, and it bears an undeniably conceptual aspect. Goethe's prism experiment with the four black-and-white rectangles in a checkerboard pattern (Fig. 2.11), for example, shows us the two possible edge spectra side by side, but it is not Urphenomenal until we recognize it as the culmination of our work, a phenomenon through which we can recognize the rest of the phenomena that have been studied as simultaneously intelligible and therefore articulable. See also the section on Urphenomenality in Chapter 5.

    In the historical part of *Zur Farbenlehre*, Goethe briefly discussed Galileo's law of falling bodies as an example of Urphenomenlity. "If natural science appeared to be forever fragmented by the dispersive method of Verulam, it was immediately brought to a focus again by Galileo; he led the doctrine of nature back again into the human being and showed already in his early youth that for the genius a single instance stands for a thousand, in that he developed for himself from swinging churchlamps the doctrine of the pendulum and falling bodies. Everything in science depends on what is called an aperçu, on an apperception of what actually lies at the foundation of the appearances. And such an apperception is fruitful ad infinitum" (*HA*, 14: 98). This example shows that the Urphenomenon is not intrinsically amathematical – Galileo's doctrine was mathematically formulated – when the mathematization summarizes and synthesizes experience without violating it. A mathematical formulation of the law of course expresses an ideal case, but Galileo's argument (which combined actual experiments with thought experiments) made explicit how certain conditions needed to be idealized so that the formula might be understood as holding strictly, something that Newton did not do for his theory of white light and colors.

20 Interestingly, Descartes's method of equivalently representing through geometry and

algebra the proportionality of the aspects or "dimensions" of things is based on a similar notion of the relativity of measure; see especially rules 13–18 in *Rules for the direction of the mind*.

21 Because the context of this study of Goethe's Farbenlehre is its relation to physical science, I refrain from more than mentioning the service Goethe did color science by systematically organizing in *Zur Farbenlehre*, and thereby rescuing from obscurity, the phenomena he called the physiological colors. Notably, the physiological part of *Zur Farbenlehre* inspired the early work of Johannes Müller and Jan Purkinje.

22 It may be helpful to reflect that one does not experience the blackest black by excluding all light; what one sees under such conditions is *Eigengrau*, brain gray. The darkest blacks require contrast; thus, a black rectangle looks blackest on a white ground. Moreover, Land (1977, 109–16) has produced experiments in which the light reflected from a black rectangle in the field of vision is greater than the light reflected simultaneously from a white rectangle in the same field, yet the former still appears black, the latter white. It is perhaps relevant that, in the wave theory of light, darkness is not evidence that there is no radiation present. Two waves arriving at a point may result in darkness owing to interference; and the wave theory explains geometric shadows not as the absence of wave activity but as space where interference produces a null effect.

23 This holds true as well for green spectral light when it is produced according to the specifications of Newton's *experimentum crucis*. Compare the discussion in Chapter 4 of Desaguliers's "proof" that it is possible to eliminate these fringes.

24 This requires a more thorough investigation of color space and its dimensions (e.g. hue, saturation, and brightness). In the eighteenth century, the mathematician and physicist Johann Heinrich Lambert developed a third dimension in his color pyramid; in the early nineteenth century, the painter Philipp Otto Runge introduced a color sphere.

25 The uselessness of Newton's theory for technicians and artists is one of the leitmotifs of the historical part of *Zur Farbenlehre*. The reader may wonder whether John Dollond's invention of an achromatic telescope does not, in its way, give evidence of the fruitfulness of Newton's theory. Although the invention proved that such a telescope was not an impossibility, contrary to Newton's claims in the *Opticks*, Dollond did employ differential indexes of refraction to help in his calculations. Goethe nevertheless believed that Dollond's invention should have been the death blow to Newton's theory, but instead it was accommodated to the theory by means of a new concept, *dispersive power*, which was not entirely consistent with Newton's original conception. Strictly speaking, Goethe was probably right: The idea that the medium, the refracting material, makes an important difference in the dispersion of the rays is contrary to Newton's understanding of what he had proved, that the refraction of each of the color rays stands in some constant relationship to the degree of refraction of the least refrangible red ray, regardless of the medium, and that the cause of the dispersion is located at the interface of air and the medium, not within the medium itself. None of Newton's work indicates he believed that the matter of the prism had anything to do with the degree of separation of the colors; instead he looked to extrinsic factors like gradients in the aether density at the interface. Goethe, on the other hand, thought that the effect of a medium on light could reveal chemical and other properties of the medium itself (see, for instance, *FL-D*, par. 491–93, 505–506, 516, and passim). It could be argued, then, that in this respect Goethe anticipated future developments better than Newton.

26 This should also help make clear that Goethe's science was not purely phenomenal: One could search for efficient causes and what is not accessible to the senses as long as one had first secured the comprehensive phenomenal base. One should compare his attribution of the development of the plant to a progressive refinement of sap in the *Metamorphosis of Plants* (*HA*, 13: 120–23).

27 Of course Goethe was not the first to notice these colors, or the first to try to collect and systematize them; but he was among the first to argue that they reveal more fundamentally than physical colors the nature of chromatic experience and are a more basic and inalienable condition of color perception. Cf. note 21.

28 Correlative with the notion of polarity is *Steigerung* (see *HA*, 13: 48), which may be

translated as "intensification," "enhancement," "heightening" (the German stem *steig* implies a climbing or ascent). It is a crucial concept in *Zur Farbenlehre* but does not appear in the early work on color. One can argue, however, that it is implicit even there. The notion is easier to illustrate than to define. Yellow and blue pigments can be mixed to yield green (this holds true even of colored light for many frequencies of yellow and blue, although the resulting green is typically very pale); this is a simple (atomistic or mechanical) mixture. But one can also intensify the yellow and blue by increasing the density of pigments (or, in colored solutions, by adding more of the coloring agent); the result is a darkening of the color that is typically also a gravitation of the hue toward magenta (i.e., yellow begins to appear orange, orange appears reddish orange, reddish orange appears purplish; among the cool colors there is a similar movement along Goethe's color circle toward the magenta). In the solar spectrum itself, the red and the violet ends can both take on a purplish cast; when they are combined, they of course produce magenta. This mutual tendency and resemblance of spectral red and violet to a common color (that is produced in full eminence by their mixture) is an example of Goethe's *Steigerung*. The mixture of red and violet is not atomistic or mechanical, argues Goethe, but rather dynamic, *gesteigert*; the components in themselves already point toward a fundamental unity that is, as it were, a fulfillment of the promise of both (in contrast to the mixture of blue and yellow, which as psychological primary colors seem to have no hue in common, no intrinsic commonality before being mixed to arrive at the psychologically quite different green).

In other contexts *Steigerung* implies an ascent to a new, higher level of being. One can carefully combine hydrogen and oxygen gas in a chamber to get a mechanical mixture; but if one adds heat, there results a fusion of the two in the compound water. In this sense *Steigerung* is fundamental to Goethe's understanding of phenomenality, in that under the right *n* conditions there may emerge something that does not occur given just 1, 2, 3, up to *n*-1 of those conditions; the phenomenon is something new that arises only when all the necessary conditions are present.

29 Groth 1972 identifies a whole constellation of polar positions that underlie the *Vorstellungsarten*. We should realize, however, that Goethe, reluctant as he was to impose a rigorous system on what has the subtler, dynamic logic of the living, did not ever claim to have produced an exhaustive listing of all possible ways of conceiving things.

30 For instance, Gögelein 1972 sees the *Vorstellungsarten* solely from the later perspective of *Zur Farbenlehre*.

CHAPTER 3
The problematics of Newton's theory of white light colors

1 Between 1 January (New Year's Day on the Continent) and 25 March (English New Year's), the English year designation was one year behind the Continental. In addition, the English old-style (Julian) calendar was ten days behind the Continental Gregorian calendar; thus 6 February 1671/72 indicates 6 February 1671 in England and 16 February 1672 on the Continent.

2 It is almost a commonplace among historians of science that eighteenth-century optics, not to speak of color theory, was strangely quiescent (note the title of Pav 1964: "Eighteenth-century optics: The age of unenlightenment"), and that as far as experimental data and mathematical techniques were concerned the wave revolution in optics might have occurred decades earlier than it did. See T. Kuhn 1978; Mason 1962, 468; Pav 1964. For a somewhat different view, see Steffens 1977.

3 The chief sources are Bechler 1974; Blay 1983; Gruner 1973; Guerlac 1983; Hall 1948 and 1960; Hendry 1980; T. Kuhn 1978; Laymon 1978; Lohne 1961, 1963, and 1968; Mamiani 1976; Marek 1969; Sabra 1967; Shapiro 1975 and 1980; Westfall 1962, 1963, 1966, and 1980; and especially Feyerabend 1970 and Goethe's historical part to *Zur Farbenlehre*.

4 Especially relevant are Sabra 1967, 231–342; Lohne 1968; Gruner 1973; Laymon 1978; and Blay 1983. Guerlac 1983 casts doubt even on whether the events described

in the letter occurred in 1666, as Newton says in the opening sentence; Guerlac suggests 1668 or 1669 as more likely.

5 Many excellent studies concern different aspects of the Letter and the controversy it touched off; the present work is an attempt to unify the phenomenological, methodological, rhetorical, and logical approaches. The scholar who pioneered raising questions about Newton's portrayal of phenomena is of course Johannes Lohne (e.g., in Lohne 1968). Perhaps most thorough in treating the argument in its entirety is Mamiani 1976; but although he clearly recognizes the refutatory intent of many of the experiments, he does not seem to realize that the refutations are almost all failures and thus that the cogency of the theory and method is undermined. Sabra 1967 gives an excellent, detailed account of the issues that divided Newton and his earliest opponents. Shapiro 1975 also considers disputed points and some of the phenomenological issues that bear on cogency. Laymon 1978 analyzes the early disputes from the perspective of how the idealization of phenomena functions in, and how it affects, the course of scientific proof and refutation. Bechler 1974 gives an acute study of the different standards of argumentation to which the disputants held. Gravander 1975 attends to Newton's argument in minute detail but accepts Newton's claims to proof at face value. Closest in spirit to Goethe's understanding of Newton's strategies is Feyerabend 1970, who is almost alone among modern philosophers and historians of science in appreciating the basic correctness of Goethe's critique. Gruner 1974, in view of Goethe's polemics, believes that the questions need reopening and re-poses them (though without providing answers).

6 The analysis I am about to present will follow along the lines set out by Goethe (especially in WA II, 4: 441–65), but at times will supplement his argument or even diverge from it for the sake of maintaining continuity or clarity or in order to take into account light others have subsequently shed on the Letter. I shall indicate by means of parenthetical remarks and footnotes major divergences; afterwards I shall reconsider the overall strategy of Goethe's critiques of Newton's theory and discuss certain details that will not have been included in my analysis of the Letter.

7 On the theory of light and colors before Newton one might consult Boyer 1959; Sabra 1967 (esp. 46–68 and 185–230); Westfall 1962; Marek 1969; Lohne 1963; Shapiro 1973; Guerlac 1986; also Blay 1983 and Goethe's history in Zur Farbenlehre.

8 This scheme is still apparent in the structure of the first book of the Opticks. In part 1, only proposition 1 includes in its statement a mention of colors; the other eight propositions avoid it (and part 1 is devoted chiefly to differential refrangibility and considers geometrical properties of the images produced). In part 2, all eleven propositions are concerned with colors.

9 Besides Newton's works cited so far there is an autograph manuscript of Newton's Cambridge lectures on optics in the Cambridge University Library, identified as ULC.Add.4002, which is an early version of the revised and augmented copy deposited in the Library that served as the basis for the 1729 Lectiones opticae (the first half of which was translated the year before as the Optical Lectures); this autograph has been published in facsimile as Newton 1973. In this first version Newton does a much more successful job of keeping the issues of color and refraction separate. The third lecture begins the treatment of color, while in the first two, which treat of differential refrangibility, there is, unlike in the Lectiones, hardly a mention of color once Newton announces his intention to treat the subjects separately (Newton 1973, 3). Unlike the Letter, it contains a long geometrical demonstration of what should happen to sunlight refracted at the position of minimum deviation according to the received law of sines. What is interesting for our purposes is that the first two chapters of Newton 1973 do not claim it is possible to prove differential refrangibility by geometry alone. In this earliest version of the Lectiones the reason for his not making the claim is fairly clear: It is only once colors are introduced that he secures the necessary criterion for discriminating between rays.

10 Recall that Gren, without giving most of the pertinent conditions and without even mentioning that he was following Newton, said that this would be the proportion obtained (Gren 1793, par. 575). Newton of course knew better; see, e.g., Opticks, 65.

In considering this and the next experiment, we are elaborating on Goethe's basic points.

11 Goethe seconded Newton's rejection of chance irregularities as the cause of refractive colors, although he criticized him for not finding out the true lawfulness governing the phenomena (*HA*, 14: 149–50; *WA* II, 4: 446); but he did not consider the textual background to this experiment that we have just been exploring.

12 Goethe frequently complained that Newton used "image," "light," and "ray" interchangeably, and that the confusion of the terminology confused the issue as well. See, e.g., *FL-P*, par. 29, 203, 208.

13 This obviously accords with the intention to distinguish primary from secondary qualities. It would be hasty to conclude, however, that Newton was therefore simply carrying out in his optics the projects of Galileo and Descartes, for Newton seems to have been trying to raise color to the status of mathematical property of light, that is, to the status of primary quality.

14 Goethe did not accept Newton's claim to have kept geometry and color separate. In *WA* II, 4: 441–65, he offered an amplifying experiment to the *experimentum crucis*. Using different colored filters in the windowshut aperture and just one prism, he obtains the same results as Newton – a much less elongated image chiefly of a single color but with differently colored fringes – and explains it according to his theory of edge-color enhancement and canceling as in the *Beiträge* (see the section on the experiments in Chapter 2) and in *FL-D*, par. 258–84. Within this *Vorstellungsart*, the result depends fundamentally on the color of the image or light; therefore the explanation of the *experimentum crucis* cannot prescind from color.

15 Minor, but not insignificant. For example, where in the *Beiträge* he had used color names or *Fläche* (surface), he often substituted *Bild* (image, a term that had no systematic or causal importance in the *Beiträge*); and in *Zur Farbenlehre* he made *Verrückung* (displacement) of the image by refraction one of the fundamental conditions for the appearance of color (of course, this harmonizes with his notion of the image as the active, causal factor).

16 Often a secondary bow, with colors in the opposite order, appears, outside the primary bow. The sky between them is noticeably darker than the parts of the sky inside the first and outside the second.

17 An example of an error (or obfuscation) bordering on self-deception (or dishonesty) is table 14 of *Zur Farbenlehre* (which should be read in conjunction with *FL-P*, par. 373–401, esp. 382): His figure shows colors appearing before there is any genuine bounding of the light. For the translation of the *Opticks*, Goethe chiefly used the fourth English edition (*FL-P*, par. 11); the errors he makes usually reveal either haste or uncertainties about syntax. In general the translation is very good, however.

18 In Newton, the degree of refraction and color dispersion is not correlated with the kind of material itself but the relative density of the material or the density gradient of the postulated aether at the boundaries of the material; see Bechler 1973.

19 He also excludes an explicit treatment of the eye (*HA*, 13: 323); or rather, he assumes both as *anerkannt* (recognized or acknowledged). The logic seems to be this: *Zur Farbenlehre* is about color; as such it necessarily incorporates phenomena relevant to the study of light and of the eye. But because color is the focus here, light and the eye must be treated as primary in different studies. That they are relevant and must eventually be incorporated to complete the study of color seems clear.

20 The opponent theories arose out of dissatisfaction with the failure of component theories to describe adequately our experience of color. They take as primary not only red, green, and blue (which are usually given as the elementary hues of component theory, though the choice of primaries is relatively arbitrary) but also yellow, white, and black, which represent unique psychological experiences (i.e., pure red is devoid of all traces of yellow, blue, and green, etc.) and can be organized into three sets of complementary or polar pairs that represent perceptual systems (red-green, blue-yellow, and black-white). The opponent theories allow a much simpler explanation of what Goethe called physiological colors than do the component theories. Ewald Hering is usually acknowledged as the founder of opponent theories; and, though Hering himself

only mentioned Goethe in passing, his followers pointed out the affinities between Goethe and their master (see Jablonski 1930). Wasserman 1978 gives excellent brief accounts of component, opponent, and zone theories. (For one schooled in Goethe's *Vorstellungsarten*, Wasserman, who holds no brief for Goethe except as a late representative of pre-Newtonian views, provides abundant evidence of how the predominance of one *Vorstellungsart* over all others can be detrimental to the progress of a science and, on the other hand, of how the fusion or cooperation of them can reanimate a science.)

CHAPTER 4
Factuality, certainty, and the organization of science

1 We should also not forget the importance of Newton's religiosity in his attitude toward natural philosophy. He believed that the great prophets had understood the mathematics and physics of the cosmos but had veiled their knowledge in symbolical and allegorical writings. Although the age of prophecy had come to an end, the age for discovering fundamental truths about God's creation through natural philosophy was opening; through the labor of discovery one might understand the cosmos as the prophets had, and so natural philosophy, in a sense, brought about a new age of revelation. The quest for this natural-philosophical truth received its greatest impetus from the piety of the quester. Natural philosophers strove for the perfection of reason and virtue so that they might live in the knowledge and harmony of the divine ordination and will. Newton even tried to coordinate the laws of nature with history: In his writings on the chronology of ancient events and prophecies, he attempted to interpret sacred history in light of his scientific knowledge. His passion for mathematics may also have had a religious significance. The surest knowledge was mathematical, and the surest knowledge about nature was the understanding of its mathematical principles, which understanding underlies the writings of the prophets. Through the phenomena of the prism, Newton had seen the glimmer of an unvarying mathematical law governing the light God had created, and he penetrated beyond the merely visible into a realm that had been known only to the prophets. To be wrong in natural philosophy, then, was to be fundamentally deceived about God and his universe. Anyone who accused Newton of error would thus indirectly be impugning his spirituality. See Manuel 1968 and 1974. Further evidence of the close link between Newton's faith and his theory of white light and colors may be sought in Query 28 of the *Opticks*, in which Newton begins by rejecting all impulse theories, the predecessors of the wave theory, as presupposing the repudiated modificationist theory of colors, and in which, after pointing up other impossibilities in these hypotheses, he ends by showing how natural philosophy leads us closer to the First Cause and creator of the universe.
2 See the entry under "fact" in the *Oxford English Dictionary*, especially definition 4, where the examples of usage reveal the eighteenth-century shift in meaning.
3 See Lessing 1838–40, 11: 645. Margarita Bowen agrees in attributing this changed notion of fact, in which "the individual observation of some occurrence is itself free of inference and therefore beyond doubt" (Bowen 1981, 176), to the period of the Enlightenment. She further claims that in Hume it represents a last remnant of the dogmatism he otherwise hoped to undermine.
4 The difficulty inherent in the modern notion of fact and its fusion of the subjective and objective aspects is no accident; it is in essence *the* question of modern epistemology and metaphysics. Though with different presuppositions, its ancestry goes back at least to the assertion of Parmenides that knowing and being are the same. It is curious, in light of the original meaning of the word, that many Anglo-American philosophers insist that fact designates not an existent reality but a proposition.
5 Burwick (1986) claims that Goethe was not favorably inclined to the new theory. Goethe certainly had reservations about the theory, for although it conceived the phenomena more dynamically than the corpuscular theory it still suffered from the same shortcoming of tending to materialize light (interestingly, in view of subsequent nineteenth-century

developments, Goethe found the hypothesis of a material aether most suspect in the wave theory). But there is little doubt that he considered it an advance over Newtonian corpuscularism, and that he thought its introduction was giving new life to optics.

6 Goethe's early work on color (before 1800) antedates that of most of the older generation of electromagnetists who are the subject of Caneva's study, and he was either a personal or a scientific acquaintance of many of them.

7 The historical part mentions only a few men whose work appeared after 1790. Herschel is one of them (*HA*, 14: 228; cf. 13: 535, where Goethe expressly renounces the task of explaining what had happened in the science of color "in the last decades"). Although we might also wish that he had included such figures as Thomas Young and William Wollaston, and the physical researches in France that led to the modern wave theory of light, this material would have moved the history ever further from its proper subject, the realm of chromatics.

CHAPTER 5
Goethe and the ethos of science

1 The phrase "Man schlägt ganze Zahlen in die Brüche" in this quotation contains an untranslatable pun. *Brüche,* which I have rendered as "breaches," also means "fractions." Thus one could read it alternatively as "one casts numbers and numbers of things into breaches" or "one changes whole numbers into fractions" (fudging the figures?).

2 Especially in the cases of Müller, Purkinje, and Seebeck, it is probable that their peers' rejection of Goethe's *Farbenlehre* made it prudent for them to fall silent; cf. Jungnickel and McCormmach 1986, 18. The question deserves further study.

3 It is interesting as well that even though he disagreed with many of Goethe's general statements and principles, H. W. Brandes, in his article "Farbe" in the revised and greatly expanded second edition of Gehler (Gehler 1825–45), organized the subject matter according to the categories of the didactic part of *Zur Farbenlehre* and had special praise for the physiological section.

4 My text for what follows is, in part, the section "Aus Makariens Archiv" from the novel *Wilhelm Meisters Wanderjahre* (Goethe 1982, 465–92, esp. 478). The afterword in Goethe 1982, by Adolf Muschg, is well worth reading for its own sake as well as in amplification of the present work.

References

Bacon, Francis. 1960. *The new organon and related writings*. Ed. F. H. Anderson. New York: Liberal Arts Press.

Bechler, Zev. 1973. Newton's search for a mechanistic model of colour dispersion: A suggested interpretation. *Archive for History of Exact Sciences* 11: 1–37.

———. 1974. Newton's 1672 optical controversies: A study in the grammar of scientific dissent. In *The interaction between science and philosophy*. Ed. Y. Elkana. Atlantic Highlands, N.J.: Humanities Press, pp. 115–42.

Blasius, Jürgen. 1979. Zur Wissenschaftstheorie Goethes. *Zeitschrift für philosophische Forschung* 33: 371–88.

Blay, Michel. 1983. *La conceptualisation newtonienne des phénomènes de la couleur*. L'Histoire des sciences: textes et études. Paris: Librairie philosophique J. Vrin.

Bowen, Margarita. 1981. *Empiricism and geographical thought: From Francis Bacon to Alexander von Humboldt*. Cambridge Geographical Studies, no. 15. Cambridge: Cambridge University Press.

Boyer, Carl B. 1959. *The rainbow: From myth to mathematics*. New York: Thomas Yoseloff.

Boyle, Robert. 1664. *Experiments and considerations touching colours. First occasionally written, among some other essays to a friend; and now suffer'd to come abroad as the beginning of an experimental history of colours*. London: H. Herringman.

Bräuning-Oktavio, Hermann. 1956. *Vom Zwischenkieferknochen zur Idee des Typus*. Nova Acta Leopoldina, n.s. 18, no. 126.

Bratranek, F. Th. 1874. *Neue Mittheilungen aus Johann Wolfgang von Goethe's handschriftlichem Nachlasse*. Vol. 1, *Goethe's naturwissenschaftliche Correspondenz I*. Leipzig: Brockhaus.

Braun, Julius W. 1883–85. *Goethe im Urteile seiner Zeitgenossen*. 3 vols. Berlin: Luckhardt.

Brücke, Ernst von. 1852. Ueber die Farben, welche trübe Medien im auffallenden und durchfallenden Lichte zeigen. *Sitzungsberichte der kaiserlichen Akademie der Wissenschaften. Mathematisch-naturwissenschaftliche Classe* 9: 530–49.

Burwick, Frederick. 1986. *The damnation of Newton: Goethe's color theory and Romantic perception*. Quellen und Forschungen zur Sprach- und Kulturgeschichte der germanischen Völker, n.s. 86 (210). Berlin and New York: de Gruyter.

Caneva, Kenneth L. 1975. Conceptual and generational change in German physics: The case of electricity, 1800–1846. Ph.D diss., Princeton University.

Cohen, I. Bernard. 1956. *Franklin and Newton: An inquiry into speculative*

Newtonian experimental science and Franklin's work in electricity as an example thereof. Memoirs of the American Philosophical Society, vol. 43. Philadelphia: American Philosophical Society.

Comte, Auguste. [1830] 1968. *Oeuvres d'Auguste Comte.* Vol. 1, *Cours de philosophie positive, premier volume: Les préliminaires généraux et la philosophie mathématique.* Paris: Editions anthropos.

Conant, James B., ed. 1964. *The overthrow of the phlogiston theory: The chemical revolution of 1775–1789.* Harvard Case Histories in Experimental Science, no. 2. Cambridge, Mass.: Harvard University Press.

Desaguliers, J. T. 1717. An account of some experiments of light and colors, formerly made by Sir Isaac Newton, and mention'd in his Opticks, lately repeated before the Royal Society by J. T. Desaguliers, F.R.S. *Philosophical Transactions of the Royal Society of London* 29: 433–47.

Dove, Heinrich Wilhelm. 1853. *Darstellung der Farbenlehre und optische Studien.* Berlin: Müller.

Eckermann, Johann Peter. 1949. *Gespräche mit Goethe in den letzten Jahren seines Lebens.* Ed. H. H. Houben. Wiesbaden: Brockhaus.

Engelhardt, Dietrich von. 1972. Grundzüge der wissenschaftlichen Naturforschung um 1800 und Hegels spekulative Naturerkenntnis. *Philosophia Naturalis* 13: 290–315.

1979. *Historisches Bewusstsein in der Naturwissenschaft, von der Aufklärung bis zum Positivismus.* Orbis Academicus: Problemgeschichten der Wissenschaft in Dokumenten und Darstellungen, no. 4. Freiburg (Breisgau) and Munich: K. Alber.

Erxleben, Johann Christian Polykarp. 1787. *Anfangsgründe der Naturlehre.* 4th ed. Ed. G. C. Lichtenberg. Göttingen: J. C. Dietrich.

Evans, Ralph M. 1974. *The perception of color.* New York: John Wiley & Sons.

Fairley, Barker. 1947. *A study of Goethe.* Oxford: The Clarendon Press.

Feyerabend, Paul K. 1970. Classical empiricism. In *The methodological heritage of Newton.* Ed. R. E. Butts and J. W. Davis. Toronto: University of Toronto Press, pp. 150–70.

1975. *Against method: Outline of an anarchistic theory of knowledge.* Atlantic Highlands, N. J.: Humanities Press.

Fischer, Ernst Gottfried. 1819. *Lehrbuch der mechanischen Naturlehre.* 2d ed. 2 vols. Berlin and Leipzig: G. C. Nauck.

Gehler, Johann Samuel Traugott. 1787–96. *Physikalisches Wörterbuch.* 6 vols. Leipzig: Schwickert.

1825–45. *Physikalisches Wörterbuch.* Ed. H. W. Brandes et al. 2d ed. 11 vols. Leipzig: Schwickert.

Gehrcke, E. 1948. Neue Versuche über Farbensehen. *Annalen der Physik,* 6th ser., 2: 345–54.

Gögelein, Christoph. 1972. *Zu Goethes Begriff von Wissenschaft auf dem Wege der Methodik seiner Farbstudien.* Munich: C. Hanser.

Goethe, Johann Wolfgang von. 1887–1919. *Goethes Werke* (Sophien-Ausgabe or Weimarer-Ausgabe). 4 divs., 143 vols. Weimar: Böhlau for the Grand Duchess Sophie of Saxony.

1907. *Maximen und Reflexionen, nach den Handschriften des Goethe- und Schiller-Archivs.* Ed. M. Hecker, Schriften der Goethe-Gesellschaft, no. 21. Weimar: Goethe-Gesellschaft.

1947–. *Die Schriften zur Naturwissenschaft* (Leopoldina-Ausgabe). Ed. R.

Matthaei et al. 2 divs., 15 vols. to date. Weimar: Böhlau for the Deutsche Akademie der Naturforscher (Leopoldina) zu Halle.

1948–60. *Goethes Werke* (Hamburger-Ausgabe). Ed. E. Trunz. 14 vols. Hamburg: C. Wegner.

1982. *Wilhelm Meisters Wanderjahre, oder die Entsagenden*. Frankfurt am Main: Insel.

Goethegesellschaft. 1952/53 ff. Goethe-Bibliographie. Goethe Jahrbuch, vols. 14/15 ff.

Gravander, Jerry Wallace. 1975. Newton's "New theory about light and colors" and the hypothetico-deductive account of scientific method: Scientific practice contra philosophic doctrine. Ph.D. diss., University of Texas at Austin.

Gren, Friedrich Albrecht Carl. 1788. *Grundriss der Naturlehre zum Gebrauch akademischer Vorlesungen*. Halle: Hemmerde & Schwetschke.

1793. *Grundriss der Naturlehre in seinem mathematischen und chemischen Theile neu bearbeitet von Friedrich Albrecht Carl Gren*. 2d ed. Halle: Hemmerde & Schwetschke.

Grimm, Jacob, and Wilhelm Grimm. 1854–1919. *Deutsches Wörterbuch*. 15 vols. Leipzig: S. Hirzel.

Groth, Angelika. 1972. *Goethe als Wissenschaftshistoriker*. Münchener Germanistische Beiträge, no. 7. Munich: Fink.

Gruner, Shirley M. 1973. Defending Father Lucas: A consideration of the Newton-Lucas dispute on the nature of the spectrum. *Centaurus* 17: 315–29.

1974. Goethe's criticism of Newton's *Opticks*. *Physis* 16: 66–82.

Guerlac, Henry. 1977. *Essays and papers in the history of modern science*. Baltimore: The Johns Hopkins University Press.

1981. *Newton on the Continent*. Ithaca, N.Y.: Cornell University Press.

1983. Can we date Newton's early optical experiments? *Isis* 74: 74–80.

1986. Can there be colors in the dark? Physical color theory before Newton. *Journal of the History of Ideas* 47: 3–20.

Hall, Alfred Rupert. 1948. Sir Isaac Newton's note-book, 1661–65. *Cambridge Historical Journal* 9: 239–50.

1960. Newton's first book. *Archives Internationales d'Histoire des Sciences* 13: 39–61.

Hanson. Norwood Russell. 1958. *Patterns of discovery: An inquiry into the conceptual foundations of science*. Cambridge: At the University Press.

Hargreave, David. 1973. Thomas Young's theory of color vision: Its roots, development, and acceptance by the British scientific community. Ph.D. diss., University of Wisconsin.

Heilbron, J. L. 1979. *Electricity in the 17th and 18th centuries: A study of early modern physics*. Berkeley and Los Angeles: University of California Press.

Heisenberg, Werner. 1952. *Philosophic problems of nuclear science*. Trans. F. C. Hayes. New York: Pantheon.

1967. Das Naturbild Goethes und die technisch-naturwissenschaftliche Welt. *Jahrbuch der Goethegesellschaft*, n.s. 29: 27–42.

Helmholtz, Hermann von. 1892. *Goethes Vorahnungen kommender naturwissenschaftlicher Ideen*. Berlin: Pastel.

1971. *Philosophische Vorträge und Aufsätze*. Ed. H. Hörz and S. Wollgast. Berlin: Akademie-Verlag.

Hendry, John. 1980. Newton's theory of colour. *Centaurus* 23: 230–51.

Hooke, Robert. 1665. *Micrographia, or some physiological descriptions of mi-*

nute bodies made by magnifying glasses, with observations and inquiries thereupon. London: Martyn & Alestry.

Hurvich, Leo M. 1981. *Color vision.* Sunderland, Mass.: Sinauer Associates.

Jablonski, Walter. 1930. Zum Einfluss der Goetheschen Farbenlehre auf die physiologische und psychologische Optik der Folgezeit. *Archiv für Geschichte der Mathematik, der Naturwissenschaften und der Technik* 13: 75–82.

Jaki, Stanley L. 1969. Goethe and the physicists. *American Journal of Physics* 37: 195–203.

Jenkins, Francis A., and Harvey E. White. 1976. *Fundamentals of optics.* 4th ed. New York: McGraw-Hill.

Judd, Deane B. 1970. Introduction to *Theory of Colours*, by Johannn Wolfgang von Goethe, trans. C. L. Eastlake. Cambridge, Mass.: MIT Press, pp. v–xvi.

Jungnickel, Christa. 1979. Teaching and research in the physical sciences and mathematics in Saxony, 1820–1850. *Historical Studies in the Physical Sciences* 10: 3–47.

Jungnickel, Christa, and Russell McCormmach. 1986. *Intellectual mastery of nature: Theoretical physics from Ohm to Einstein.* Vol. 1, *The torch of mathematics, 1800–1870.* Chicago: University of Chicago Press.

Klein, Jacob. 1940. Phenomenology and the history of science. In *Philosophical essays in memory of Edmund Husserl,* ed. M. Farber. Cambridge, Mass.: Harvard University Press, pp. 143–63.

Kuhn, Dorothea. 1967. *Empirische und ideelle Wirklichkeit: Studien über Goethes Kritik des französischen Akademiestreites.* Neue Hefte zur Morphologie, no. 5. Graz, Vienna, and Cologne: Böhlau.

1972, Goethe und die Chemie. *Medizinhistorisches Journal* 7: 264–78.

Kuhn, Thomas S. 1970. *The structure of scientific revolutions.* 2d ed. Chicago: University of Chicago Press.

1977. *The essential tension: Selected studies in scientific tradition and change.* Chicago: University of Chicago Press.

1978. Newton's optical papers. In *Isaac Newton's papers and lectures on natural philosophy and related documents,* ed. I. B. Cohen. Cambridge, Mass.: Harvard University Press, pp. 27–45.

Lakatos, Imre. 1978. Newton's effect on scientific standards. In *Philosophical papers.* Vol. 1, *The methodology of scientific research programmes.* Cambridge: Cambridge University Press, pp. 193–222.

Land, Edwin H. 1959a. Color vision and the natural image. *Proceedings of the National Academy of Sciences* 45 (January): 115–29.

1959b. Experiments in color vision. *Scientific American* 200 (May): 84–99.

1977. The retinex theory of color vision. *Scientific American* 237 (December): 108–28.

1978. Our "polar partnership" with the world around us. *Harvard Magazine,* January-February: 23–26.

Land, Edwin, and John McCann. 1971. Lightness and retinex theory. *Journal of the Optical Society of America* 61 (January): 1–11.

Lavoisier, Antoine Laurent. 1952. *Elements of chemistry.* Trans. R. Kerr. In *Great books of the western world,* ed. R. M. Hutchins, vol. 45, *Lavoisier, Fourier, Faraday.* Chicago: William Benton, Encyclopeadia Britannica, Inc. pp. 1–159.

Laymon, Ronald. 1978. Newton's *experimentum crucis* and the logic of idealization and theory refutation. *Studies in History and Philosophy of Science* 9: 51–77.

Lessing, Gotthold Ephraim. 1838–40. *Gotthold Ephraim Lessings Sämmtliche Schriften.* New ed. 13 vols. Berlin: Voss.

Lohne, Johannes A. 1961. Newton's "proof" of the sine law and his mathematical principles of color. *Archive for History of Exact Sciences* 1: 389–405.

———. 1963. Zur Geschichte des Brechungsgesetzes. *Sudhoffs Archiv für Geschichte der Medizin und der Naturwissenschaften* 47:152–72.

———. 1967. The increasing corruption of Newton's diagrams. *History of Science* 6: 69–89.

———. 1968. Experimentum crucis. *Notes and Records of the Royal Society of London* 23: 169–99.

Londey, David. 1969. On the uses of fact-expressions. *Theoria* (Sweden) 35: 70–79.

MacAdam, David L., ed. 1970. *Sources of color science.* Cambridge, Mass.: MIT Press.

Malus, Etienne Louis. 1811. Traité des couleurs; par M. Goethe (1810). *Annales de Chimie,* ser. 1, 79: 199–219.

Mamiani, Maurizio. 1976. *Isaac Newton filosofo della natura: le lezioni giovanili di ottica e la genesi del metodo newtoniano.* Università degli Studi di Parma, Pubblicazioni della Facoltà di Magistero, no. 2. Florence: La Nuova Italia.

Manuel, Frank E. 1968. *A portrait of Isaac Newton.* Cambridge, Mass.: Belknap Press for Harvard University Press.

———. 1974. *The religion of Isaac Newton.* Oxford: Oxford University Press.

Marek, Jiří. 1969. Newton's report ("New theory about light and colours") and its relation to results of his predecessors. *Physis* 11: 390–407.

Mason, Stephen F. 1962. *A history of the sciences.* Rev. ed. New York: Collier Books.

Matthaei, Rupprecht. 1941. *Die Farbenlehre im Goethe-Nationalmuseum: Eine Darstellung auf Grund des gesamten Nachlasses in Weimar mit der vollständigen Bestandsaufnahme.* Jena: G. Fischer.

———. 1949. Ueber die Anfänge von Goethes Farbenlehre. *Goethe Jahrbuch,* n.s. 11: 249–62.

Mundle, C. W. K. 1971. *Perception: Facts and theories.* London: Oxford University Press.

Nelson, John O. 1967. The ontological emergence of FACT in the twentieth century. *Darshana International* (India) 7:33–38.

Newton, Isaac. 1728. *Optical lectures read in the publick schools of the university of Cambridge, anno domini, 1669.* London: Fayram.

———. 1729. *Lectiones opticae.* London: Innys.

———. 1744. *Opuscula mathematica, philosophica et philologica.* Trans. and ed. G. F. M. M. S. di Castiglione. 3 vols. Lausanne and Geneva: Marc-Michael Bousquet.

———. 1934. *Sir Isaac Newton's mathematical principles of natural philosophy and his system of the world.* Trans. A. Motte, rev. F. Cajori. Berkeley and Los Angeles: University of California Press.

———. 1952. *Opticks.* New York: Dover.

———. 1959–76. *The correspondence of Isaac Newton.* Ed. H. W. Turnbull et al. 7 vols. Cambridge: Cambridge University Press for the Royal Society.

[1779–85] 1964. *Opera quae exstant omnia.* Ed. Samuel Horsley. 5 vols. London: Johannes Nichols. Reprint. Stuttgart-Bad Cannstatt: Friedrich Frommann (Günther Holzboog).

1973. *The unpublished first version of Isaac Newton's Cambridge lectures on optics, 1670–1672.* Ed. D. T. Whiteside. Cambridge: University Library.

1984. *The optical papers of Isaac Newton.* Vol. 1, *The optical lectures, 1670–1672.* Ed. A. E. Shapiro. Cambridge: Cambridge University Press.

Pav, Peter Anton. 1964. Eighteenth-century optics: The age of unenlightenment. Ph. D. diss., Indiana University.

Pfaff, C. H. 1813. *Ueber Newton's Farbentheorie, Herrn von Goethe's Farbenlehre und den chemischen Gegensatz der Farben: Ein Versuch in der experimentalen Optik.* Leipzig: Vogel.

Popkin, Richard H. 1964. *The history of scepticism from Erasmus to Spinoza.* Rev. ed. Berkeley and Los Angeles: University of California Press.

Priestley, Joseph. 1772. *The history and present state of discoveries relating to vision, light, and colours.* London: J. Johnson.

1776. *Dr. Joseph Priestleys Geschichte und gegenwärtigen Zustand der Optik, vorzüglich in Absicht auf den physikalischen Teil dieser Wissenschaft.* Trans. G. S. Klügel. Leipzig: J. F. Junius.

Pyritz, Hans. 1965. *Goethe-Bibliographie.* Ed. P. Raabe, H. Nicolai, and G. Burkhardt. Heidelberg: C. Winter.

Raman. C. V. 1968. *The physiology of vision.* Bangalore: Indian Academy of Sciences.

Richter, Manfred. 1938. *Das Schrifttum über Goethes Farbenlehre mit besonderer Berücksichtigung der naturwissenschaftlichen Probleme.* Berlin: R. Pfau.

Ronchi, Vasco. 1970. *The nature of light.* Trans. V. Barocas. London: Heinemann.

Sabra, A. I. 1967. *Theories of light from Descartes to Newton.* London: Oldbourne.

Schmid, Gunther. 1940. *Goethe und die Naturwissenschaften.* Halle: Emil Abderhalden in the name of the Kaiserlich Leopoldinisch-Carolinisch Deutsche Akademie der Naturforscher.

Schrimpf, Hans Joachim. 1963. Ueber die geschichtliche Bedeutung von Goethes Newton-Polemik und Romantik-Kritik. In *Gratulatio: Festschrift für Christian Wegner zum 70. Geburtstag am 9. September 1963.* Ed. M. Honeit and M. Wegner. Hamburg: C. Wegner, pp. 63–82.

Sepper, Dennis L. 1981. Goethe, Newton, and color: The background and rationale of an unrealized scientific controversy. Ph.D. diss., University of Chicago.

1987. Goethe against Newton: Towards saving the phenomenon. In *Goethe and the sciences: A reappraisal,* ed. F. Amrine, F. J. Zucker, and H. Wheeler. Boston Studies in the Philosophy of Science, no. 97. Dordrecht and Boston: Reidel, pp. 175–93.

Shapiro, Alan E. 1973. Kinematic optics: A study of the wave theory of light in the seventeenth century. *Archive for History of Exact Sciences* 11: 134–266.

1975. Newton's definition of a light ray and the diffusion theories of chromatic dispersion. *Isis* 66: 194–210.

1979. Newton's "achromatic" dispersion law: Theoretical background and experimental evidence. *Archive for History of Exact Sciences* 21: 91–128.

1980. The evolving structure of Newton's theory of white light and color. *Isis* 70: 211–35.

Shklar, Judith. 1981. Jean d'Alembert and the rehabilitation of history. *Journal of the History of Ideas* 42: 643–64.

Steffens, Henry John, 1977. *The development of Newtonian optics in England.* New York: Science History Publications.

Turner, R. Stephen. 1974. University reform and professorial scholarship in Germany, 1760–1806. In *The university in society*, ed. Lawrence Stone, vol. 2. Princeton: Princeton University Press, pp. 495–531.

Wagner, Karl. 1935. Goethes Farbenlehre und Schopenhauers Farbentheorie. *Jahrbuch der Schopenhauer-Gesellschaft* 22: 92–176.

Wasserman, Gerald S. 1978. *Color vision: An historical introduction.* New York: John Wiley & Sons.

Weinhandl, Ferdinand. 1932. *Die Metaphysik Goethes.* Berlin: Junker & Dünnhaupt.

Wells, George A. 1968. Goethe's scientific method and aims in the light of his studies in physical optics. *Publications of the English Goethe Society*, n.s. 38: 69–113.

Westfall, Richard S. 1962. The development of Newton's theory of color. *Isis* 53: 339–58.

1963. Newton's reply to Hooke and the theory of colors. *Isis* 54: 82–96.

1966. Newton defends his first publication: The Newton-Lucas correspondence. *Isis* 57: 299–314.

1973. Newton and the fudge factor. *Science* 179 (23 February): 751–58.

1980. *Never at rest: A biography of Isaac Newton.* Cambridge: Cambridge University Press.

Wünsch, Christian Ernst. 1792. *Versuche und Beobachtungen über die Farben des Lichtes.* Leipzig: Breitkopf.

Young, Thomas. 1814. Review of *Zur Farbenlehre*, by Johann Wolfgang von Goethe. *Quarterly Review* (Edinburgh) 10: 427–41.

Index

Lightning Source UK Ltd.
Milton Keynes UK
27 October 2009

145456UK00002BA/14/A